Rings and Fields

Rings and Fields

59

Graham Ellis

Department of Mathematics
University College Galway, Ireland

CLARENDON PRESS • OXFORD
1992

Oxford University Press, Walton Street, Oxford OX2 6DP

Oxford   New York   Toronto
Delhi   Bombay   Calcutta   Madras   Karachi
Kuala Lumpur   Singapore   Hong Kong   Tokyo
Nairobi   Dar es Salaam   Cape Town
Melbourne   Auckland   Madrid
and associated companies in
Berlin   Ibadan

Oxford is a trade mark of Oxford University Press

Published in the United States
by Oxford University Press Inc., New York

A catalogue record for this book is available from the British Library

Library of Congress Cataloging in Publication Data
Ellis, Graham.
  Rings and fields/Graham Ellis.
    p.   cm.
  Includes bibliographical references and index.
  1. Rings (Algebra)   2. Fields, Algebraic.   I. Title.
QA247.E39   1992
512'.4–dc20   92-15556

CIP

ISBN 0–19–853455–8
ISBN 0–19–853454–X (pbk.)

Typeset by Apek Typesetters Ltd, Bristol
Printed in Great Britain by Biddles Ltd, Guildford and King's Lynn

Preface

This book is a slightly expanded version of a course of forty lectures on rings and fields which I have given to final year undergraduate students at University College Galway. It aims to provide a well-motivated introduction to the subject that will give the reader an appreciation of the power of algebraic techniques to handle diverse and difficult problems. The only absolute prerequisite is a standard undergraduate first course in linear algebra: the reader is assumed to have a basic knowledge of matrices and systems of linear equations; all of the necessary definitions and results on vector spaces are however recalled in Chapter 0. No acquaintance with group theory is assumed.

The interdependence of the various chapters is shown in the following chart.

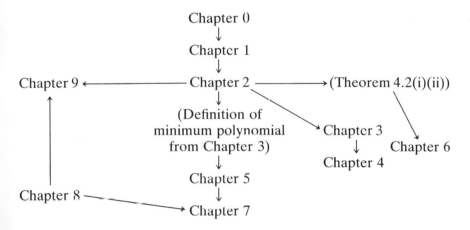

Chapter 8 is essentially independent of the other chapters, and can be omitted by students who have already followed a standard undergraduate first course in group theory. The reader without a knowledge of group theory can choose to read Chapter 8 either before or after Chapter 7. The material in Chapters 1, 6, and 9 is perhaps more demanding and less essential than that in the other chapters.

The exercises at the end of chapters contain much material that would, in more traditional books, be included in the main body of the text. For instance, ring homomorphisms and quotient rings are dealt with in the exercises for Chapter 2. The exercises vary considerably in difficulty and, in keeping with real life mathematical problems, no measure of this difficulty is indicated. Readers are advised to at least look at all of the problems and to make a genuine attempt at a fair few of them.

I would like to take this opportunity to thank the anonymous mathematician who, on behalf of Oxford University Press, read the various versions of the manuscript and suggested many worthwhile improvements.

Galway   G.E.
March 1992

Contents

0 Preliminaries

There are many occurrences in mathematics of sets whose objects can, in some natural way, be added and multiplied. For instance we have the integers $\mathbb{Z}$, the even integers $2\mathbb{Z}$, the rational numbers $\mathbb{Q}$, the real numbers $\mathbb{R}$, and the complex numbers $\mathbb{C}$. Not all of the occurrences are as sets of numbers. We have for example the set of all 2×2 matrices over $\mathbb{R}$

$$M_2(\mathbb{R}) = \left\{ \begin{pmatrix} a & b \\ c & d \end{pmatrix} : a, b, c, d \in \mathbb{R} \right\},$$

and, more generally, the set $M_n(R)$ of all $n \times n$ matrices over R for R equal to any of $\mathbb{Z}$, $2\mathbb{Z}$, $\mathbb{Q}$, $\mathbb{R}$ or $\mathbb{C}$. The set of real continuous functions

$$C(\mathbb{R}) = \{ f : \mathbb{R} \to \mathbb{R} : f \text{ is continuous} \}$$

also possesses a natural addition and multiplication defined, for f, g in $C(\mathbb{R})$, by

$$f + g : x \mapsto f(x) + g(x), \qquad fg : x \mapsto f(x)g(x).$$

This same addition and multiplication works equally well in the subset of $C(\mathbb{R})$ consisting of the real polynomial functions $f(x) = a_0 + a_1 x + \cdots + a_n x^n$, $a_i \in \mathbb{R}$. There is a corresponding (well-known) addition and multiplication on the set

$$\mathbb{R}[x] = \{ a_0 + a_1 x + a_2 x^2 + \cdots + a_n x^n : a_i \in \mathbb{R} \text{ and } n \geq 0 \}$$

of real polynomials. Several important algebraic features, such as the associativity of the multiplication

$$(xy)z = x(yz) \qquad \text{for all } x, y, z,$$

are common to all these examples. Other features, such as the commutativity of the multiplication

$$xy = yx \qquad \text{for all } x, y,$$

and the existence of a multiplicative identity element 1 satisfying

$$1x = x1 = x \qquad \text{for all } x,$$

are not common to all the examples. The ramifications of this kind of algebraic similarity and difference between sets with addition and multiplication will be the focus of our attention in this book.

0.1 Rings, integral domains, and fields

The basic algebraic structure common to all of the above examples is that of a non-empty set R with two binary operations $+$ and $\circ$ satisfying, for any elements a, b, c in R:

(1) $a + b = b + a$;

(2) $(a + b) + c = a + (b + c)$;

(3) there is a *zero* element 0 in R such that $a + 0 = a$;

(4) there is an element $-a$ in R such that $a + (-a) = 0$;

(5) $a \circ (b + c) = a \circ b + a \circ c$;

(6) $(b + c) \circ a = b \circ a + c \circ a$;

(7) $(a \circ b) \circ c = a \circ (b \circ c)$.

Any such R we shall call a *ring*. (We shall often omit the symbol $\circ$ and write ab for the product of two ring elements a and b.)

A ring R may have additional algebraic properties. Some of these are captured in the following definitions.

1. A ring R is *commutative* if $a \circ b = b \circ a$ for all a, b in R.

2. A ring R has an *identity* if there is an element 1 in R such that $1 \circ a = a \circ 1 = a$ for all a in R.

3. A ring R is an *integral domain* if it is commutative and if, for all a, b in R, the equality $a \circ b = 0$ implies that $a = 0$ or $b = 0$.

4. An element u in a ring R with identity is a *unit* if there is an element u^{-1} in R such that $u \circ u^{-1} = u^{-1} \circ u = 1$. We call u^{-1} the (*multiplicative*) *inverse* of u.

A ring R is a *field* if it has an identity $1 \neq 0$, is commutative, and every non-zero element is a unit. It is a simple exercise to show that every field is an integral domain.

In order to get a feel for these definitions we need to consider a few examples. Certainly $\mathbb{Z}$, $\mathbb{Q}$, $\mathbb{R}$, $\mathbb{C}$, and $\mathbb{R}[x]$ are all integral domains with identity. The units in $\mathbb{Z}$ are ± 1. In $\mathbb{Q}$, $\mathbb{R}$, and $\mathbb{C}$ every non-zero element is a unit, and these are thus fields. In $\mathbb{R}[x]$ the units are the constant polynomials.

For any integer d the sets $\mathbb{Z}[\sqrt{d}] = \{m + n\sqrt{d}: m, n \in \mathbb{Z}\}$ and $\mathbb{Q}[\sqrt{d}] = \{u + v\sqrt{d}: u, v \in \mathbb{Q}\}$, with the usual addition and multiplication of complex numbers, are integral domains with identity. The even integers $2\mathbb{Z}$ form an integral domain without identity; more generally for any integer $m \geqslant 2$ the set $m\mathbb{Z}$ of integer multiples of m forms an integral domain without identity.

The set $C(\mathbb{R})$ is an example of a commutative ring with identity which is not an integral domain. A function f is a unit in this ring if $f(x) \neq 0$ for all $x \subset \mathbb{R}$.

The set $M_n(\mathbb{R})$ is a ring with identity which, for $n \geqslant 2$, is not commutative. The units in $M_n(\mathbb{R})$ are those matrices with non-zero determinant.

All of the above examples of rings contain infinitely many elements. A finite ring $\mathbb{Z}_m$ of m elements can be constructed as follows. For each integer a let $\bar{a}$ denote the set of integers $\{a + km: k \in \mathbb{Z}\}$. There are m such sets, and these sets are to be the elements of $\mathbb{Z}_m$. Addition and multiplication is defined by

$$\bar{a} + \bar{b} = \overline{a+b} \qquad \text{and} \qquad \bar{a} \circ \bar{b} = \overline{ab}.$$

For instance, suppose $m = 7$. Then

$$\bar{3} = \{\ldots, -11, -4, 3, 10, 17, \ldots\}$$
$$\bar{5} = \{\ldots, -9, -2, 5, 12, 19, \ldots\}$$

and

$$\bar{3} + \bar{5} = \bar{8} = \bar{1} = \{\ldots, -13, -6, 1, 8, 15, \ldots\}.$$

There is a question of well-definedness which needs to be considered here: if $\bar{a} = \bar{a}'$ and $\bar{b} = b'$ then this definition of addition and multiplication (for arbitrary m) only makes sense if

$$\bar{a} + \bar{b} = \bar{a}' + \bar{b}' \quad \text{and} \quad \bar{a} \circ \bar{b} = \bar{a}' \circ \bar{b}'.$$

The reader should check that these equalities do indeed hold.

The ring $\mathbb{Z}_m$ is a commutative ring with identity which, for certain m, is a field. For instance $\mathbb{Z}_3$ and $\mathbb{Z}_5$ are fields, but $\mathbb{Z}_4$ and $\mathbb{Z}_6$ are not. (In $\mathbb{Z}_4$ we have $\bar{2} \circ \bar{2} = \bar{4} = \bar{0}$, and in $\mathbb{Z}_6$ we have $\bar{2} \circ \bar{3} = \bar{6} = \bar{0}$. Since $\mathbb{Z}_4$ and $\mathbb{Z}_6$ are not integral domains they cannot be fields.)

Each of the chapters in this book is devoted to a particular aspect of the algebraic theory of rings and fields. Each chapter begins with a discussion of a concrete problem (mathematical or otherwise) and then just enough theory is introduced in order to solve the problem. This approach emphasizes an important phenomenon: general mathematical theories usually grow out of quite specific problems. The concrete problems used to motivate the theory in this way have been chosen so as to convey some idea of the wide range of mathematical areas that are now dependent on the theory of rings and fields.

All too often introductory texts on algebra begin with a list of unmotivated axioms, go on to deduce as quickly and elegantly as possible a collection of abstract theorems stated in their most general form, and finally offer the reader a few specific applications with which the theory is miraculously able to cope. In this way the amount of theory covered in a given number of pages is maximized, and the logical order of the theory is optimized. The student, however, gains little appreciation of how new mathematics is discovered.

The remaining sections of this preliminary chapter contain brief accounts of some necessary background material. The reader is advised to skim these sections lightly, and return to them later when necessary.

0.2 Linear algebra

Let K be a field (such as $\mathbb{R}$, $\mathbb{Q}$, or $\mathbb{C}$). The set of all triples

$$K^3 = \{(k_0, k_1, k_2): k_i \in K\}$$

has a natural addition.

$$(k_0, k_1, k_2) + (k'_0, k'_1, k'_2) = (k_0 + k'_0, k_1 + k'_1, k_2 + k'_2).$$

Any triple in K^3 can also be multiplied by any element λ in K:

$$\lambda(k_0, k_1, k_2) = (\lambda k'_0, \lambda k'_1, \lambda k'_2).$$

To differentiate between the elements of K^3 and the elements of K we call the former *vectors*, and the latter *scalars*. Each triple (k_0, k_1, k_2) can be thought of as representing an 'arrow' starting at the origin $(0, 0, 0)$ and ending at the point (k_0, k_1, k_2). The addition and scalar multiplication of vectors satisfies, for all $u, v, w \in K^3$ and $\lambda, \mu \in K$:

(1)$'$ $u + v = v + u$;

(2)$'$ $(u + v) + w = u + (v + w)$;

(3)$'$ there is a *zero* element 0 such that $u + 0 = u$;

(4)′ there is an element $-u$ such that $u+(-u)=0$;

(5)′ $\lambda(u+v)=\lambda u+\lambda v$;

(6)′ $(\lambda+\mu)u=\lambda u+\mu u$;

(7)′ $(\lambda\mu)u=\lambda(\mu u)$;

(8)′ $1u=u$.

We can abstract from this description of K^3 the fundamental definition of linear algebra: any set V which admits an addition and a scalar multiplication by elements of the field K is called a *vector space over K* if axioms (1)′ to (8)′ hold for all $u, v, w \in V$ and $\lambda, \mu \in K$. The elements of a vector space are called *vectors*.

The similarity between axioms (1)–(7) and axioms (1)–(7)′ leads us to the important observation that any field K is a vector space over itself. Another similar, and important, example of a vector space over K is the ring of polynomials $K[x]=\{a_0+a_1x+\cdots a_nx^n: a_i \in K \text{ and } n \geq 0\}$.

For any fixed elements a, b, c in K the subset

$$W=\{(x, y, z)\in K^3: ax+by+cz=0\}$$

of K^3 represents a 'plane' in K^3. The subset W is itself a vector space as it is closed under addition and scalar multiplication. In particular:

(9) $0 \in W$;

(10) $u+v \in W$ for all $u, v \in W$;

(11) $\lambda u \in W$ for all $u \in W, \lambda \in K$.

Because W satisfies (9)–(11) we say that W is a *subspace* of K^3.

More generally, any subset W of a vector space V is called a *subspace* if properties (9)–(11) hold.

In the vector space K^3 it is possible to find a set of three vectors $E=\{e_1, e_2, e_3\}$ with the property that any vector v in K^3 can be expressed uniquely in the form $v=\lambda_1e_1+\lambda_2e_2+\lambda_3e_3$ with $\lambda_i \in K$ (for instance, take $e_1=(1,0,0)$, $e_2=(0,1,0)$, $e_3=(0,0,1)$). We call any such set E a *basis*. This notion of a basis can be extended to an arbitrary vector space.

A subset E of a vector space V is said to be a *basis of V* if:

1. the set E is *linearly independent*; that is, for any subset $\{e_1, \ldots, e_n\}$ of E, if $\lambda_1, \ldots, \lambda_n \subset K$ satisfy

$$\lambda_1e_1+\cdots\lambda_ne_n=0,$$

then $\lambda_1=\lambda_2=\cdots\lambda_n=0$;

2. the set E *generates* V; that is, for any $v \in V$ there exist $\lambda_1, \ldots, \lambda_n \in K$ and $e_1, \ldots, e_n \in E$ such that

$$v = \lambda_1 e_1 + \cdots + \lambda_n e_n.$$

Essentially we need just one result on vector spaces.

Theorem 0.1. *Let S be a finite subset of a vector space V that generates V. Then some subset of S is a basis of V. Moreover, if V possesses a finite basis of n vectors, then any other basis of V also consists of n vectors.*

Proof. Let $s_1, \ldots, s_n$ be the non-zero elements of S. We first have to construct a subset E of S which is a basis of V. Let s_1 be in E. Let s_2 be in E if and only if the set $\{s_1, s_2\}$ is linearly independent. Inductively let s_i be in E if and only if the set $\{s_i\} \cup \{s_j: j < i$ and $s_j \in E\}$ is linearly independent. This defines for us a linearly independent set E. We leave as an exercise the proof that E generates V, and is thus a basis of V.

Suppose now that E is a basis of V consisting of n vectors.

Claim. *No subset of V consisting of more than n vectors can be linearly independent.*

If we prove this claim, it will follow that any subset E' of V consisting of n' vectors can only be linearly independent if $n' \leq n$. If E' is a basis then, interchanging E' and E in this argument, it will also follow that $n \leq n'$, and hence that $n = n'$. It remains to prove the claim.

Suppose $E = \{e_1, \ldots, e_n\}$ and consider a set of m vectors $X = \{w_1, \ldots, w_m\}$ in V with $m > n$. We need to show that X is *linearly dependent* (that is, not linearly independent). If $w_1 = 0$ then certainly X is linearly dependent, so suppose $w_1 \neq 0$. Since E generates V we can write

$$w_1 = \lambda_1 e_1 + \cdots + \lambda_n e_n$$

with $\lambda_i \in K$. As $w_1 \neq 0$, it follows that one of the λ_i is non-zero. After renumbering if necessary we can assume that $\lambda_1 \neq 0$. Solving for e_1 we get

$$e_1 = \lambda_1^{-1} w_1 - \lambda_1^{-1}\lambda_2 e_2 - \cdots - \lambda_1^{-1}\lambda_n e_n.$$

The subspace of V generated by $w_1, e_2, \ldots, e_n$ contains e_1, and hence must be all of V since E generates V. This argument can be continued and $e_2, e_3, \ldots$ can be replaced, one at a time, by $w_2, w_3, \ldots$ until all the elements $e_1, \ldots, e_n$ are exhausted and $w_1, \ldots, w_n$ generate V. Thus we can find λ_i in K such that

$$w_m = \lambda_1 w_1 + \cdots \lambda_n w_n$$

thereby proving that $w_1, \ldots, w_n$ are linearly dependent. ∎

The number of elements in a basis of a vector space V over K is called the *dimension* of V over K. For instance, K^3 is of dimension 3 over K. The vector space of complex numbers $\mathbb{C}$ is of dimension 2 over $\mathbb{R}$, but of dimension 1 over $\mathbb{C}$. The vector space $\mathbb{R}[x]$ is infinite dimensional over $\mathbb{R}$.

The three-dimensional vector space K^3 has an n-dimensional analogue K^n. The vectors in K^n can usefully be thought of as $n \times 1$ matrices (that is, n rows by 1 column matrices). For any fixed $m \times n$ matrix A over K, an arbitrary vector v in K^n can be multiplied on the left by A to produce a vector Av in K^m; this yields a function

$$\phi \colon K^n \to K^m, \qquad v \mapsto Av$$

which, thanks to the properties of matrix multiplication, satisfies:

(1) $\phi(u + v) = \phi u + \phi v$;

(2) $\phi(\lambda v) = \lambda(\phi v)$;

for all $u, v \in V$ and $\lambda \in K$. We call ϕ a *linear transformation* or *linear homomorphism*. More generally, given any two vector spaces V and V' over K, a function

$$\phi \colon V \to V'$$

is said to be a *linear transformation* or *linear homomorphism* if it satisfies properties (1) and (2).

0.3 Equivalence relations

Notions of 'equivalence' abound in mathematics: the geometrical properties of a triangle (such as the ratio between the lengths of its sides) are completely determined by its three angles, and so from a geometrical point of view two triangles are 'equivalent' if their corresponding angles are equal; the two systems of linear equations

$$
\begin{array}{ll}
x+\ 2y-2z+\ 3w=2 & x+2y-2z+3w=2 \\
2x+\ 4y-3z+\ 4w=5 & z-2w=1 \\
5x+10y-8z+11w=12 &
\end{array}
$$

have the same real-numbered solutions and thus, from a numerical point of view, are 'equivalent'; the assertion that a given triangle is right-angled and the assertion that the sum of the squares of two sides of the triangle is equal to the square of the third side are 'equivalent' assertions since either one can be deduced from the other. In these three uses of the term 'equivalent' we have, for all X, Y, Z under consideration (i.e. all triangles, all systems of real equations, or all mathematical assertions),

reflexivity: X is equivalent to X;
symmetry: if X is equivalent to Y then Y is equivalent to X;
transitivity: if X is equivalent to Y and Y is equivalent to Z then X is equivalent to Z.

We say that a binary relation between elements of a set S is an *equivalence relation on S* if the relation is reflexive, symmetric, and transitive. For any element x in S we let $[x]$ denote the set of all elements of S equivalent to x. We call $[x]$ the *equivalence class* of x.

We have given three examples of equivalence relations on infinite sets. As an example of an equivalence relation on a finite set let us consider the ring $\mathbb{Z}_{12} = [\bar{0}, \bar{1}, \bar{2}, \ldots, \overline{11}\}$ and define the relation ρ on $\mathbb{Z}_{12}$ by

$$\bar{a}\rho\bar{b} \qquad \text{if and only if} \qquad \bar{a}-\bar{b}\in\{\bar{0},\bar{4},\bar{8}\}.$$

(Read $\bar{a}\rho\bar{b}$ as $\bar{a}$ is equivalent to $\bar{b}$.) Certainly $\bar{a}\rho\bar{a}$; and if $\bar{a}\rho\bar{b}$ then $\bar{b}\rho\bar{a}$; and if both $\bar{a}\rho\bar{b}$ and $\bar{b}\rho\bar{c}$ then $\bar{a}\rho\bar{c}$. Thus ρ is an equivalence relation on $\mathbb{Z}_{12}$. There are just four equivalence classes in this example:

$$[\bar{0}]=\{\bar{0},\bar{4},\bar{8}\}, \qquad [\bar{1}]=\{\bar{1},\bar{5},\bar{9}\}, \qquad [\bar{2}]=\{\bar{2},\bar{6},\overline{10}\},$$
$$[\bar{3}]=\{\bar{3},\bar{7},\overline{11}\}.$$

Note that for $\bar{a}$, $\bar{b}$ in $\mathbb{Z}_{12}$ we either have $[\bar{a}]=[\bar{b}]$ (for instance $[\bar{1}]=[\bar{5}]$) or $[\bar{a}]\cap[\bar{b}]=\varnothing$.

For any equivalence relation ρ on a set S the union of the equivalence classes is obviously equal to S, and the intersection of any two distinct equivalence classes can be shown to be empty. In other words, the equivalence classes form a *partition* of S. Conversely any partition of S determines an equivalence relation on S: two elements are equivalent if and only if they belong to the same set in the partition.

For any ring R with identity we let R^* denote the set of units in R. It is readily checked that the product of two units is always a unit. Hence the ring multiplication restricts to a multiplication on R^*. (The ring addition does not however restrict to an addition on R^*.) Any unit u in R^* determines an equivalence relation on the set R^* for which the equivalence class of any unit a is defined to be

$$[a] = \{x \in R^* : x = au^n \text{ for some integer } n\}.$$

We leave as a worthwhile exercise the proof that the sets $[a]$ for $a \in R^*$ form a partition of R^*. (It needs to be shown that for any a, b in R^* either $[a] = [b]$ or $[a] \cap [b] = \varnothing$.) For any a, b in R^* there is a one-to-one correspondence between the elements of the sets $[a]$ and $[b]$: an element x in $[a]$ corresponds to the element $ba^{-1}x$ in $[b]$ where a^{-1} is the multiplicative inverse of a.

Suppose that R^* is a finite set, say with n elements. Then the number of elements in the equivalence class $[1]$ is a finite number m. In fact each equivalence class $[a]$ for a in R^* has the same number, m, of elements. We call m the *order* of u. (We leave as an exercise the proof that m is the least positive integer such that $u^m = 1$.) Since R^* is the union of disjoint sets of size m, it follows that m divides n. We have thus proved the following theorem due in essence to Lagrange.

Theorem 0.2. (Lagrange) *Let R be a ring with identity which has only a finite number n of units. Then the order of any unit divides n.*

As an illustration of the sort of result that can be inferred from Lagrange's theorem, consider the ring $M_3(\mathbb{Z}_5)$ of 3×3 matrices over the field $\mathbb{Z}_5$. A matrix is invertible (or in other words is a unit in $M_3(\mathbb{Z}_5)$) if and only if its rows, considered as vectors in the vector space $(\mathbb{Z}_5)^3$, are linearly independent. There are $5^3 - 1$ ways to choose a first non-zero row of a matrix; there are $5^3 - 5$ ways to choose a second non-zero row which is linearly independent of the first, there are $5^3 - 5^2$ ways to choose a third non-zero row which is linearly independent of the preceding two rows. In all then, there are $(5^3 - 1) \times (5^3 - 5) \times (5^3 - 5^2) = 1\,488\,000$ invertible matrices in the ring $M_3(\mathbb{Z}_5)$. It follows that the order of any one of these invertible matrices divides 1 488 000. Hence for any 3×3 invertible matrix A over $\mathbb{Z}_5$ there is an integer k such that $1\,488\,000 = (\text{order } A) \times k$, and therefore the 1 488 000th power of A is equal to the identity matrix: $A^{1\,488\,000} = A^{(\text{order } A) \times k} = I^k = I$.

0.4 Set theory

We have used the term 'set' several times already in this book, most importantly in the definition of a ring. It would be difficult to state precisely what we mean by this term, and so we shall rely on the reader's intuitive understanding of it. Basic facts about sets (such as the union of sets being a set, and the existence of the set of subsets of a given set) will be assumed. One has to be careful, however, when working intuitively with sets. Bertrand Russell's famous paradox highlights this. In 1902 Russell pointed out that although most sets are not members of themselves (the set of cats, for example, is not a member of itself because the set of cats is not a cat), there may be sets that do belong to themselves (for example the set of all sets). Russell's paradox asks us to consider the set X consisting of all those sets S such that S is not a member of S. Is X a member of itself? If we assume X is a member of itself we are led to a contradiction; unfortunately, assuming X is not a member of itself also leads to a contradiction!

One way around this, and other related paradoxes, is based on an axiomatic treatment of set theory. There is some debate as to what axioms should be included in such a treatment. However, with one exception, the 'obvious' facts that have implicitly been assumed about sets in this book are undisputed and are common to all treatments of set theory. The one exception concerns only Exercise 10 in Chapter 1. Any reader not intending to attempt this exercise can safely omit the rest of this subsection on set theory.

Imagine a scene in which there is an endless queue of people, each person holding a pair of shoes and a pair of socks. (We are assuming a one-to-one correspondence between the queue of people and the natural numbers $\mathbb{N} = \{1, 2, 3, \ldots\}$.) No mathematician would object to us talking about a set S of shoes consisting of exactly one shoe from each person; a pair of shoes always consists of one right shoe and one left shoe, so we could take S to be the set of all right shoes. There are, however, mathematicians who would object to us talking about a set S' of socks consisting of exactly one sock from each person; there is no way of distinguishing between right socks and left socks, and thus no algorithmic way of choosing the elements of S'. Mathematicians who accept the existence of S' need the following axiom of choice in their treatment of set theory.

Axiom of choice. *Given any set X of pairwise disjoint sets, there is a set Y that contains exactly one element in common with each set in X.*

The axiom of choice is known to be consistent with, and independent of, the list of basic and universally accepted axioms of set theory due to Zermelo and Fraenkel. (It should perhaps be pointed out that no one has yet succeeded in showing the Zermelo–Franenkel axioms themselves to be consistent. In fact, there is to date no plausible framework within which consistency could be shown. This is a fundamental philosophical problem which, due to its intractability, is not dwelt upon too much by most mathematicians). A large number of important results have been obtained from the axiom of choice in many branches of mathematics. Indeed, many branches, such as general topology, would be virtually void of results without it. On the other hand, it is known that the negation of the axiom of choice is also consistent with the Zermelo–Fraenkel axioms. (The negation states that there is a collection X of pairwise disjoint sets for which no set Y, containing exactly one element in common with each set in X, exists). So it would seem to be merely a matter of taste whether we work with the axiom of choice, its negation, or neither. Most mathematicians accept the axiom of choice. The axioms we accept will of course determine the theorems we can prove!

There are several equivalent versions of the axiom of choice. The version needed in Exercise 10 of Chapter 1 is a rather technical one known as Zorn's lemma. To state this lemma we need some preliminary terminology.

A binary relation $\leqslant$ on a set X is said to be a *partial order* on X if it is reflexive and transitive and if $x = y$ whenever elements x, y in X satisfy both $x \leqslant y$ and $y \leqslant x$. For example, set inclusion $\subseteq$ is a partial order on the set of subsets of $\mathbb{Z}$.

A binary relation $\leqslant$ on X is said to be a *total order* on X if it is a partial order and if for every pair of elements x, y in X either $x \leqslant y$ or $y \leqslant x$. For example, the usual ordering $\leqslant$ of the integers is a total order on $\mathbb{Z}$. Set inclusion is not a total order on the set of subsets of $\mathbb{Z}$.

If X is a partially ordered set, S a subset of X, and b an element in X, we say that b is an *upper bound* for S if $x \leqslant b$ for all x in S. For example, the set of even integers is an upper bound for the set of finite sets of even integers, with respect to the partial ordering given by set inclusion $\subseteq$.

If X is a partially ordered set, S a subset of X, and m an element in S, we say that m is a *maximal element* of S if there is no x in S such that $m \leq x$ and $x \neq m$.

Zorn's Lemma.   *Any non-empty partially ordered set X, in which every totally ordered subset has an upper bound, has a maximal element.*

We shall not prove the equivalence between Zorn's lemma and the axiom of choice.

1 Diophantine equations

A basic property of integers is that they can be expressed uniquely as a product of prime numbers. In this chapter we investigate other rings having a similar type of unique factorization property.

As a means of motivating our investigation, let us begin by considering two number theoretic puzzles involving so-called *Diophantine equations*. The first is: are there any odd intgers x, y which satisfy the equation

$$y^2 - 4 = x^3? \tag{1.1}$$

Note that we can rewrite the equation as

$$(y-2)(y+2) = x^3.$$

Since y is odd, the integers $y-2$ and $y+2$ must be *coprime*; that is, their highest common factor must be 1. (To see this, note that if an integer d divides both $y-2$ and $y+2$, then d divides their difference which is 4. The only odd devisor of 4 is 1. As $y-2$ and $y+2$ are both odd we must have $d=1$.) Since the product $(y-2)(y+2)$ is a cube, the following general property of coprime integers implies that both $y-2$ and $y+2$ are cubes.

The general property invoked here is that the product of two coprime integers a and b is a cube only if both a and b are cubes. To see this suppose

$$a = p_1 p_2 \ldots p_m,$$
$$b = p_1' p_2' \ldots p_n',$$
$$ab = (q_1)^3 (q_2)^3 \ldots (q_k)^3,$$

where p_i, p_i' and q_i are primes. Since the p_i are distinct from the p_i' it follows from the uniqueness of prime factorization that at least three of the p_i, or at least three of the p_i', are equal to $\pm q_1$. Relabelling the primes q_i if necessary, we can assume $p_1 = p_2 = p_3 = q_1$. Repeating the argument, it follows that for a suitable relabelling of the primes q_i we have

$$p_1 = p_2 = p_3 = q_1, \qquad p_4 = p_5 = p_6 = q_2, \qquad \ldots, \qquad p_{m-2} p_{m-1} p_m = q_{m/3},$$
$$p_1' = p_2' = p_3' = q_{m/3+1}, \qquad \ldots, \qquad p_{n-2}' p_{n-1}' p_n' = q_k.$$

Hence both a and b are cubes.

Returning to the initial problem, we have shown that $y+2=a^3$ and $y-2=b^3$ for some integers a, b. There are, however, no integers a, b such that $a^3-b^3=4$, and so we are forced to conclude that equation (1.1) has no odd integer solutions.

The second number theoretic puzzle is a bit more difficult: find all pairs of (odd or even) integers x, y which satisfy the equation

$$y^2+2=x^3. \tag{1.2}$$

Certainly $y=5$, $x=3$ satisfies this equation, and so does $y=-5$, $x=3$. As there are no other obvious integer solutions to the equation, we might try proving that $y=\pm5$, $x=3$ are the only integer solutions.

It is not too difficult to see that there is no integer solution with y even. (For if $y=2y'$ then $4y'^2+2=x^3$. Thus x^3 would be even, and consequently x would have to be even, say $x=2x'$. Thus we would have $4y'^2+2=8x'^3$. But $4y'^2+2$ is not divisible by 8, whereas $8x'^3$ is divisible by 8. This is a contradiction.) We can conclude then that y, and x, have to be odd integers.

We might now try handling equation (1.2) as we did equation (1.1). Certainly we can rewrite it as

$$(y+\sqrt{-2})(y-\sqrt{-2})=x^3.$$

To continue the analogy we need to prove that $y+\sqrt{-2}$ and $y-\sqrt{-2}$ are 'coprime'. To do this we first have to give a meaning to 'coprime' in this context.

Let $\mathbb{Z}[\sqrt{-2}]$ be the set of complex numbers of the form

$$m+n\sqrt{-2}$$

where m, n are integers. Note that under the usual addition and multiplication of complex numbers, $\mathbb{Z}[\sqrt{-2}]$ satisfies the axioms of an integral domain with identity. For $a, b, d \in \mathbb{Z}[\sqrt{-2}]$ we say that d *divides* b (and write $d|b$) if there is an element $c \in \mathbb{Z}[\sqrt{-2}]$ such that $b=cd$. We say that d is a *common factor* of a and b if d divides both a and b. We say that a and b are *coprime* if the only common factors are ±1. The reason that we allow only ±1 as common factors is that these are the only two units in $\mathbb{Z}[\sqrt{-2}]$. The best way to see that these are the only units is to use the *norm* $|a|^2$ of an element $a=m+n\sqrt{-2}$, by which we mean the integer

$$|a|^2=m^2+2n^2.$$

(We are thinking of $\mathbb{Z}[\sqrt{-2}]$ as a subset of the complex numbers, and so $|a| = \sqrt{(m^2 + 2n^2)}$ is just the modulus of the number a. A basic property of the modulus of complex numbers is that $|ab| = |a||b|$.) If u is a unit in $\mathbb{Z}[\sqrt{-2}]$ then it has an inverse u^{-1} in $\mathbb{Z}[\sqrt{-2}]$, and $|u|^2|u^{-1}|^2 = |uu^{-1}|^2 = |1|^2 = 1$. It follows that $|u|^2 = 1$, since $|u|^2$ and $|u^{-1}|^2$ have both to be integers. Clearly the only elements u with $|u|^2 = 1$ are $u = 1$ and $u = -1$.

To show that $y + \sqrt{-2}$ and $y - \sqrt{-2}$ are coprime, suppose that $r + s\sqrt{-2}$ is a common factor. So $r + s\sqrt{-2}$ divides both their sum $2y$ and their difference $2\sqrt{-2}$. It follows that $|r + s\sqrt{-2}|^2$ divides both $|2y|^2$ and $|2\sqrt{-2}|^2$. In other words $r^2 + 2s^2$ divides $4y^2$, and $r^2 + 2s^2$ divides 8. Since y is not even, we can deduce that $r^2 + 2s^2$ divides 4. Therefore the only possibilities for r and s are: $r = \pm 1$, $s = 0$; $r = 0$, $s = \pm 1$; $r = \pm 2$, $s = 0$. Only for the first of these possibilities is $r + s\sqrt{-2}$ a common divisor of $y + \sqrt{-2}$ and $y - \sqrt{-2}$. Hence $y + \sqrt{-2}$ and $y - \sqrt{-2}$ are coprime.

Since the product $(y + \sqrt{-2})(y - \sqrt{-2})$ is a cube, it is tempting to conclude that each of $(y + \sqrt{-2})$ and $(y - \sqrt{-2})$ must be cubes. (Such a conclusion is valid, but maybe not so obvious. We'll come back to it later.) Suppose that

$$y + \sqrt{-2} = (i + j\sqrt{-2})^3$$

where i and j are integers. By equating the coefficients of $\sqrt{-2}$ we find that

$$1 = j(3i^2 - 2j^2).$$

Thus $j = 1$ and $i = \pm 1$. It follows that $y = \pm 5$ and $x = 3$. So we have almost proved the following result (due originally to Fermat).

Theorem 1.1.   *The only integer solutions of $y^2 + 2 = x^3$ are $y = \pm 5$ and $x = 3$.*

The gap in our proof is that we have not justified the claim that the product of two coprime elements a, b in $\mathbb{Z}[\sqrt{-2}]$ is a cube only if both a and b are cubes. Our justificiation of the analogous claim for a, b two coprime elements of $\mathbb{Z}$ relied on the fact that any integer can be written as a product of prime integers, and that (up to the sign and order of the primes) this product is unique. We need to show that this unique factorization property of $\mathbb{Z}$ is also possessed by $\mathbb{Z}[\sqrt{-2}]$.

There are several ways to define a prime integer in $\mathbb{Z}$. One definition is that p is prime if $p \neq \pm 1$ and if the only way to write p as a product of integers $p = ab$ is to choose either $a = \pm 1$ or $b = \pm 1$. So p is *prime* means that p is in some sense *irreducible*. We shall say that an element p in $\mathbb{Z}[\sqrt{-2}]$ is *irreducible* if $p \neq \pm 1$ and $p = ab$ with $a, b \in \mathbb{Z}[\sqrt{-2}]$ only if $a = \pm 1$ or $b = \pm 1$. The gap in our proof of Theorem 1.1 will be bridged if we can show that any element $a \neq \pm 1$ of $\mathbb{Z}[\sqrt{-2}]$ can be written as a product of irreducible elements, and that this product is unique (up to sign and order).

To see that there really is something to prove, let us consider the set of complex numbers $\mathbb{Z}[\sqrt{-5}] = \{m + n\sqrt{-5}: m, n \in \mathbb{Z}\}$. This set, like $\mathbb{Z}[\sqrt{-2}]$, is an integral domain with identity. Note that 6, 2, 3, $1 + \sqrt{-5}$, $1 - \sqrt{-5}$ are all in $\mathbb{Z}[\sqrt{-5}]$, and that

$$6 = 2.3 = (1 + \sqrt{-5})(1 - \sqrt{-5}).$$

Our definition of *irreducible element* which we gave for $\mathbb{Z}[\sqrt{-2}]$ works equally well for $\mathbb{Z}[\sqrt{-5}]$. In $\mathbb{Z}[\sqrt{-5}]$ the element $1 + \sqrt{-5}$ is irreducible. For, suppose that $1 + \sqrt{-5} = ab$ with $a, b \in \mathbb{Z}[\sqrt{-5}]$. Then $6 = |1 + \sqrt{-5}|^2 = |a|^2|b|^2$, where

$$|m + n\sqrt{-5}|^2 = m^2 + 5n^2.$$

It follows, by considering the possible values of $|a|^2$ and $|b|^2$, that either $|a| = 1$ or $|b| = 1$. Hence either $a = \pm 1$ or $b = \pm 1$. A similar argument shows that the elements 2, 3, $1 - \sqrt{-5}$ are also irreducible in $\mathbb{Z}[\sqrt{-5}]$. Therefore in $\mathbb{Z}[\sqrt{-5}]$ the element 6 can be written as a product of irreducibles in two quite different ways.

The usual proof of the unique factorization property of $\mathbb{Z}$, due to Euclid, is based on the fact that for any two integers a, b there exist integers q, r such that

$$a = qb + r \qquad \text{with} \qquad |r| < |b|. \tag{1.3}$$

The idea behind the proof is to use this division property to produce an algorithm which, for any two integers a, b, yields their highest common factor d together with two integers s, t such that $d = sa + tb$. From this it is deduced that if a prime integer p divides a product of integers ab, then either p divides a or p divides b. This last result is then used to prove that essentially there is only one way to express an integer as a product of primes. The details of Euclid's proof can be found in any introductory text on number theory, and in essence are contained in our proof of Theorem 1.3 below.

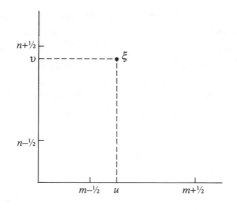

Fig. 1.1.

If we are to modify Euclid's proof so that it works for $\mathbb{Z}[\sqrt{-2}]$, we must first show that for any a, b in $\mathbb{Z}[\sqrt{-2}]$ there exist elements q, r in $\mathbb{Z}[\sqrt{-2}]$ such that a version of equation (1.3) holds. For an element $x \in \mathbb{Z}[\sqrt{-2}]$ the modulus $|x|$ is not in general an integer. The quantity $|x|^2$ is however always an integer, and so it will be convenient to use $|x|^2$ instead of $|x|$.

Theorem 1.2. *For any non-zero elements a, b in $\mathbb{Z}[\sqrt{-2}]$ there are elements q, r in $\mathbb{Z}[\sqrt{-2}]$ such that $a = qb + r$ with $|r|^2 < |b|^2$.*

Proof. Consider the subset $\mathbb{Q}[\sqrt{-2}] = \{u + v\sqrt{-2}: u, v \in \mathbb{Q}\}$ of the complex numbers. This subset, under the usual addition and multiplication of complex numbers, is a commutative ring with identity. Moreover, note that for any non-zero element ξ in $\mathbb{Q}[\sqrt{-2}]$ the inverse ξ^{-1} is also in $\mathbb{Q}[\sqrt{-2}]$. So $\mathbb{Q}[\sqrt{-2}]$ is in fact a field. Consider the following claim.

Claim. *For all ξ in $\mathbb{Q}[\sqrt{-2}]$ there is an element c in $\mathbb{Z}[\sqrt{-2}]$ such that $|\xi - c| < 1$.*

If the claim is true then, by putting $\xi = ab^{-1}$, we are assured of an element c in $\mathbb{Z}[\sqrt{-2}]$ such that $|ab^{-1} - c|^2 < 1$. Multiplying both sides of this inequality by $|b|^2$ we find $|a - bc|^2 < |b|^2$. The theorem then follows by setting $q = c$ and $r = a - bc$.

To prove the claim let ξ be any element in $\mathbb{Q}[\sqrt{-2}]$. Then $\xi = u + v\sqrt{-2}$, say, with u, v in $\mathbb{Q}$. We can certainly find integers m, n such that $|u - m| \leqslant \frac{1}{2}$ and $|v - n| \leqslant \frac{1}{2}$, as illustrated in Fig. 1.1. Let $c = m + n\sqrt{-2}$. Then

$$|\xi - c|^2 = |(u - m) + (v - n)\sqrt{-2}|^2 = (u - m)^2 + 2(v - n)^2 \leqslant \tfrac{1}{4} + \tfrac{1}{2} < 1. \blacksquare$$

There are two things to notice about the proof of Theorem 1.2. Firstly, it can be adapted to provide an analogous theorem in which $\mathbb{Z}[\sqrt{-2}]$ is replaced by the ring $\mathbb{Z}[\sqrt{-1}]$ known as the *Gaussian integers*. Secondly, the proof cannot be adapted to the situation in which $\mathbb{Z}[\sqrt{-2}]$ is replaced by $\mathbb{Z}[\sqrt{-5}]$. (The reader should justify these two assertions.) This gives us reason to hope that $\mathbb{Z}[\sqrt{-2}]$, and also $\mathbb{Z}[\sqrt{-1}]$, will have the unique factorization property, even though $\mathbb{Z}[\sqrt{-5}]$ does not have it.

Instead of merely adapting Euclid's proof of unique factorization in $\mathbb{Z}$ to a proof of unique factorization in $\mathbb{Z}[\sqrt{-2}]$ we shall be a bit more ambitious. We shall aim for a general result which simultaneously implies unique factorization in $\mathbb{Z}$, $\mathbb{Z}[\sqrt{-2}]$, and $\mathbb{Z}[\sqrt{-1}]$. In fact we shall be even more ambitious. For, consider the ring $\mathbb{R}[x]$ of real polynomials in the indeterminate x. Such a polynomial has the form

$$a(x) = a_0 + a_1 x + a_2 x^2 + \cdots + a_n x^n$$

where $a_0, \ldots, a_n \in \mathbb{R}$; if $a_n \neq 0$ we say that the *degree* of $a(x)$ is n, and write $\deg(a(x)) = n$. We have already noted in Chapter 0 that $\mathbb{R}[x]$ is an integral domain with identity. The long division algorithm, which is the usual method for dividing one number by another (in the absence of an electronic calculator!) can be applied in $\mathbb{R}[x]$. For instance, if

$$a(x) = 2x^5 + x^4 + x^3 + 2x^2 + 2x + 4$$
$$b(x) = x^3 + 1$$

then, to divide $a(x)$ by $b(x)$ we proceed as follows:

$$
\begin{array}{r}
2x^2 + x + 1 \\
x^3+1 \overline{)\,2x^5 + x^4 + x^3 + 2x^2 + 2x + 4} \\
\underline{2x^5 \qquad\qquad\quad + 2x^2} \\
x^4 + x^3 \qquad\quad + 2x + 4 \\
\underline{x^4 \qquad\qquad\quad + x} \\
x^3 \qquad\quad + x + 4 \\
\underline{x^3 \qquad\qquad\quad + 1} \\
x + 3
\end{array}
$$

This calculation shows that

$$\frac{a(x)}{b(x)} = 1 + x + 2x^2 + \frac{3+x}{1+x^3}.$$

The long division algorithm ensures that for any two real polynomials $a(x)$, $b(x)$ there exist real polynomials $q(x)$, $r(x)$ such that

$$a(x) = q(x)b(x) + r(x) \qquad \text{with } r(x) = 0 \quad \text{or} \quad \deg(r(x)) < \deg(b(x)).$$

So it would be realistic (and useful for later purposes) to aim for a version of Euclid's result which is sufficiently general to imply unique factorization in $\mathbb{Z}$, $\mathbb{Z}[\sqrt{-1}]$, $\mathbb{Z}[\sqrt{-2}]$, and in $\mathbb{R}[x]$. To do this we need a few abstract algebraic definitions.

Recall that an element u in a ring R with identity is a *unit* if there is an element u^{-1} in R such that $u \circ u^{-1} = u^{-1} \circ u = 1$. We shall say that an element c in R is *irreducible* if c is not a unit and if $c = a \circ b$ implies that either a or b is a unit.

A ring R is a *unique factorization domain* if it is an integral domain with identity such that:

(UFD1) any non-zero element is either a unit or a product of irreducible elements; and

(UFD2) if $p_1, \ldots, p_m, q_1, \ldots, q_n$ are irreducible elements such that $p_1 \circ \cdots \circ p_m = q_1 \circ \cdots \circ q_n$, then $m = n$ and there is a permutation ρ of the first n natural numbers such that $p_i = u_i q_{\rho(i)}$ with u_i a unit for each i.

A ring R is a *Euclidean domain* if it is an integral domain containing at least one non-zero element such that there is a function $\phi: R \backslash \{0\} \to \mathbb{N}$ from the non-zero elements of R into the natural numbers $\mathbb{N} = \{1, 2, 3, \ldots\}$ which, for all $a, b \in R \backslash \{0\}$, satisfies:

(E1) $\phi(a) \leqslant \phi(a \circ b)$;

(E2) there are elements q, r in R such that

$$a = q \circ b + r \qquad \text{with } r = 0 \quad \text{or} \quad \phi(r) < \phi(b).$$

The rings $\mathbb{Z}$, $\mathbb{Z}[\sqrt{-1}]$, and $\mathbb{Z}[\sqrt{-2}]$ are examples of Euclidean domains with $\phi = |\ |^2$. The ring $\mathbb{R}[x]$ is a Euclidean domain with, for $a(x)$ any non-zero polynomial, $\phi(a(x)) = \text{degree}(a(x)) + 1$.

To complete our proof of Theorem 1.1 we need to prove the following theorem. We give the proof as a sequence of seven claims.

Theorem 1.3. *Every Euclidean domain is a unique factorization domain.*

To make the proof more elegant we shall use the notion of an *ideal*, by which we mean a non-empty subset I of a ring R with the property that for all elements a, b in I and all elements r in R the sum $a + b$ is in I, and the products ra, ar are in I. We write $I \trianglelefteq R$ to mean I is an ideal in R. For example, $2\mathbb{Z} \trianglelefteq \mathbb{Z}$. More generally for any commutative ring R and any element a in R the set

$$(a) = \{ra : r \in R\}$$

is an ideal in R; the ideal (a) is said to be *generated* by the element a. The ideal $(0) = \{0\}$ is called the *zero ideal*.

In all the following claims R denotes an arbitrary Euclidean domain. A non-zero element a in an ideal I in R is said to be *minimal* in I if $\phi(a) \leqslant \phi(b)$ for all non-zero b in I.

Claim 1. *Every ideal I in R, other than the zero ideal, contains a minimal element. An element a generates I if and only if it is minimal in I.*

Proof. The set $\{n \in \mathbb{N} : n = \phi(a) \text{ for some } a \in I\}$ is non-empty if I is not the zero ideal, and hence contains a least integer n_0. Any a in I satisfying $\phi(a) = n_0$ is a minimal element in I.

Let a be any minimal element in I. Certainly $(a) \subseteq I$. Let b be an arbitrary element in I. If $b = 0$ then $b = 0a \in (a)$. Suppose $b \neq 0$. Then there exist $q, r \in R$ such that $b = qa + r$ with $r = 0$ or $\phi(r) < \phi(a)$. Now $r = b - qa$ is an element in I since it is the sum of two elements, b and $(-q)a$, both in I. Since a is minimal, we must have $r = 0$. Hence $b \in (a)$. Therefore $I \subseteq (a)$ and consequently $I = (a)$.

Conversely if $I = (a)$ then for any b in I we have $b = ra$ and so $\phi(a) \leqslant \phi(ra) = \phi(b)$. Thus a is minimal. ∎

Claim 2. *There is an identity element in R. Moreover, an element a in R is a unit if and only if a is minimal in R.*

Proof. As R is an ideal of itself, it follows from Claim 1 that there is a minimal element u in R such that any element b in R is of the form $b'u$. In particular $u = u'u$. So for any b we have $u'b = u'b'u = u'ub' = ub' = b'u = b$. Thus u' is the identity element 1.

For any unit a in R we have $\phi(a) \leqslant \phi(aa^{-1}) = \phi(1)$. Since 1 is minimal in R it follows that a is minimal in R. Conversely, if a is minimal in R then a generates R and, since 1 is in R, there must be an element a^{-1} in R such that $aa^{-1} = 1$. Hence a is a unit. ∎

Claim 3. *Let a, b be non-zero elements in R and suppose that b is not a unit. Then $\phi(a) < \phi(ab)$.*

Proof. Certainly $\phi(a) \le \phi(ab)$. If $\phi(a) = \phi(ab)$ then ab is a minimal element in the ideal (a). It follows from Claim 1 that $(ab) = (a)$. Thus $a = uab$ for some u in R. Since R is an integral domain the identity $(1 - ub)a = 0$ implies that $1 = ub$. This in turn implies that b is a unit. This is a contradiction, and so $\phi(ab) \ne \phi(a)$. ∎

Claim 4. *Any non-zero element in R is either a unit or a finite product of irreducible elements.*

Proof. Let u be a minimal element in R. Then by Claim 1 we have $R = (u)$. So in particular $1 = u'u$ for some u' in R. This implies that u is a unit. We shall work by induction on $\phi(u)$, the inductive hypothesis being that the claim is true for all elements u in R with $\phi(u) < n$. Let c be an element with $\phi(c) = n$. Suppose c is reducible. Then $c = ab$ with a, b non-units in R. It follows from Claim 3 that $\phi(a) < n$ and $\phi(b) < n$. Hence both a and b are finite products of irreducibles. Therefore $c = ab$ is a finite product of irreducibles. The claim follows by induction. ∎

For elements a, b, d in R we shall say that d *divides* a if there is an element c in R such that $a = cd$; we shall say that d is a *highest common factor* of a and b if d divides both a and b and if, in addition, any other element d' which divides both a and b also divides d. For example, in $\mathbb{Z}$ the integers 4 and -4 are both highest common factors of 8 and 12.

Claim 5. *Any non-zero elements a, b in R have a highest common factor d. Moreover there exist elements r, s in R such that $d = ra + sb$.*

Proof. The set $I = \{ra + sb : r, s \in R\}$ is an ideal in R. By Claim 1 there is an element d in R such that $I = (d)$. We need to prove that d is a highest common factor of a and b. Certainly a and b are both in I, and are thus both multiples of d. So d divides both a and b. Suppose d' also divides a and b, say $a = a'd'$ and $b = b'd'$. For some r, s we have $d = ra + sb = (ra' + sb')d'$, and hence d' divides d. ∎

Claim 6. *Let p, a, b be elements in R such that p is an irreducible element which divides ab. Then p divides either a or b.*

Proof. Suppose p does not divide a. Then 1 is a highest common factor of p and a. Therefore there exist elements r, s in R such that $1 = rp + sa$. Suppose $tp = ab$ for some t in R. Then $b = brp + bsa = brp + tps = (br + ts)p$. That is, p divides b.

Claim 7. *If $p_1, \ldots, p_m, q_1, \ldots, q_n$ are irreducible elements such that $p_1 p_2 \cdots p_m = q_1 q_2 \cdots q_n$, then $m = n$ and there is a permutation ρ of the first n natural numbers such that $p_i = u_i q_{\rho(i)}$ with u_i a unit for each i.*

Proof. If $m = 1$ then, since p_1 is irreducible, we must have $n = 1$ and $p_1 = q_1$. Suppose, for some natural number M, the claim is true for all $m < M$. Suppose $p_1, \ldots, p_M, q_1, \ldots, q_n$ are irreducible elements such that $p_1 p_2 \cdots p_M = q_1 q_2 \cdots q_n$. Certainly p_M divides $q_1(q_2 \cdots q_n)$. By Claim 6 either p_M divides q_1 or p_M divides $(q_2 \cdots q_n)$. If the latter is the case then either p_M divides q_2 or p_M divides $(q_3 \cdots q_n)$. Continuing the argument we see that p_M divides some q_j. Without loss of generality we can assume that $j = n$. Thus $p_M = u_M q_n$ say. The irreducibility of p_M implies u_M is a unit. We now have

$$p_1 p_2 \cdots p_M = (q_1 q_2 \cdots q_{n-1}) u_M^{-1} p_M.$$

Consequently

$$(p_1 p_2 \cdots p_{M-1} - (u_M^{-1} q_1) q_2 \cdots q_{n-1}) p_M = 0.$$

This means that $p_1 p_2 \cdots p_{M-1} = (u_M^{-1} q_1) q_2 \cdots q_{n-1}$. By the inductive hypothesis $M - 1 = n - 1$ and there is a permutation ρ such that $p_i = u_i q_{\rho(i)}$ with u_i a unit for $1 \leqslant i \leqslant n - 1$. The claim follows by induction. ∎

Claims 4 and 7 together prove Theorem 1.3. We leave as an exercise for the reader the proof, based on Theorem 1.3, that the product ab of two coprime elements a and b in a Euclidean domain is a cube only if both a and b are cubes. (*Coprime* can be taken to mean that all common divisors of a and b are units.) Since $\mathbb{Z}[\sqrt{-2}]$ is a Euclidean domain, this completes the proof of Theorem 1.1.

Exercises

1. By factoring 6 show that $\mathbb{Z}[\sqrt{-6}]$ is not a unique factorization domain. Prove in a similar way that $\mathbb{Z}[\sqrt{-10}]$ is not a unique factorization domain.

2. In $\mathbb{Z}[\sqrt{-2}]$ express $1 + 4\sqrt{-2}$ and 11 as products of irreducible elements. Find a single element which generates the ideal $I = \{11r + (1 + 4\sqrt{-2})s : r, s \in \mathbb{Z}[\sqrt{-2}]\}$.

3. In $\mathbb{Z}[x]$ find a highest common factor of $x^3 - 1$ and $x^3 + x^2 - x - 1$.

4. Show that 5 factorizes uniquely into irreducibles in $\mathbb{Z}[\sqrt{-5}]$ even though $\mathbb{Z}[\sqrt{-5}]$ is not a unique factorization domain.

5. Let $p \geq 2$ be an integer and $I = (p)$ the ideal in $\mathbb{Z}$ generated by p. Show that p is a prime number if and only if I has the following property: a product ab of integers is in I implies either $a \in I$ or $b \in I$.

6. Let R be an integral domain with identity. In view of Exercise 5 we say that a non-zero element $p \in R$ is *prime* in R if the ideal $I = (p)$ does not contain 1, and has the following property: for $a, b \in R$ the product ab is in I only if either $a \in I$ or $b \in I$. Prove that any prime element is irreducible.

7. Find an irreducible element in $\mathbb{Z}[\sqrt{-5}]$ which is not prime.

8. An integral domain R with identity is said to be a *principal ideal domain* if every ideal I in R is of the form $I = (a)$ for some $a \in I$. (Claim 1 states that every Euclidean domain is a principal ideal domain.) Prove that an element in a principal ideal domain is prime if and only if it is irreducible.

9. An ideal I in a ring R is *maximal* if $I \neq R$ and the only ideals $J \trianglelefteq R$ containing I are $J = I$ and $J = R$. In a principal ideal domain R show that an element $a \in R$ is prime if the ideal (a) generated by a is maximal.

10. Prove that every principal ideal domain is a unique factorization domain. (Hint: since the proof of Claims 5, 6, and 7 remain valid for any principal ideal domain R, it only needs to be shown that every non-zero non-unit x is a finite product of prime elements. Suppose x is not a product of primes. Zorn's lemma, which is stated in the preliminary chapter, can be used to show that x is contained in a maximal ideal $I_1 = (p_1)$. So $x = x_1 p_1$ with p_1 a prime. For any natural number n we can write $x = x_n p_n p_{n-1} \cdots p_1$ with each p_i a prime. Let I_∞ be the union of the ideals $(x_1) \subseteq (x_2) \subseteq (x_3) \cdots$. Since I_∞ is an ideal we have $I_\infty = (b)$ for some $b \in I$. Show that $b \in (x_n)$ for some n and deduce a contradiction.)

11. Let $\theta = (1 + \sqrt{-19})/2$ and let $\mathbb{Z}[\theta] = \{m + n\theta : m, n \in \mathbb{Z}\}$. The ring $\mathbb{Z}[\theta]$ is a principal ideal domain but is not a Euclidean domain. A readable proof of this is contained in the *American Mathematical Monthly*, **95**, No. 9, p. 868.

12. Show that the only integer solutions of $y^2 + 4 = z^3$ are $y = \pm 11$, $z = 5$ or $y = \pm 2$, $z = 2$. (Hint: first do the case y odd. Factorize the equation $(2 + y\sqrt{-1})(2 - y\sqrt{-1}) = z^3$ and deduce that $2 + y\sqrt{-1} = (a + b\sqrt{-1})^3$, $2 - y\sqrt{-1} = (a - b\sqrt{-1})^3$ for some integers a, b. For the case y even suppose that $y = 2Y$, $z = 2Z$ and consider the equation $Y^2 + 1 = 2Z^3$. Deduce that Y is odd and that $1 + Y\sqrt{-1} = (1 + \sqrt{-1})(a + b\sqrt{-1})$ for some integers a, b.)

2 Construction of projective planes

In this chapter we turn our attention to rings with only a finite number of elements, and in particular to finite fields. (Recall that a field is a commutative ring with identity $1 \neq 0$ in which each non-zero element has a multiplicative inverse.) Finite fields play an important role in many branches of mathematics. We begin by showing how the existence of certain finite fields leads, via projective geometry, to the solution of a particular problem in combinatorial mathematics. We then go on to investigate the existence of finite fields. Several of the concepts that we introduce in connection with finite fields will be of use when we later turn our attention to infinite fields. For this reason we give definitions in more generality than at first glance seems necessary.

The combinatorial problem we consider is the following. Suppose that an agricultural agency wants to compare a number v of fertilizers. The agency invites the same number v of farmers to participate in a comparative test. It is not practicable to ask each farmer to assess every fertilizer, and it is decided that for a feasible and meaningful test:

(1) each farmer should be asked to assess a number of fertilizers, the number being the same for each farmer;

(2) each pair of fertilizers should be assessed by exactly one common farmer;

(3) each pair of farmers should assess exactly one common fertilizer.

The problem is to find values of v for which such a test can be carried out. (This type of problem is of great interest to statisticians, and belongs to a branch of mathematics known as combinatorial design theory.)

Suppose for instance that $v = 7$ in the problem, that the farmers are numbered from 1 to 7, and that the fertilizers are labelled from A to G. Then the test can be run by giving three fertilizers to each farmer as follows:

1: $\{A, B, C\}$ 2: $\{A, D, F\}$ 3: $\{B, D, E\}$ 4: $\{A, E, G\}$
5: $\{C, E, F\}$ 6: $\{B, F, G\}$ 7: $\{C, D, G\}$.

This assignment has the nice pictorial representation shown in Fig. 2.1 in which farmers are represented by lines (six straight lines and one circular line) and fertilizers by points. Note that each pair of points lies

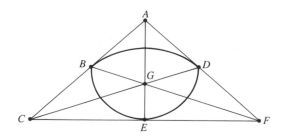

Fig. 2.1.

on exactly one line, and that each pair of lines has exactly one point in common. In general, our combinatorial problem is just one of drawing v lines between v points such that each pair of points has exactly one line in common, and each pair of lines has exactly one point in common. This is related to projective geometry.

Roughly speaking, projective geometry is the study of geometric properties that are preserved under projections. The impetus for the formal development of the subject came from Renaissance artists. In the process of depicting objects and scenes on canvas, considerable distortion takes place. Lengths, areas, and angles may be changed, yet still the identity of the original is unmistakable. Projective geometry is concerned with those geometric properties retained by the canvas image.

To get a feel for which geometric properties are, or are not retained, imagine that on some plane M in three-dimensional space $\mathbb{R}^3$ an equilateral triangle is inscribed in a circle. If another plane M' is placed between M and the origin $(0, 0, 0)$, as shown in Fig. 2.2, then the image on M' of the inscribed triangle, when viewed from the origin, may be that of a non-equilateral triangle inscribed in an ellipse. This illustrates for example that triangles and conics are preserved by projections and are thus allowable notions in projective geometry, whereas equilateral triangles and circles are not always preserved and are therefore not notions used in projective geometry.

Any point P on the plane M corresponds to a point P' on M', the correspondence being such that the straight line containing P and P' passes though the origin. We can thus think of any line in $\mathbb{R}^3$ through the origin as being a *projective point*. (A more precise definition will follow.) Any geometric figure on M gives rise to a corresponding set of projective points. In particular a straight line on M gives rise to a set of projective points constituting a plane in $\mathbb{R}^3$ containing the origin. Thus we can think of planes in $\mathbb{R}^3$ containing the origin, as being *projective lines*. (A more precise definition will follow.) After a little practice at visualizing projective lines and points it becomes clear that every pair of distinct projective lines is incident with a unique projective point, and every pair of distinct projective points is incident with a unique projective line. Lines in $\mathbb{R}^3$ through the origin which are parallel to M can be thought of as *projective points at infinity*.

The projective points and lines obtained from $\mathbb{R}^3$ have obvious properties in common with the points and lines in our pictorial representation of the assignment of fertilizers to farmers. We shall exploit this similarity.

The ring $\mathbb{R}$ of real numbers has infinitely many elements, and consequently we obtain infinitely many projective points and lines from $\mathbb{R}^3$. In order to construct a finite set of projective points and lines it should be possible to replace $\mathbb{R}$ by a suitable finite ring K and work in K^3 instead of in $\mathbb{R}^3$. It is known from linear algebra that much of the theory of linear equations over $\mathbb{R}$ (and in particular the theory of lines and planes in $\mathbb{R}^3$) can be extended to linear equations over an arbitrary field K. We should therefore be able to construct projective points and lines from an arbitrary field K, and in particular from an arbitrary finite field K.

For any positive integer m we have seen in Chapter 0 how to construct the finite ring $\mathbb{Z}_m$ of m elements. It was observed that for some m, such as $m = 3$ and $m = 5$, the ring $\mathbb{Z}_m$ is a finite field. It follows from parts (i) and (ii) of Exercise 1 at the end of this chapter that $\mathbb{Z}_m$ is a

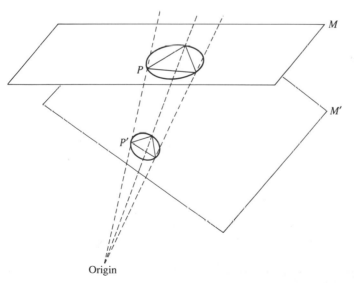

Fig. 2.2.

field if and only if m is a prime number. (No reader should attempt to read past this point before tackling both parts of this exercise.)

Our hope then, is that by taking $K = \mathbb{Z}_p$ with p a prime, we should be able to construct finite sets of projective points and lines.

Let K be a field. Given an ordered triple (x_0, x_1, x_2) with each x_i an element of K, and with at least one $x_i \neq 0$, we shall let $[x_0, x_1, x_2]$ denote the set $\{(ax_0, ax_1, ax_2): a \in K\}$ of ordered triples. We shall call $[x_0, x_1, x_2]$ a *projective point* over K.

Note that for any non-zero b in K the projective point $[x_0, x_1, x_2]$ is equal to the projective point $[bx_0, bx_1, bx_2]$. To see this, note that any element (abx_0, abx_1, abx_2) of $[bx_0, bx_1, bx_2]$ is also an element of $[x_0, x_1, x_2]$. Conversely any element $(ax_0, ax_1, ax_2) = (ab^{-1}bx_0, ab^{-1}bx_1, ab^{-1}bx_2)$ of $[x_0, x_1, x_2]$ is also an element of $[bx_0, bx_1, bx_2]$. Hence $[x_0, x_1, x_2] = [bx_0, bx_1, bx_2]$.

By a *projective line* over K we shall mean a collection of projective points $[x_0, x_1, x_2]$ whose coordinates simultaneously satisfy an equation of the form $ax_0 + bx_1 + cx_2 = 0$ for some fixed elements a, b, c in K not all of which are zero. That is, the set of projective points $\{[x_0, x_1, x_2]: ax_0 + bx_1 + cx_2 = 0\}$ is a projective line if a, b, c are not all zero. Note that the equation $ax_0 + bx_1 + cx_2 = 0$ represents the same projective line as the equation $dax_0 + dbx_1 + dcx_2 = 0$ for any non-zero d in the field K.

We shall denote by PG(2, K) the collection of projective lines and projective points over K. In this notation PG stands for projective geometry, and the 2 is there because we are dealing with (projective) planes.

As an example let us take $K = \mathbb{Z}_2$. This is a field since 2 is prime. We let 0 and 1 denote the two elements of $\mathbb{Z}_2$. There are just seven distinct projective points:

$A = [0, 0, 1]$ $B = [0, 1, 0]$ $C = [0, 1, 1]$ $D = [1, 0, 0]$

$E = [1, 1, 0]$ $F = [1, 0, 1]$ $G = [1, 1, 1]$.

There are also seven distinct projective lines, each containing three projective points. For instance, the equation $x_2 = 0$ represents the projective line $\{B, D, E\}$, the equation $x_0 = 0$ represents the projective line $\{A, B, C\}$, and the equation $x_0 + x_1 + x_2 = 0$ represents the projective line $\{C, E, F\}$. We denote a projective line such as $\{B, D, E\}$ more succinctly by BDE. In this notation the projective lines of PG(2, $\mathbb{Z}_2$) are:

ABC ADF BDE AEG CEF BFG CDG.

Compare these projective lines with our solution to the fertilizer assignment problem for $v = 7$.

As another example let us take $K = \mathbb{Z}_3 = \{0, 1, 2\}$, which again is a field because 3 is prime. There are 13 projective points in PG(2, $\mathbb{Z}_3$):

$A = [0, 0, 1]$ $B = [0, 1, 0]$ $C = [0, 1, 1]$ $D = [0, 1, 2]$ $E = [1, 0, 0]$

$F = [1, 0, 1]$ $G = [1, 0, 2]$ $H = [1, 1, 0]$ $I = [1, 1, 1]$

$J = [1, 1, 2]$ $K = [1, 2, 0]$ $L = [1, 2, 1]$ $M = [1, 2, 2]$.

There are also 13 projective lines over $\mathbb{Z}_3$, each containing four projective points. For instance, the equation $x_2 = 0$ represents the projective line $BEHK$, the equation $x_1 - 0$ represents the projective line $AEFG$, and the equation $x_0 + 2x_1 + 2x_2 = 0$ represents the projective line $DHFM$. The projective lines of PG(2, $\mathbb{Z}_3$) are:

BEHK,   AEFG,   ABCD,   DEJL,   CEIM,   BGJM,   BFIL,

AKLM,   DGIK,   CFJK,   AHIJ,   CGHL,   DHFM.

We can represent PG(2, $\mathbb{Z}_3$) pictorially, as shown in Fig. 2.3. Note that in this picture each 'line' contains four points, each pair of lines has exactly one common point, and each pair of points has exactly one common line. Thus PG(2, $\mathbb{Z}_3$) explains how 13 fertilizers can be assigned to 13 farmers subject to the given constraints, each farmer being assigned four fertilizers.

At this point in our discussion of the fertilizer assignment problem we should prove that, for any finite field K, the collection of projective points and lines PG(2, K) represents a solution to the problem for some value of v. For this it will be convenient to have some abstract definitions.

A *projection plane* π consists of a set whose elements are called *points*, together with a set whose elements are called *lines*, and also a relation, called *incidence*, between points and lines which satisfies the following axioms:

(1) every pair of distinct lines is incident with a unique point;

(2) every pair of distinct points is incident with a unique line;

(3) there exist four points such that no three of them are incident with a single line.

We use terminology such as 'point P is on line L' and 'line L passes through point P' to mean that P and L are incident.

Axiom (3), in the presence of axioms (1) and (2), is equivalent to the following axiom:

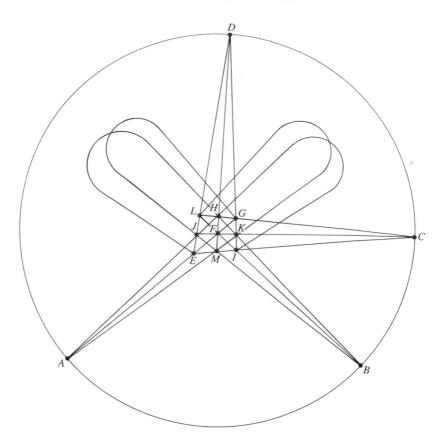

Fig. 2.3.

(4) there exist four distinct lines in a projective plane, no three of
which pass through the same point.

The reader should verify this claim!

Every statement concerning a projective plane has a *dual* statement
obtained by replacing the word 'point' by the word 'line', replacing
'line' by 'point', and replacing expressions such as 'point P is on line L'
by 'line L passes through point P'. If a theorem about projective planes
can be deduced from axioms (1), (2) and (3), then the dual theorem can
also be deduced from these axioms (thanks to the equivalence of (3)
and (4)).

Therorem 2.1.　*If K is a (possibly infinite) field then* PG $(2, K)$ *is a
projective plane.*

Proof. We first have to show that every pair of distinct lines L and L' is incident with a unique point. Suppose that the two lines are represented by the equations $ax_0 + bx_1 + cx_2 = 0$ and $a'x_0 + b'x_1 + c'x_2 = 0$. That is, $L = \{[x_0, x_1, x_2]: ax_0 + bx_1 + cx_2 = 0\}$ and $L' = \{[x_0, x_1, x_2]: a'x_0 + b'x_1 + c'x_2 = 0\}$. Since L and L' are distinct, the triple (a, b, c) is not a scalar multiple of (a', b', c'). A basic result in the theory of linear equations (see any text on linear algebra) asserts that the subset $W = \{(x, y, z): ax + by + cz = 0$ and $a'x + b'y + c'z = 0\}$ of the vector space K^3 is a subsapce generated by a single vector (z_0, z_1, z_2), say. Thus any vector in W is of the form $(\lambda z_0, \lambda z_1, \lambda z_2)$ for λ in K. It follows that $[z_0, z_1, z_2]$ is the unique point of intersection of the line L and L'.

Next we have to show that any two distinct points $[z_0, z_1, z_2]$ and $[z_0', z_1', z_2']$ determine a unique line. Let V be the subspace of K^3 generated by the two vectors (z_0, z_1, z_2) and (z_0', z_1', z_2'). A basic result in the theory of linear equations (again see any text on linear algebra) asserts the existence of an equation $ax_0 + bx_1 + cx_2 = 0$ such that $V = \{(x_0, x_1, x_2) \in K^3: ax_0 + bx_1 + cx_2 = 0\}$. The unique line determined by the two points is thus $L = \{[x_0, x_1, x_2]: ax_0 + bx_1 + cx_2 = 0\}$.

Finally, since any field K contains both a zero element 0 and identity element 1, we have the four points: $A = [1, 0, 0]$, $B = [0, 1, 0]$, $C[0, 0, 1]$, $D = [1, 1, 1]$. The equation $x_2 = 0$ represents line AB, and point C does not satisfy this equation; hence points A, B, and C are not incident with a common line. Similarly it can be checked that no other three of the four points are incident with a common line. ∎

In order to complete the proof that, for any finite field K, the projective plane $PG(2, K)$ provides a solution to our problem of assigning fertilizers to farmers, we need to show that each line in $PG(2, K)$ is incident with the same number v of points. The following theorem does this.

Theorem 2.2 *Let P and P' be two distinct points and let L and L' be two distinct lines in an arbitrary projective plane π. There are bijections between the points on L and the points on L', between the lines through P and the lines through P', and between the points on L and the lines through P.*

Proof. For points Q and Q' in π let QQ' denote the unique line through Q and Q'. We shall begin the proof by showing that there exists a point O not on L or L'. Suppose all points of π were on L or L'. Then there would be points A, B on L and points C, D on L' such that A, B, C, D satisfy axiom (3). Let E be the unique point of intersection of AC and BD. By supposition E would have to lie on L or L'. Without loss of generality, suppose E were on L. Axiom (1) would then imply $A = E$, and thus contradict axiom (3). Our supposition has to be false. Therefore we can take O to be a point incident with neither L nor L'.

If Q is a point on L then the line OQ passes through a unique point Q' on L'. This gives us a bijection $Q \leftrightarrow Q'$ between the points on L and the points on L'. The second assertion of the theorem is the dual of the first, and thus needs no proof.

The third assertion is proved by first considering the case when P is a point not on the line L. Then every point Q on L determines a unique line PQ, and conversely every line through P determines by intersection with L a unique point Q on L. If P does lie on L then choose a point O not on L. The lines through P are bijective with the lines through O, and as we have already seen, the lines through O are bijective with the points on L.   ∎

A projective plane π is said to be *finite* of *order q* if there are only a finite number of points in π, and the totality of points on some line of π is $q + 1$. For example, PG$(2, \mathbb{Z}_3)$ is finite of order 3. The next theorem and corollary tell us those values of v for which we have solved our problem of assigning fertilizers to farmers.

Theorem 2.3.   *Let π be a projective plane of order q. Then the total number of points (resp. lines) incident with an arbitrary line (resp. point) is $q + 1$. Moreover π has exactly $q^2 + q + 1$ points (resp. lines).*

Proof.   The first assertion (resp. its dual) follows from the preceding theorem. Let O be a point in π. There are exactly $q + 1$ lines through O, and there are exactly q points on each of these lines in addition to O. Hence π has exactly $q(q + 1) + 1$ points. Dually π has exactly $q^2 + q + 1$ lines.   ∎

Corollary 2.4.   *For any prime p the projective plane PG$(2, \mathbb{Z}_p)$ is finite of order p.*

Proof.   In PG$(2, \mathbb{Z}_p)$ the equation $x_2 = 0$ represents the projective line $\{(0, 1, 0), (1, a, 0): a \in \mathbb{Z}_p\}$. There are $p + 1$ projective points in this projective line.   ∎

Theorems 2.1 and 2.3 together with Corollary 2.4 solve our problem of assigning v fertilizers to v farmers for $v = p^2 + p + 1$ with p any prime number. One way of solving the problem for other values of v is to find finite fields which contain q elements with q not a prime. The remainder of this chapter is devoted to the quest for such fields. We begin by looking for certain necessary restrictions on q.

Let K be an arbitrary field. Then K contains the identity element 1. For any positive integer n the sum $1+1+\cdots+1$ of n copies of the identity element is also contained in K; we denote this sum by $\bar{n}$. It is possible that $\bar{n}=0$ for some positive integer n (consider $\bar{3}$ in $K=\mathbb{Z}_3$). If $\bar{n}\neq 0$ for all positive integers n, then K is said to have *characteristic* 0. Otherwise K is said to have *characteristic* p where p is the least positive integer such that $\bar{p}=0$. The fields $\mathbb{Q}$, $\mathbb{R}$, and $\mathbb{C}$ are examples of fields of fields of characteristic 0. For p a prime, the field $\mathbb{Z}_p$ is an example of a field of characteristic p.

If K has characteristic 0 we can identify the rational number m/n in $\mathbb{Q}$, where m, n are positive integers, with the element $\bar{m}\bar{n}^{-1}$ in K, we can identify the rational number $-m/n$ with $-\bar{m}\bar{n}^{-1}$. (The element $\bar{n}^{-1}$ lies in K because every non-zero element of K has a multiplicative inverse, and $-\bar{m}\bar{n}^{-1}$ lies in K because every element of K has an additive inverse.) We can therefore think of $\mathbb{Q}$ as a subset of K and, as $\mathbb{Q}$ is a field, we say that $\mathbb{Q}$ is a *subfield* of K.

In general a subset S of any field K is a *subfield* if it is a field under the operations of addition and multiplication in K. It can be checked (and it is worthwhile doing so) that a subset S of K is a subfield if and only if $a-b$ and ab^{-1} are in S for all a, b in S. The fields $\mathbb{Q}$, $\mathbb{R}$, and $\mathbb{Q}[\sqrt{-2}]$ are all examples of subfields of $\mathbb{C}$.

If K has characteristic p then for any positive integer n we can identify the element $\bar{n}$ in K with the element $\bar{n}$ in $\mathbb{Z}_p$. In this way we can think of $\mathbb{Z}_p$ as a subfield of K. Note that p is necessarily a prime number, for if $p=mn$ with $m,n\geq 2$ then $\bar{m}\bar{n}=0$ and thus, since every field is an integral domain, $\bar{m}-0$ or $\bar{n}=0$. This would contradict the fact that p is the least positive integer such that $\bar{p}=0$.

Note that we have shown that any field K contains either $\mathbb{Q}$ as a subfield, or $\mathbb{Z}_p$ as a subfield for some prime number p. It follows that K can be considered as a vector space over either $\mathbb{Q}$ or $\mathbb{Z}_p$.

More generally, suppose that R is a ring with identity $1\neq 0$ and that S is a *subring* of R. By this we mean that S is a subset of R containing the identity, and that S is a ring under the operations of addition and multiplication in R. If S is a field then we can consider R as a vector space over S. As a concrete illustration of this consider the ring $M_2(\mathbb{Z}_p)$ of 2×2 matrices over $\mathbb{Z}_p$ with p a prime. The subset

$$S=\left\{\begin{pmatrix}\lambda & 0\\ 0 & \lambda\end{pmatrix}:\lambda\in\mathbb{Z}_p\right\}$$

of $M_2(\mathbb{Z}_p)$ is a ring under matrix addition and multiplication; by identifying the matrix $\begin{pmatrix}\lambda & 0\\ 0 & \lambda\end{pmatrix}$ with the element λ, we see that S is just a copy of $\mathbb{Z}_p$ and is thus a field. We can therefore think of $M_2(\mathbb{Z}_p)$ as a vector space over $\mathbb{Z}_p$. The addition in this vector space is just the ring addition. Scalar multiplication of a vector by an element λ in $\mathbb{Z}_p$ is just ring multiplication:

$$\lambda \begin{pmatrix} a & b \\ c & d \end{pmatrix} = \begin{pmatrix} \lambda & 0 \\ 0 & \lambda \end{pmatrix} \begin{pmatrix} a & b \\ c & d \end{pmatrix} = \begin{pmatrix} \lambda a & \lambda b \\ \lambda c & \lambda d \end{pmatrix}.$$

As a vector space over $\mathbb{Z}_p$, the dimension of $M_2(\mathbb{Z}_p)$ is 4; one basis consists of the four matrices

$$e_1 = \begin{pmatrix} 1 & 0 \\ 0 & 0 \end{pmatrix}, \qquad e_2 = \begin{pmatrix} 0 & 1 \\ 0 & 0 \end{pmatrix}, \qquad e_3 = \begin{pmatrix} 0 & 0 \\ 1 & 0 \end{pmatrix}, \qquad e_4 = \begin{pmatrix} 0 & 0 \\ 0 & 1 \end{pmatrix}.$$

Any matrix v in $M_2(\mathbb{Z}_p)$ can be uniquely expressed as

$$v = \lambda_1 e_1 + \lambda_2 e_2 + \lambda_3 e_3 + \lambda_4 e_4$$

with $\lambda_i \in \mathbb{Z}_p$. There are precisely p^4 such expressions since there are p possible choices for each λ_i in the expression. This corresponds to the fact that there are p^4 matrices in $M_2(\mathbb{Z}_p)$.

The above analysis of the particular ring $M_2(\mathbb{Z}_p)$ carries over to the case of an arbitrary finite field $\mathbb{F}$. Since the field $\mathbb{Q}$ has infinitely many elements, and since any field must contain either $\mathbb{Q}$ or $\mathbb{Z}_p$ as a subfield, it is clear that any finite field $\mathbb{F}$ must contain $\mathbb{Z}_p$ as a subfield for some prime p. We can therefore consider $\mathbb{F}$ as a vector space over the field $\mathbb{Z}_p$. As $\mathbb{F}$ has only finitely many elements it must be of finite dimension over $\mathbb{Z}_p$, with basis $e_1, \ldots, e_n$ say. The elements of $\mathbb{F}$ can be uniquely expressed in the form

$$\lambda_1 e_1 + \lambda_2 e_2 + \cdots + \lambda_n e_n$$

with $\lambda_i \in \mathbb{Z}_p$. There are p choices for each of the n coefficients λ_i, and so we have the following result.

Theorem 2.5. *A finite field $\mathbb{F}$ contains precisely p^n elements for some prime number p and integer $n \geqslant 1$.*

We now aim to prove that for any prime p and positive integer n there exists a field with $q = p^n$ elements. In other words, we aim to show that there is a field $\mathbb{F}$ containing $\mathbb{Z}_p$ as a subfield such that, as a vector space over $\mathbb{Z}_p$, the dimension of $\mathbb{F}$ is n. (The equivalence of these two aims is a consequence of the following exercise: if K is a field of p elements and L is a vector space of dimension n over K, then L has p^n elements.)

In general a field L containing a subfield K is said to be a *field extension* of K of *degree n* if the dimension of L as a vector space over K is n. For example, $\mathbb{C}$ is a field extension of $\mathbb{R}$ of degree 2. We let $L:K$ denote a field extension, and $[L:K]$ the degree. So, for example, we write $\mathbb{C}:\mathbb{R}$ and $[\mathbb{C}:\mathbb{R}]=2$. In this terminology our aim is to construct field extensions of $\mathbb{Z}_p$ of arbitrary degree n.

The construction of field extensions is best motivated by a detailed analysis of the familiar extension $\mathbb{C}:\mathbb{R}$ of degree 2. We can think of the complex numbers as real polynomials in the indeterminate i 'modulo the identity $i^2 = -1$'. The identity $i^2 = -1$ implies the more general identity

$$a_0 + a_1 i + a_2 i^2 + \cdots + a_n i^n = (a_0 - a_2 + a_4 + \cdots) + (a_1 - a_3 + a_5 + \cdots)i$$

for $a_0, \ldots, a_n \in \mathbb{R}$. It follows that any element of $\mathbb{C}$ can be represented by a real constant or a real polynomial in i of degree 1.

This 'construction' of $\mathbb{C}$ from $\mathbb{R}$ can be generalized. To do this we first need to give a precise meaning to the phrase 'modulo the identity $i^2 = -1$'. Consider the ring $\mathbb{R}[x]$ of all real polynomials in the indeterminate x. Let I be the ideal in the ring $\mathbb{R}[x]$ generated by the polynomial $p(x) = x^2 + 1$. That is

$$I = (p(x)) = \{r(x)p(x) : r(x) \in \mathbb{R}[x]\}.$$

For any polynomial $f(x) \in \mathbb{R}[x]$ we can form the *coset*

$$f(x) + I = \{f(x) + r(x)p(x) : r(x) \in \mathbb{R}[x]\}.$$

Thus a coset is a set of polynomials. Note that $p(x) + I = I$. In fact, given polynomials $f(x)$ and $g(x)$ such that $f(x) = g(x) + r(x)p(x)$ for some polynomial $r(x)$, the reader should verify the coset identity $f(x) + I = g(x) + I$. It follows that any two cosets are either identical or have no elements in common. (That is, the cosets form a partition of $\mathbb{R}[x]$ and, as explained in Chapter 0, correspond to an equivalence relation on $\mathbb{R}[x]$.) The reader should also verify that if $f(x) + I = g(x) + I$, then $f(x) = g(x) + r(x)p(x)$ for some polynomial $r(x)$.

We can define an addition and multiplication of cosets as follows:

$$f(x) + I + g(x) + I = (f(x) + g(x)) + I,$$
$$(f(x) + I)(g(x) + I) = f(x)g(x) + I.$$

For example

$$(2+3x)+I+(1+2x)+I=(3+5x)+I,$$

$$((2+3x)+I)((1+2x)+I)=(2+5x+6x^2)+I$$
$$=(-4+5x+6(x^2+1))+I$$
$$=(-14+8x)+I.$$

The addition and multiplication satisfy the axioms of a commutative ring with identity. We denote this ring of cosets by $\mathbb{R}[x]/(x^2+1)$, and refer to it as the ring of real polynomials in x *modulo the identity* $x^2+1=0$. The coset $x+I$ can be identified with the complex number $\sqrt{-1}$; the ring $\mathbb{R}[x]/(x^2+1)$ is thus 'just a copy' of the field of complex numbers $\mathbb{C}$.

It is now fairly routine to generalize the construction of $\mathbb{C}$ from $\mathbb{R}$ to the construction of an extension L of an arbitrary field K of given degree. Let $K[x]$ be the ring of polynomials in the indeterminate x over K. Choose some polynomial $p(x)$ in $K[x]$ of degree n and let $I=(p(x))$ be the ideal generated by $p(x)$. For $f(x)$ in $K[x]$ define the *coset*

$$f(x)+I=\{f(x)+r(x)p(x): r(x)\in K[x]\},$$

and define addition and multiplication of cosets by

$$f(x)+I+g(x)+I=f(x)+g(x)+I,$$
$$(f(x)+I)(g(x)+I)=f(x)g(x)+I.$$

It is readily checked that this addition and multiplication are well defined in the following sense: if $f(x)+I=f(x)'+I$ and $g(x)+I=g(x)'+I$ then

$$f(x)+I+g(x)+I=f(x)+g(x)+I,$$
$$f(x)g(x)+I=f(x)'g(x)'+I.$$

The set of cosets, under this addition and multiplication, form a commutative ring with identity which we denote by $K[x]/(p(x))$.

Note that for any $f(x)$ in the Euclidean domain $K[x]$ we can (by definition of a Euclidean domain) find polynomials $q(x)$ and $r(x)$ in $K[x]$ such that

$$r(x)=f(x)-q(x)p(x)$$

with $r(x) = 0$ or $\deg(r(x)) < \deg(p(x)) = n$, and hence such that

$$f(x) + I = r(x) + I.$$

Note also that if $r(x)$ and $r'(x)$ are two distinct polynomials of degree $<n$ then their difference cannot be a multiple of $p(x)$ and hence the cosets $r(x) + I$ and $r'(x) + I$ must be distinct. This means that the elements of $K[x]/(p(x))$ are represented by the polynomials of degree $<n$ in $K[x]$. Since each element of K can be considered as a constant polynomial, the ring $K[x]/(p(x))$ contains K as a subfield. Therefore $K[x]$ can be considered as a vector space over K (of dimension n).

So as to keep notation simple, we shall usually denote a coset $r(x) + I$ simply by the polynomial $r(x)$.

Readers who have not previously met the concept of a coset will certainly need some concrete examples to help them grasp the difficult ideas that have just been introduced. Before giving these examples, let us summarize the situation.

Theorem 2.6. *Let K be a field and $p(x)$ a polynomial in $K[x]$ of degree n. The cosets of the ideal $(p(x))$ in $K[x]$ form a commutative ring with identity which we denote by $K[x]/(p(x))$. This ring contains a copy of K as a subfield, and can be considered as a vector space over K of dimension n. If K is a finite field of q elements then $K[x]/(p(x))$ is a finite ring of q^n elements.*

To illustrate the ideas summarized in Theorem 2.6 take $K = \mathbb{Z}_2$, $p(x) = x^2 + x + 1 \in \mathbb{Z}_2[x]$, and $I = (p(x))$. The ring $\mathbb{Z}_2[x]/(x^2 + x + 1)$ consists of four cosets: $0 + I, 1 + I, x + I, 1 + x + I$. For simplicity we denote these cosets by $0, 1, x, 1 + x$. The addition and multiplication tables for $\mathbb{Z}_2[x]/(x^2 + x + 1)$ are:

$+$	0	1	x	$1+x$
0	0	1	x	$1+x$
1	1	0	$1+x$	x
x	x	$1+x$	0	1
$1+x$	$1+x$	x	1	0

$\circ$	0	1	x	$1+x$
0	0	0	0	0
1	0	1	x	$1+x$
x	0	x	$1+x$	1
$1+x$	0	$1+x$	1	x

From the multiplication table we see that every non-zero element of the ring $\mathbb{Z}_2[x]/(x^2 + x + 1)$ has a multiplicative inverse. Hence this ring is a field. As a vector space over $\mathbb{Z}_2$, the dimension of $\mathbb{Z}_2[x]/(x^2 + x + 1)$ is 2, a basis being the set $\{1, x\}$. Thus

$$\mathbb{Z}_2[x]/(x^2 + x + 1): \mathbb{Z}_2$$

is a field extension of degree 2.

Consider now the multiplication table of the ring $\mathbb{Z}_2[x]/(x^2+1)$:

$\circ$	0	1	x	$1+x$
0	0	0	0	0
1	0	1	x	$1+x$
x	0	x	1	$1+x$
$1+x$	0	$1+x$	$1+x$	0

The ring $\mathbb{Z}_2[x]/(x^2+1)$ is not a field since $1+x$ has no multiplicative inverse. The lack of an inverse is due essentially to the fact that $x^2+1=(x+1)(x+1)$ is not an irreducible element in the ring $\mathbb{Z}_2[x]$. This observation leads us to the following theorem.

Theorem 2.7. *Let K be a field and $p(x)$ a polynomial in $K[x]$ of degree ≥ 1. The ring $K[x]/(p(x))$ is a field if and only if $p(x)$ is an irreducible element of $K[x]$.*

Proof. Let $I=(p(x))$. Suppose that $p(x)$ is reducible, say $p(x)=f(x)g(x)$ with $f(x)$ and $g(x)$ polynomials of degree ≥ 1. Then the cosets $f(x)+I$ and $g(x)+I$ are non-zero elements in the ring $K[x]/(p(x))$, but their product $f(x)g(x)+I=0+I$ is the zero element. Hence $K[x]/(p(x))$ is not an integral domain. Since every field is an integral domain it follows that $K[x]/(p(x))$ is not a field.

Conversely, suppose that $p(x)$ is an irreducible element in $K[x]$. We need to show that every non-zero element $f(x)+I$ in $K[x]/(p(x))$ is invertible. Now $f(x)+I$ is non-zero, that is, $f(x)+I \neq 0+I$, only if $f(x)$ is not a multiple of $p(x)$. Note that $K[x]$ is a Euclidean domain. Since $p(x)$ is irreducilbe it follows that, in $K[x]$, any common factor of $p(x)$ and $f(x)$ is a unit; in particular 1 is a highest common factor. It follows from Claim 5 of Theorem 1.3 that there are polynomials $r(x)$, $s(x)$ in $K[x]$ such that $1=r(x)f(x)+s(x)p(x)$. Therefore $(r(x)+I)(f(x)+I)=1+I$ which proves that $f(x)+I$ is invertible. ∎

So one way to construct a field with p^n elements is to find an irreducible polynomial $p(x)$ in $\mathbb{Z}_p[x]$ of degree n, and form the field $\mathbb{Z}_p[x]/(p(x))$. In practice it is not so easy to decide whether or not a given polynomial is irreducible. However, irreducible polynomials of degree 2 or 3 can be identified using the following definition and theorem.

Let K be a field, and $p(x)$ a polynomial in $K[x]$. An element α in K is called a *root* or *zero* of $p(x)$ if $p(\alpha)=0$.

Theorem 2.8. *Let α be an element of a field K. The linear polynomial $x - \alpha$ divides a polynomial $p(x)$ in $K[x]$ if and only if α is a root of $p(x)$.*

Proof. Suppose $x - \alpha$ divides $p(x)$. Then there is a polynomial $r(x)$ in $K[x]$ such that $p(x) = (x - \alpha)r(x)$. It follows that $p(\alpha) = (\alpha - \alpha)r(\alpha) = 0$.

Conversely suppose that $p(\alpha) = 0$. Since $K[x]$ is a Euclidean domain there exist polynomials $q(x)$, $r(x)$ such that $p(x) = (x - \alpha)q(x) + r(x)$ with $\deg(r(x)) = 0$ or $r(x) = 0$. In other words, $r(x) = r$ is an element of K. In fact $0 = p(\alpha) = 0q(\alpha) + r = r$. Hence $x - \alpha$ divides $p(x)$. ∎

As an application of Theorem 2.8 consider the polynomial $p(x) = x^3 + x^2 + x + 4$ in $\mathbb{Z}_5[x]$. Since $p(0) = 4$, $p(1) = 2$, $p(2) = 3$, $p(3) = 3$, and $p(4) = 3$ it follows that $p(x)$ has no roots in $\mathbb{Z}_5$. Consequently $p(x)$ has no linear factors in $\mathbb{Z}_5[x]$. Since the polynomial $p(x)$ is of degree 3, it must be an irreducible element in $\mathbb{Z}_5[x]$. Hence the ring $\mathbb{Z}_5[x]/(x^3 + x^2 + x + 4)$ is a finite field of 125 elements.

It is not so easy to show directly, for an arbitrary prime p and integer $n \geq 1$, the existence of an irreducible polynomial $p(x)$ in $\mathbb{Z}_p[x]$ of degree n. A simpler way of proving the existence of a field with p^n-elements is to show that certain field extensions, called *splitting fields*, always exist.

A polynomial $p(x)$ in $K[x]$ is said to *split* over the field K if there are elements $\alpha_1, \ldots, \alpha_n, k$ in K such that

$$p(x) = k(x - \alpha_1)(x - \alpha_2) \ldots (x - \alpha_n).$$

For instance, the polynomial $x^2 - 2$ splits over $\mathbb{R}$; it does not split over $\mathbb{Q}$ since $\sqrt{2}$ is not rational.

A *splitting field* for a polynomial $p(x)$ over K is a field L such that:

(1) L contains K as a subfield;

(2) $p(x)$ splits over L;

(3) there is no proper subfield M of L containing K such that $p(x)$ splits over M. (Here *proper* means $M \neq L$.)

For instance, the field $\mathbb{Q}(\sqrt{-2}) = \{x + y\sqrt{-2}: x, y \in \mathbb{Q}\}$ is a splitting field for $x^2 + 2$ over $\mathbb{Q}$. The field $\mathbb{C}$ is not a splitting field for $x^2 + 2$ over $\mathbb{Q}$ since it contains $\mathbb{Q}(\sqrt{-2})$ as a proper subfield, and $x^2 + 2$ splits over $\mathbb{Q}(\sqrt{-2})$. However, $\mathbb{C}$ is a splitting field for $x^2 + 2$ over $\mathbb{R}$. (Why?) Note also that $x^2 + 2$ splits over $\mathbb{Z}_3$ as $x^2 + 2 = (x + 2)(x + 1)$, and hence $\mathbb{Z}_3$ is a splitting field for $x^2 + 2$ over $\mathbb{Z}_3$.

We now aim to show that for any power $q = p^n$ of a prime p there exists a splitting field for $x^q - x$ over $\mathbb{Z}_p$ and, moreover, that this splitting field contains precisely q elements. We shall begin by proving the existence, in general, of splitting fields; to illustrate the ideas in this existence proof, let us first consider a specific example.

Suppose that we wish to construct a splitting field for the polynomial

$$f(x) = x^9 + x^8 + x^7 + x^6 + x^4 + 2x^2 + 1$$

over the field $\mathbb{Z}_3 = \{0, 1, 2\}$. This polynomial factorizes as

$$f(x) = (x^3 + 2x + 1)(x^2 + 1)^2(x + 2)^2.$$

Both of the factors $x^3 + 2x + 1$ and $x^2 + 1$ are irreducible over $\mathbb{Z}_3$ as neither have a root in $\mathbb{Z}_3$ (and both are of degree ≤ 3). Let us set

$$f_0(x) = x^2 + 1.$$

Consider now the ring $\mathbb{Z}_3[\alpha]$ of polynomials in the indeterminate α over the $\mathbb{Z}_3$. Since $f_0(\alpha) = \alpha^2 + 1$ is an irreducible polynomial in $\mathbb{Z}_3[\alpha]$, the ring of cosets

$$K' = \mathbb{Z}_3[\alpha]/(\alpha^2 + 1)$$

is a field. For simplicity we shall denote the coset $\alpha + I$, where I is the ideal $(\alpha^2 + 1)$, by α. The polynomial $f_0(x)$ splits over the field K':

$$f_0(x) = x^2 + 1 = (x + \alpha)(x - \alpha).$$

However, the polynomial $f(x)$ does not split over K' because none of the nine elements in K' is a root of the factor $x^3 + 2x + 1$. (For example, the element $\alpha + 1$ in K' is not a root of $x^3 + 2x + 1$ because $\alpha^2 + 1 = 0$ implies

$$(\alpha + 1)^3 + (\alpha + 1) + 1 = \alpha + 1 \neq 0.$$

The reader should verify that the other eight elements of K' are not roots.) Consider now the ring $K'[\beta]$ of polynomials in the indeterminate β over K'. Since $x^3 + 2x + 1$ is irreducible over K' (it has no roots in K'), the ring of cosets

$$L = K'[\beta]/(\beta^3 + 2\beta + 1)$$

is a field. For simplicity we denote the coset $\beta + J$, where J is the ideal $(\beta^3 + 2\beta + 1)$, by β. The polynomial $f(x)$ splits over L if the factor $x^3 + 2x + 1$ splits. Certainly β is a root of this factor, and so we have the factorization

$$x^3 + 2x + 1 = (x + \beta)(x^2 + 2\beta x + \beta^2 + 2)$$

over L. It can be checked that $2 - \beta$ is also a root of the factor $x^3 + 2x + 1$. It follows that this factor splits over L (why?). Hence $f(x)$ splits over L. Since L was obtained from $\mathbb{Z}_3$ by only 'adding what was essential' we see that L is a splitting field for $f(x)$ over $\mathbb{Z}_3$.

The ideas of this example generalize to the following theorem.

Theorem 2.9. *For any field K and polynomial $f(x)$ in $K[x]$ there exists a splitting field L for $f(x)$ over K.*

Proof. If $\deg(f(x)) = 0$ or 1 then K itself is the required splitting field. Suppose the result is true for all polynomials of degree less than n for some $n \geqslant 2$, and suppose $\deg(f(x)) = n$. There must be a factor $f_0(x)$ of $f(x)$ which is irreducible and of degree $\geqslant 1$. Let $K' = K[\alpha]/(f_0(\alpha))$, where α is an indeterminate. Then $f(x)$ is a reducible element in the ring $K'[x]$ (since the field K' contains the root α of $f(x)$). So we can write $f(x) = r(x)s(x)$ where $r(x)$ and $s(x)$ are polynomials in $K'[x]$ of degree less than n. Without loss of generality suppose that α is a root of $r(x)$. By the inductive hypothesis there is a splitting field R for $r(x)$ over K'. We can consider $s(x)$ as an element in $R[x]$ and so, again by the inductive hypothesis, there is a splitting field L for $s(x)$ over R. Certainly L contains K as a subfield, and $f(x)$ splits over L. There are inclusions:

$$K \subseteq K' \subseteq R \subseteq L.$$

We have to show that L is the 'smallest possible' extension of K over which $f(x)$ splits. Suppose that M is a subfield of L containing K over which $f(x)$ splits. Then $r(x)$ splits over M since $M[x]$ is a unique factorization domain. The intersection of any two subfields of L is a subfield. In particular $R \cap M$ is a subfield of L which, moreover, is a subfield of M. Note that $R \cap M$ contains α and K. But any subfield containing α and K must contain the subfield K'. Hence $R \cap M = R$ since R is a splitting field over K'. Thus M is a subfield of L containing R over which $s(x)$ splits. Hence $M = L$ since L is a splitting field over R. It follows that L is a splitting field for $f(x)$ over K. The theorem follows by induction. ∎

Theorem 2.10.   *Let p be a prime number, let $q = p^n$ for some $n \geqslant 1$, and let L be a splitting field for $x^q - x$ over $\mathbb{Z}_p$. Then every element of L is a root of $x^q - x$.*

Proof.   Let S be the subset of L consisting of all those elements which are roots of $x^q - x$. We can show that S is a subfield of L. To do this suppose that $a, b \in S$. Then

$$(a-b)^q - (a-b) = a^q - \binom{q}{1} a^{q-1} b + \cdots + (-1)^{q-1} \binom{q}{q-1} ab^{q-1}$$
$$+ (-1)^q b^q - (a-b).$$

Since L has characteristic p and since $\binom{q}{i}$ is divisible by p for $1 \leqslant i \leqslant q - 1$ (this is an exercise for the reader), it follows that $(a-b)^q + a - b = 0$. Thus $a - b$ is in S. Also $(ab^{-1})^q - ab^{-1} = a^q b^{-q} - ab^{-1} = ab^{-1} - ab^{-1} = 0$, and so ab^{-1} is in S. Hence S is a subfield of L. Certainly $x^q - x$ splits over S, and certainly S contains $\mathbb{Z}_p$. It follows that $L = S$.   ∎

We must now show that $x^q - x$ has precisely q roots in a splitting field.

Theorem 2.11.   *A polynomial $f(x)$ in $K[x]$ of degree n has at most n distinct roots in the field K. If $f(x)$ splits over K with no repeated linear factors (i.e. no factors $(x - \alpha)^j$ for α in K and $j \geqslant 2$) then there are precisely n roots of $f(x)$ in K.*

Proof.   Let $\alpha_1, \ldots, \alpha_m \in K$ be the distinct roots of $f(x)$. Then $(x - \alpha_i)$ divides $f(x)$ for each root α_i. Since the $x - \alpha_i$ are coprime elements in $K[x]$ it follows (why?) that $(x - \alpha_1)(x - \alpha_2) \ldots (x - \alpha_m)$ divides $f(x)$. But if a polynomial of degree m divides a polynomial of degree n we must have $m \leqslant n$. If $f(x) = k(x - \alpha_1) \ldots (x - \alpha_m)$ with $k \in K$ then $m = \deg(f(x)) = n$.   ∎

So the polynomial $x^q - x$ has at most q roots in any splitting field. To show that it has precisely q roots, we use the notion of a formal derivative.

For any field K and polynomial $f(x) = a_0 + a_1 x + \cdots + a_n x^n$ in $K[x]$, the *formal derivative* of $f(x)$ is defined to be

$$\frac{\mathrm{d}}{\mathrm{d}x} f(x) = a_1 + 2a_2 x + \cdots + n a_n x^{n-1}.$$

It is easily checked that for any $f(x)$, $g(x)$ in $K[x]$ the formulae

$$\frac{d}{dx}(f(x)+g(x)) = \frac{d}{dx}f(x) + \frac{d}{dx}g(x)$$

$$\frac{d}{dx}f(x)g(x) = g(x)\frac{d}{dx}f(x) + f(x)\frac{d}{dx}g(x)$$

hold.

Theorem 2.12. *A polynomial $f(x)$ in $K[x]$ is divisible by $(x-\alpha)^2$ for some α in K only if α is a root of both $f(x)$ and $\frac{d}{dx}f(x)$.*

Proof. If $f(x) = (x-\alpha)^2 g(x)$ then

$$\frac{d}{dx}f(x) = (x-\alpha)\left\{2g(x) + (x-\alpha)\frac{d}{dx}g(x)\right\}$$

and so α is a root of $f(x)$ and $\frac{d}{dx}f(x)$. ∎

We at least come to the proof of the existence of finite fields.

Theorem 2.13. *For any prime number p and integer $n \geq 1$ there is a finite field of p^n elements.*

Proof. Let $q = p^n$ and let L be a splitting field for $x^q - x$ over $\mathbb{Z}_p$. The field L consists of the distinct roots of $x^q - x$. Since $x^q - x$ and $\frac{d}{dx}(x^q - x) = qx^{q-1} - 1 = -1$ have no common roots it follows that $x^q - x$ splits in L with no repeated linear factors. Hence there are q distinct roots of $x^q - x$. Thus L is a field of q elements. ∎

Theorem 2.13 implies a solution to our problem of assigning fertilizers to farmers for $v = q^2 + q + 1$ with q any prime power. This is because we can find a field K with q elements and hence construct the projective plane $PG(2, K)$. A slight generalization of the proof of Corollary 2.4 shows that $PG(2, K)$ contains $q^2 + q + 1$ lines (and the same number of points).

At this stage of our understanding of finite fields it is natural to ask: for a given prime power q, how many different fields of q elements are there? The answer to this depends on a precise meaning for the term 'different'. In the terminology which we are about to introduce, two fields or rings are different if they are not isomorphic.

Let R and R' be two rings (or fields). We say that R is *isomorphic* to R' if there is a function $\phi: R \rightarrow R'$ which is injective (i.e. for all $a, b \in R$, $\phi(a) = \phi(b)$ implies $a = b$) and surjective (i.e. for every $c \in R'$ there is an $a \in R$ such that $c = \phi(a)$) and which preserves the ring structures in the following sense:

$$\phi(a + b) = \phi(a) + \phi(b) \qquad \text{and} \qquad \phi(ab) = (\phi a)(\phi b)$$

for all a, b in R. We call such a function an *isomorphism*. We write $R \cong R'$ when R is isomorphic to R'.

One example of an isomorphism is the function

$$\phi: \mathbb{C} \rightarrow \mathbb{R}[x]/(x^2 + 1)$$

which sends the complex number $u + v\sqrt{-1}$ to the coset represented by $u + vx$, for all $u, v \in \mathbb{R}$. Another example of an isomorphism is complex conjugation

$$\psi: \mathbb{C} \rightarrow \mathbb{C}$$

which sends each complex number $u + v\sqrt{-1}$ to its complex conjugate $u - v\sqrt{-1}$.

Isomorphism is a very natural notion: intuitively, two rings are isomorphic if and only if 'their addition tables are the same and their multiplication tables are the same'.

The reader should verify that isomorphism is an equivalence relation. That is:

(1) if $R \cong R'$ then $R' \cong R$;

(2) always $R \cong R$;

(3) if $R \cong R'$ and $R' \cong R''$ then $R \cong R''$.

Other useful (and easily checked) properties of an isomorphism $\phi: R \rightarrow R'$ are:

(1) $\phi(0) = 0$;

(2) if R contains an identity 1 then $\phi(1)$ is an identity in R';

(3) if R is a field then R' is a field.

Theorem 2.14. *Any two finite fields with the same number of elements are isomorphic.*

This theorem together with Theorem 2.13 tells us that for each prime power q there is essentially only one finite field of q elements. Theorem 2.5 tells us that these are the only finite fields. Thus we have a complete classification of finite fields.

Theorem 2.14 is an immediate consequence of the following two propositions.

Proposition 2.15 *Any field L of $q = p^n$ elements is a splitting field for $x^q - x$ over $\mathbb{Z}_p$.*

Proof. It follows from Lagrange's theorem in Chapter 0 that any element α in L satisfies $\alpha^q - \alpha = 0$. This implies that every element of L is a root of the polynomial $x^q - x$, and thus that all q roots of $x^q - x$ are in L. In other words, $x^q - x$ splits over L, and so L is a splitting field (since obviously $x^q - x$ can't split over a subfield of L). ∎

Note that if $\phi: K \to K'$ is an isomorphism of fields, then there is an 'induced' ring isomorphism

$$\phi: K[x] \to K'[x],$$
$$a_0 + a_1 x + \cdots + a_n x^n \mapsto (\phi a_0) + (\phi a_1)x + \cdots + (\phi a_n)x^n.$$

Proposition 2.16. Let $\phi: K \to K'$ be an isomorphism of fields, and let $f(x)$ be a polynomial in $K[x]$ of degree ≥ 1. Then any splitting field of $f(x)$ over K is isomorphic to any splitting field of $\phi(f(x))$ over K', by an isomorphism extending ϕ.

Proof. This will be our heaviest proof so far. The idea is to construct the diagram of fields given towards the end of the proof, and then to use the fact that isomorphism is a transitive relation.

If $\deg(f(x)) = 1$ then K is a splitting field for $f(x)$ over K, and K' is a splitting field for $\phi(f(x))$ over K', and hence the proposition is true. Suppose the proposition is true for all polynomials of degree less than n for some $n \geq 2$, and for all fields. Suppose that $\deg(f(x)) = n$. Then $f(x) = f_0(x)g(x)$ where $f_0(x)$ and $g(x)$ are polynomials in $K[x]$ and $f_0(x)$ is irreducible of degree ≥ 1. Let L be a splitting field for $f(x)$ over K, and let $\alpha \in L$ be a root of $f_0(x)$. Let L_0 be the intersection of all those subfields of L that contain K and α. Then L_0 is a subfield of L. (We say that L_0 is *generated* by K and α). Form the ring $K[y]$ of polynomials in the indeterminate y. Let $I = (f_0(y))$ be the ideal of $K[y]$ generated by $f_0(y)$, and let M_0 be the field $K[y]/(f_0(y))$. Consider the function

$$\psi: M_0 \to L_0, \qquad h(y) + I \mapsto h(\alpha).$$

This function is well defined since, if $h(y)+I=h'(y)+I$ then $h(y)=h'(y)+r(y)f_0(y)$ and consequently $h(\alpha)=h'(\alpha)+r(\alpha)f_0(\alpha)=h'(\alpha)+0=h'(\alpha)$. The reader should check that ψ is in fact an isomorphism.

Now $f(x)=f_0(x)g(x)$ and, since K is a subfield of both L_0 and M_0, we can consider $g(x)$ as a polynomial of degree $<n$ in $L_0[x]$ or in $M_0[x]$. Let M be a splitting field for $g(x)$ over M_0. Since L is a splitting field for $g(x)$ over L_0 it follows from the inductive hypothesis that $M\cong L$.

Let L' be any splitting field for $\phi(f(x))$ over K', let $\alpha'\in L'$ be a root of $\phi(f(x))$, and let L_0' be the subfield of L' generated by K' and α'. It is routinely checked that the function

$$\psi': M_0\to L_0', \qquad h(y)+I\mapsto\phi(h(\alpha'))$$

is an isomorphism. Note that L' is a splitting field for $\phi(g(x))$ over L_0'. Hence by the inductive hypothesis there is an isomorphism $M\cong L'$.

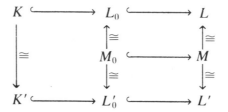

Since isomorphism is a transitive relation we have $L\cong L'$, and the proposition follows by induction. ∎

We have shown that, up to isomorphism, there is only one finite field of q elements. We shall denote 'this' field by GF (q). The letters G and F stand for Galois field, after the French mathematician Evariste Galois.

Exercises

1. (i) Show that the ring $\mathbb{Z}_m$ is an integral domain if and only if m is a prime number.
   (ii) Let R be an integral domain with only finitely many elements. Prove that R has an identity and that every non-zero element of R is a unit. (Hint: first show that for each non-zero element $a\in R$ the ideal (a) contains the same number of elements as R.)

2. If A, B, C, D are four points in a projective plane, no three of which are collinear, then they determine a 'complete quadrangle', the *diagonal points* of which are the points of intersection of AB and CD, of AC and BD, and of BC and AD.

Let $GF(4) = \{0, 1, x, 1+x\}$ be the field of four elements. In $PG(2, GF(4))$ consider the complete quadrangle determined by the four points $[1, 1, 1+x]$, $[0, 1, x]$, $[1, 1, x]$, $[1, 1+x, x]$. Find its diagonal points and verify that they are collinear.

3. List the points and lines of $PG(2, GF(4))$ and attempt the task of representing them pictorially. (The author knows of no nice pictorial representation.)

4. Show that for no field K is the ring $K[x]/(x^5 + x^4 + x^3 + 1)$ a field.

5. Which of the following rings R are fields?
   (i) $R = \mathbb{Z}_3[x]/(x^4 + x - 1)$.
   (ii) $R = \mathbb{Q}[x]/(x^4 + 1)$.
   (iii) $R = \mathbb{R}[x]/(x^4 + 1)$.
   (iv) $R = \mathbb{Z}_{17}[x]/(x^4 + 7)$.
   (v) $R = \mathbb{Z}_{11}[x]/(x^3 - 5)$.
   (vi) $R = GF(4)\,[x]/(x^3 - ax + 1 + a)$ where $GF(4) = \{0, 1, \alpha, 1 + \alpha\}$
         is the field of four elements.

6. Find a polynomial $f(x)$ in $\mathbb{Z}_7[x]$ such that $\mathbb{Z}_7[x]/(f(x))$ is a field with 343 elements.

7. Find a polynomial $f(x)$ in $GF(4)[x]$ such that $GF(4)[x]/(f(x))$ is a field of 16 elements.

8. Show that if L is a set of points of $PG(2, GF(q))$ such that every line of $PG(2, GF(q))$ contains a point of L, then $|L| \geq q+1$ with equality if and only if L is a line.

9. A schoolmistress takes nine girls for a daily walk, the girls arranged in rows of three girls. Use $PG(2, \mathbb{Z}_3)$ to plan the walk for four consecutive days so that no girl walks with any of her classmates in any triplet more than once.

10. Let p be a prime number. For all integers a not divisible by p, show that p divides $a^{p-1} - 1$. (This is Fermat's little theorem.)

11. For any field L with subfield K, and any elements $\alpha_1, \ldots, \alpha_n$ in L, we let $K(\alpha_1, \ldots, \alpha_n)$ be the intersection of all those subfields of L that contain K and $\alpha_1, \ldots, \alpha_n$. We say that $K(\alpha_1, \ldots, \alpha_n)$ is the subfield of L generated K by and the α_i.
    (i)   Show that for $\alpha = \sqrt{2} + \sqrt{3}$ we have $\mathbb{Q}(\alpha) = \mathbb{Q}(\sqrt{2}, \sqrt{3})$.
    (ii) What is the degree of the extension $\mathbb{Q}(\alpha): \mathbb{Q}$?
    (iii) Find a polynomial $f(x)$ in $\mathbb{Q}[x]$ such that there is a field isomorphism $\mathbb{Q}(\alpha) \cong \mathbb{Q}[x]/(f(x))$.

12. Find an element β in $\mathbb{R}$ such that $\mathbb{Q}(\beta) = \mathbb{Q}(\sqrt{2}, \sqrt{3}, \sqrt{5})$. What is the degree of the extension $\mathbb{Q}(\beta): \mathbb{Q}$? If $f(x)$ is a polynomial in $\mathbb{Q}[x]$

such that there is an isomorphism $\mathbb{Q}(\beta) \cong \mathbb{Q}[x]/(f(x))$, what must the degree of $f(x)$ be?

13. Prove that $\mathbb{Z}_{11}[x]/(x^2+1)$ and $\mathbb{Z}_{11}[y]/(y^2+y+4)$ are isomorphic rings.

14. Show that the sum of all the elements of a finite field is 0 if the field is not $\mathbb{Z}_2$. (This exercise will be eaiser after the reader has digested Theorem 3.5.)

15. Show that in a finite field of p^n elements any element α has exactly one pth root (i.e. there is exactly one element β such that $\beta^p = \alpha$). Deduce that if α, γ are elements in GF(27) satisfying $\alpha^2 + \alpha\gamma + \gamma^2 = 0$, then $\alpha = \beta$.

16. Let R be a commutative ring and I an ideal in R. The set $N(I) = \{a \in R: a^n \in I$ for some integer $n\}$ is called the *radical* of I.
    (i)   Show that $N(I)$ is an ideal in R containing I.
    (ii) Show that $N(N(I)) = N(I)$.
    (iii) Determine $N(I)$ for $R = \mathbb{Z}$ and $I = 72\mathbb{Z}$.

17. Let R be a ring and I an ideal in R.
    (i) Verify that the set of *cosets* $R/I = \{a + I: a \in R\}$ is a ring under the operations $(a+I)+(b+I)=a+b+I$, $(a+I)(b+I)=ab+I$.
    (ii) Show that the ideals in R containing I are in one-to-one correspondence with the ideals of R/I.

18. A function $\phi: R \to R'$ is a (*ring*) *homomorphism* if R and R' are rings and $\phi(a+b)=\phi(a)+\phi(b)$, $\phi(ab)=\phi(a)\phi(b)$ for all a, b in R. The *image* of ϕ is the set $\mathrm{im}(\phi)=\{c \in R': c = \phi(a)$ for some $a \in R\}$, and the *kernel* of ϕ is the set $\ker(\phi)=\{a \in R: \phi(a)=0\}$.
    (i)   Show that $\mathrm{im}(\phi)$ is a subring of R', and that $\ker(\phi)$ is an ideal in R.
    (ii) Show that there is an isomorphism $\mathrm{im}(\phi) \cong R/\ker(\phi)$.
    (iii) Show that for any ideal I in R there is a surjective homomorphism $\pi: R \to R/I$ such that $\ker(\pi) = I$.

19. Let I be an ideal in a ring R. Let $M_n(R)$ be the ring of $n \times n$ matrices over R.
    (i) Show that $M_n(I)$ is an ideal in $M_n(R)$.
    (ii) Show that $M_n(R/I)$ is isomorphic to $M_n(R)/M_n(I)$.

3 Error codes

In this chapter we study some applications of finite fields to coding theory. This is a theory concerned with the efficient transmission of digital information, and is essential for the proper functioning of electronic equipment such as computers and compact disk players. To explain the basic ideas behind the theory we begin by looking at a simple code used every-day by bookshops when ordering books.

All modern books can be identified by their International Standard Book Number. For instance, the ISBN of *A First Course In Abstract Algebra* by J. B. Fraleigh is 0-201-16847-2. The first four digits determine the publisher Addison-Wesley. The next five digits are the publisher's code number for the book. The last digit is a *safety check-digit*. The hyphens are unimportant. An ISBN always consists of a string of ten digits $x_1 x_2 \ldots x_{10}$, and the last digit is chosen so that the sum

$$x_1 + 2x_2 + 3x_3 + \cdots + 10x_{10}$$

is an integer multiple of 11. The digits x_i can thus be thought of as elements in the field $\mathbb{Z}_{11}$. Sometimes it is necessary to put $x_{10} = 10$, and when this is the case, an X is put as the last digit. For example the ISBN of *Modern Algebra* by I. N. Herstein is 0-471-02371-X.

If an ISBN is quoted with an error in exactly one of its digits, this error can be detected. For suppose that the kth digit x_k is accidentally changed to $x_k + e$ with e a non-zero element of $\mathbb{Z}_{11}$. Then $\Sigma_{i=1}^{10} i x_i = ke$ and ke is non-zero since $\mathbb{Z}_{11}$ is a field and hence an integral domain.

If the ISBN is quoted with two of its digits interchanged, then this error too can be detected. For suppose that x_k and $x_{k'}$ are interchanged. Then $\Sigma_{i=1}^{10} i x_i = (k' - k)(x_k - x_{k'})$.

To illustrate the advantages of the check-digit in the ISBN, let us suppose that the average bookshop employee, when quoting a digit of a reference number, gets the digit right 98 times out of 100. So $p = 0.98$ is the probability that a particular digit in an ISBN is quoted correctly, and $q = 0.02$ is the probability that it is incorrectly quoted. If the check-digit of the ISBN were not used by publishers, the resulting 9-digit number would be correctly quoted only $p^9 \times 100 \approx 83$ times out of a hundred. Since however the check-digit is used, and consequently all single errors (and some additional errors) are detected, more than

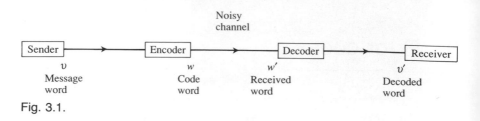

Fig. 3.1.

$(p^{10} + 10p^9 q) \times 100 \simeq 98$ in 100 ISBNs received by publishers contain no undetectable errors (given our initial supposition).

The ISBN is an example of a simple but useful *error-detecting* code. There are many other situations, mostly connected with electronic digital equipment, where digital information needs to be encoded in order to reduce the risk of errors. In all of these situations there is a *sender*, a *receiver*, and an imperfect *communications channel*. The sender encodes her *message* and transmits the *encoded message*. The *received message* is decoded in such a way that transmission errors are likely to be detected or corrected. This is illustrated in Fig. 3.1

A message consists of *message words*, and these words are just strings of digits $x_1 x_2 \ldots x_k$ made from a finite alphabet $\mathbb{F}$. We shall assume that $\mathbb{F}$ is a finite field, and that each message word has the same length k. When dealing with binary digital information the field $\mathbb{F}$ is usually taken to be the field $\mathbb{Z}_2$ of two elements (or possibly some other field of characteristic 2). Message words can be considered to be elements of the vector space $\mathbb{F}^k$. An *encoding function* is an injective function $E\colon \mathbb{F}^k \to \mathbb{F}^n$, where $n \geq k$. The image of the funciton E is called a *code* of *length n*, and the elements of the image are called *codewords*. If E is a linear homomorphism, the code is said to be a *linear (n, k)-code* over $\mathbb{F}$, and k is the *dimension* of the code. In other words, a linear (n, k)-code over $\mathbb{F}$ is just a subspace C of $\mathbb{F}^n$ of dimension k.

An example of a linear (12, 3)-code over any field $\mathbb{F}$ is given by the linear homomorphism

$$E\colon \mathbb{F}^3 \to \mathbb{F}^{12}, \qquad (a, b, c) \mapsto (a, b, c, a, b, c, a, b, c, a, b, c).$$

This is a *repetition code* and can be used to detect all single, double, or triple errors which occur in the transmission of a codeword. For instance, if two errors occur, the received word might have the form

$$(a, b, c, a, a, c, a, b, a, a, b, c);$$

as this is not a codeword the error can be detected. If four errors occur they might not be detectable. This code can also be used to correct any single errors. For instance, if the word

$$w = (a, a, c, a, b, c, a, a, c, a, a, c)$$

is received then, since w is not a codeword, at least one error must have occurred. We always assume that single errors are more probable than double errors, and so the transmitted codeword was most likely

$$w' = (a, a, c, a, a, c, a, a, c, a, a, c).$$

The number of errors that can be detected and the number of errors that can be corrected by a code are important features of the code. They are determined by the 'minimum distance' between codewords. To make this precise we define the *distance* $d(u, v)$ between any two vectors u, v in $\mathbb{F}^n$ to be the number of coordinates in which u and v differ. For instance, $d(w, w') = 1$ for the words w and w' above. The *minimum distance* d_C of a code C is defined as

$$d_C = \min_{u \neq v \in C} d(u, v).$$

So for example the minimum distance of the $(12, 3)$-repetition code is 4.

The reader should verify that any code with minimum distance equal to $t + 1$ can be used to detect up to t errors. (Perhaps begin with the specific examples of the $(12, 3)$-repetition code which has $d_c = 3 + 1$: this can detect all single, double, or triple errors, but certain quadruple errors will be undetectable.) Also, any code with minimum distance equal to $2t + 1$ can be used to correct up to t errors. (Again consider the $(12, 3)$-repetition code, which has $d_c > 2(1) + 1$: all single errors can be corrected, but certain double errors will be uncorrectable.)

We say that a code C is *t-error-detecting* if $d_C \geq t + 1$. We say that C is *t-error-correcting* if $d_C \geq 2t + 1$.

The increased reliability resulting from transmitting with a code has a price: there is a decrease in the rate at which information can be transmitted. By definition each digit of a binary message word (that is a message word over $\mathbb{F} = \mathbb{Z}_2$) contains one *bit of information*. The term bit is derived form *bi*nary dig*it*. There are eight bits of information in a *byte*. The *information rate* R_C of an (n, k)-binary code C is by definition k/n. So for instance the $(12, 3)$-repetition code has information rate $R_c = \frac{1}{4}$.

More generally, the *information rate* of an arbitrary code C of length n over the field of q elements is

$$R_C = (1/n) \log_q |C|$$

where $|C|$ denotes the number of codewords in the code. It follows from this definition that the information rate of a code is always between 0 and 1. A good code will have both a high information rate and a high error-correction/detection potential.

One of the main problems of coding theory is the construction of codes to given specifications. Suppose for instance that a four-dimensional 1-error-correcting binary code is required. One possibility is the $(12, 4)$-binary repetition code, which has information rate $\frac{1}{3}$. However, this is not the most efficient code. For, consider the *null space* C of the following matrix over $\mathbb{F} = \mathbb{Z}_2$:

$$H = \begin{pmatrix} 0 & 0 & 0 & 1 & 1 & 1 & 1 \\ 0 & 1 & 1 & 0 & 0 & 1 & 1 \\ 1 & 0 & 1 & 0 & 1 & 0 & 1 \end{pmatrix},$$

That is, C consists of all those vectors $w = (a_1, a_2, \ldots, a_7)$ in $\mathbb{F}^7$ such that

$$\begin{pmatrix} 0 & 0 & 0 & 1 & 1 & 1 & 1 \\ 0 & 1 & 1 & 0 & 0 & 1 & 1 \\ 1 & 0 & 1 & 0 & 1 & 0 & 1 \end{pmatrix} \begin{pmatrix} a_1 \\ \vdots \\ a_7 \end{pmatrix} = \begin{pmatrix} 0 \\ 0 \\ 0 \end{pmatrix},$$

or more succinctly, such that $Hw^t = 0$. There is an encoding function

$$E: \mathbb{F}^4 \to C, \qquad (a_1, a_2, a_3, a_4) \mapsto w = (a_1, a_2, a_3, a_4, c_1, c_2, c_3)$$

for which the *check-digits* c_i are determined by the equation $Hw^t = 0$:

$$c_1 = a_2 + a_3 + a_4,$$
$$c_2 = a_1 + a_3 + a_4$$
$$c_3 = a_1 + a_2 + a_4.$$

This code is called the *Hamming (7, 4)-binary code*. The reader can (and should) check that its minimum distance is 3. It is therefore a 1-error-correcting code. Its information rate is 4/7, a substantial improvement on the information rate of the $(12, 4)$-repetition code.

In fact the Hamming $(7, 4)$-binary code has the lowest information rate possible for a four-dimensional 1-error-correcting linear binary code. To see this, suppose that C is any four-dimensional code over $\mathbb{F} = \mathbb{Z}_2$ with minimum distance 3. So C is a subspace of $\mathbb{F}^n$ for some n. There are 2^4 codewords in C, and for any given codeword there are n

words in $\mathbb{F}^n$ of distance 1 from it. Since the minimum distance of the code is 3 it follows that there must be at least $2^4(n+1)$ words in $\mathbb{F}^n$. For this, we require $2^4(n+1) \leq 2^n$. But this inequality holds only if $n \geq 7$. Therefore the information rate is $4/n \leq 4/7$.

A generalization of this argument leads to the following result.

Theorem 3.1. *Let C be a code of length n over the field $\mathbb{F} = GF(q)$ of q elements with minimum distance $d_C \geq 2t+1$ and information rate R_C. Then*

$$R_C \leq 1 - \frac{1}{n} \log_q \left(\sum_{i=0}^{t} \binom{n}{i} (q-1)^i \right).$$

Proof. Applying $\log_q$ to both sides of the inequality established in Lemma 3.2 below, we find

$$\log_q |C| + \log_q \left(\sum_{i=0}^{t} \binom{n}{i} (q-1)^i \right) \leq n.$$

The theorem follows immediately from the definition of R_C. ∎

Lemma 3.2. (Hamming Bound) *Let C be a code as in the preceding theorem. Then*

$$|C| \left(\sum_{i=0}^{t} \binom{n}{i} (q-1)^i \right) \leq q^n.$$

Proof. For a word u in $\mathbb{F}^n$ let $B(u,t) = \{v \in \mathbb{F}^n : d(u,v) \leq t\}$. So $B(u,t)$ can be thought of as a ball of radius t and centre u. For distinct codewords w and w' the intersection $B(w,t) \cap B(w',t)$ is empty since $d_C \geq 2t+1$. The vectors in the ball $B(w,t)$ are determined by their difference with w; that is, they correspond to the vectors in $\mathbb{F}^n$ with t or fewer non-zero coordinates. A vector with precisely i non-zero coordinates is said to be of *weight i*. In $\mathbb{F}^n$ there are $\binom{n}{i}(q-1)^i$ words of weight i, and so

$$|B(w,t)| = \sum_{i=0}^{t} \binom{n}{i} (q-1)^i.$$

The lemma follows from the inequality $|\cup_{w \in C} B(w, t)| \leq |\mathbb{F}^n|$.   ∎

A code C is said to be *perfect* if for some t we have $B(w, t) \cap B(w', t) = \emptyset$ for any pair of distinct codewords w, w', and $\cup_{w \in C} B(w, t) = \mathbb{F}^n$. (In other words, the balls of radius t, centred on codewords, form a partition of $\mathbb{F}^n$.) The Hamming $(7, 4)$-binary code is an example of a perfect code.

At this point we should demonstrate that error-correcting codes really do decrease the probability of transmission errors. We shall just consider the binary case. Suppose that binary messages are transmitted across a communications channel and that each digit of a word has equal probability $p \geq \frac{1}{2}$ of correct transmission, and probability $q = 1 - p$ of incorrect transmission. This is called a *binary symmetric channel*. (For many situations, such as when errors occur in bursts, this model is not realistic.) If, say, a 4-digit message word is transmitted without the use of a code, then the probability of correct transmission is p^4. If however the Hamming $(7, 4)$-code is used, all single errors can be corrected but no double errors can be corrected. As there are seven possible digits in which a single error may occur, the probability of correct transmission is $p^7 + 7p^6 q$. For $p = 0.99$ we have $p^4 = 0.9601$ and $p^7 + 7p^6 q = 0.9980$; the Hamming code thus reduces the frequency of errors in decoded words from 4 in 100 to 2 in 1000.

Suppose now that the $(12, 4)$-repetition code is used instead of the Hamming code to send a 4-digit binary message word. Then all single errors (there are 12 possibilities), and no quintuple errors can be corrected. Certain double, triple, and quadruple errors can be detected. To see this consider an arbitrary code word

$$w = (a, b, c, d, a, b, c, d, a, b, c, d).$$

Double errors can be corrected if and only if they occur in distinct letters. (So for instance, if two of the a's were transmitted incorrectly, the error could not be corrected.) There are $3^2 \times \binom{4}{2} = 54$ such double errors. Triple errors can be corrected if and only if they occur in distinct letters. There are $3^3 \times \binom{4}{3} = 108$ such triple errors. Quadruple errors can be corrected if and only if they occur in distinct letters. There are $3^4 = 81$ such quadruple errors. The probability of correct transmission with the repetition code is therefore

$$p^{12} + 12p^{11}q + 54p^{10}q^2 + 108p^9 q^3 + 81p^8 q^4.$$

For $p = 0.99$ this probability is 0.9988. This is a negligibly better probability than that of the Hamming code gained at the cost of almost halving the information rate.

Much of coding theory is concerned with the problem of construct-ing, for given values of n and t, efficient t-error-correcting/detecting codes of length n. Field theory helps with the construction of such codes.

The vector space $\mathbb{F}^n$ can be identified with the vector space

$$\mathbb{F}[x]_n = \{a_0 + a_1 x + a_2 x^2 + \cdots + a_m x^m : m < n, a_i \in \mathbb{F}\}$$

of polynomials in $\mathbb{F}[x]$ of degree less than n. The identification is given by the *linear isomorphism* (that is, surjective and injective linear homomorphism).

$$\mathbb{F}^n \xrightarrow{\cong} \mathbb{F}[x]_n, \qquad (a_0, a_1, \ldots, a_{n-1}) \mapsto a_0 + a_1 x + \cdots + a_{n-1} x^{n-1}.$$

Let $g(x)$ be a polynomial in $\mathbb{F}[x]$ of degree $n-k$. Such a polynomial represents an injective linear homomorphism $g: \mathbb{F}[x]_k \to \mathbb{F}[x]_n$, $a(x) \mapsto g(x)a(x)$. Thus $g(x)$ represents an encoding function $g: \mathbb{F}^k \to \mathbb{F}^n$.

To illustrate this, take $\mathbb{F} = \mathbb{Z}_2$, $k = 3$, $n = 6$, $g(x) = 1 + x + x^3$. Then the encoding function g is described by the following table:

Message word			Code word					
0	0	0	0	0	0	0	0	0
0	0	1	0	0	1	1	0	1
0	1	0	0	1	1	0	1	0
0	1	1	0	1	0	1	1	1
1	0	0	1	1	0	1	0	0
1	0	1	1	1	1	0	0	1
1	1	0	1	0	1	1	1	0
1	1	1	1	0	0	0	1	1

A linear code arising from a polynomial $g(x)$ in this way is called a *polynomial code*, and $g(x)$ is called the *generating polynomial*.

A powerful class of polynomial codes was discovered independently around 1960 by Bose and Chaudhuri and by Hoquenghem. To under-stand these *BCH codes* we need to introduce the notion of the 'minimum polynomial' of an element in a field extension.

Let $L:K$ be a field extension. An element α in L is said to be *algebraic* over K if there is a non-zero polynomial $f(x)$ in $K[x]$ such that $f(\alpha) = 0$. For instance, the real number $\sqrt{2}$ is algebraic over $\mathbb{Q}$ since $\sqrt{2}$ is a root of $x^2 - 2$. If every element of L is algebraic over K then the extension $L:K$ is said to be *algebraic*. The extension $\mathbb{C}:\mathbb{R}$ is an example of an algebraic extension. The extension $\mathbb{R}:\mathbb{Q}$ is not algebraic; it can be shown that certain real numbers, such as π, are not algebraic over $\mathbb{Q}$.

A polynomial in $K[x]$ is said to be *monic* if the coefficient of the highest power of x in the polynomial is 1. If an element α of L is algebraic over K then there must exist a monic polynomial $m_\alpha(x)$ in $K[x]$ such that α is a root of $m_\alpha(x)$, and such that α is not a root of any non-zero polynomial in $K[x]$ of lower degree. We call $m_\alpha(x)$ the *minimum polynomial* of α over K. We can show that this minimum polynomial is unique: if $m_\alpha(x)$ and $m_\alpha(x)'$ are both minimum polynomials of α then they must have the same degree and hence $m_\alpha(x) - m_\alpha(x)'$ is a polynomial of lesser degree having α as a root; thus $m_\alpha(x) - m_\alpha(x)'$ must be the zero polynomial and so $m_\alpha(x) = m_\alpha(x)'$.

As an example note that $m_\alpha(x) = x^2 - 2$ is the minimum polynomial of $\alpha = \sqrt{2}$ over $\mathbb{Q}$. The minimum polynomial of $\sqrt{2}$ over $\mathbb{R}$ is however $x - \sqrt{2}$. A more complicated example, the verification of which we leave as an exercise, is that

$$m_\alpha(x) = x^4 - 10x^2 + 1$$

is the minimum polynomial of $\alpha = \sqrt{2} + \sqrt{3}$ over $\mathbb{Q}$. From the point of view of finite fields it is important to consider the case where α is the coset represented by x in the field $K' = K[x]/(f(x))$ constructed from a field K and an irreducible polynomial $f(x)$ in $K[x]$; the minimum polynomial of α over K' is $f(x)$.

For an algebraic element α over any field K the minimum polynomial $m_\alpha(x)$ divides any polynomial $f(x)$ in $K[x]$ having α as a root. This is proved by noting that there must exist polynomials $q(x)$, $r(x)$ in the Euclidean domain $K[x]$ such that

$$f(x) = q(x)m_\alpha(x) - r(x)$$

with $r(x)$ of lesser degree than $m_\alpha(x)$ or $r(x) = 0$. Since $r(x) = q(x)m_\alpha(x) - f(x)$ has α as a root it follows necessarily that $r(x) = 0$. Hence $m_\alpha(x)$ divides $f(x)$.

We can now explain the various steps in the construction of a generator polynomial for a *BCH code of designated distance d over* $\mathbb{F} = \mathrm{GF}(q)$.

1. Choose an integer r such that $q^r \geqslant d + 1$.

2. We shall show subsequently (Theorems 3.5 and 3.6) that $\mathrm{GF}(q^r)$ contains $\mathbb{F}$ as a subfield, and that there is always at least one element α in $\mathrm{GF}(q^r)$ of order $n = q^r - 1$ (see Chapter 0 for the definition of order); the powers α, $\alpha^2, \ldots, \alpha^n$ are thus the $n = q^r - 1$ distinct

non-zero elements of GF(q). Such an α is said to be a *primitive element*. Choose one primitive element α.

3. For $i = 1, 2, \ldots, d-1$ determine the minimum polynomial of α^i over $\mathbb{F}$; denote this minimum polynomial by $m^i(x)$.

4. The generator polynomial $g(x)$ of the code is taken to be the lowest common multiple of the $m^i(x)$:

$$g(x) = lcm(m^1(x), \ldots, m^{d-1}(x)).$$

Lowest common multiples in $\mathbb{F}[x]$ are only unique up to a constant factor; to ensure uniqueness of $g(x)$ we always take $g(x)$ to be monic. This polynomial $g(x)$ can be used to generate a linear code of length $n = q^r - 1$ and dimension $k = q^r - 1 - \deg(g(x))$. (See the proof of Theorem 3.4 below for an explanation of why $k \geq 0$.)

A BCH code is completely determined by the three parameters d, n, and q, where n has to satisfy $n = q^r - 1 \geq d$ for some r.

As an illustration, suppose we want to construct a generator polynomial for a BCH code of designated distance 5, and length 15 over $\mathbb{F} = \mathbb{Z}_2$. So we want $q^r - 1 = 15$ with $q = 2$. We must therefore choose $r = 4$. The field of 16 elements can be represented by

$$GF(2^4) = \mathbb{Z}_2[x]/(x^4 + x^3 + 1)$$

since $x^4 + x^3 + 1$ is irreducible over $\mathbb{Z}_2$. (Verify that $x^4 + x^3 + 1$ has no roots in $\mathbb{Z}_2$, and cannot be expressed as the product of two quadratic polynomials.) It turns out that any root of $x^4 + x^3 + 1$ in $GF(2^4)$ is a primitive element. To see this let α be one of its roots and compute the powers of α:

α	$\alpha^9 = \alpha^2 + 1$
α^2	$\alpha^{10} = \alpha^3 + \alpha$
α^3	$\alpha^{11} = \alpha^3 + \alpha^2 + 1$
$\alpha^4 = \alpha^3 + 1$	$\alpha^{12} = \alpha + 1$
$\alpha^5 = \alpha(\alpha^3 + 1) = \alpha^3 + \alpha + 1$	$\alpha^{13} = \alpha^2 + \alpha$
$\alpha^6 = \alpha^3 + \alpha^2 + \alpha + 1$	$\alpha^{14} = \alpha^3 + \alpha^2$
$\alpha^7 = \alpha^2 + \alpha + 1$	$\alpha^{15} = 1$
$\alpha^8 = \alpha^3 + \alpha^2 + \alpha$	

The minimum polynomial of α over $\mathbb{Z}_2$ is $m^1(x) = x^4 + x^3 + 1$. The following lemma will be helpful in computing $m^i(x)$ for $i = 2, 3, 4$.

Lemma 3.3. *Let β be an element in a field L of characeristic p. The minimum polynomial $m_\beta(x)$ of β over $\mathbb{Z}_p$ is the same as the minimum polynomial $m_{\beta^p}(x)$ of β^p over $\mathbb{Z}_p$.*

Proof. Since we are in characteristic p there is an injective field homomorphism $\phi : L \to L$, $a \mapsto a^p$ known as the *Frobenius homomorphism*. (The reader should use the results in the proof of Theorem 2.10 to prove that ϕ is a homorphism, and then establish injectivity.) The Frobenius homomorphism restricts to the identity homomorphism on the subfield $\mathbb{Z}_p$ of L. Suppose $m_{\beta^p}(x) = a_0 + a_1 x + \cdots + a_n x^n$. Then

$$\phi(m_{\beta^p}(\beta)) = \phi(a_0 + a_1\beta + \cdots a_n\beta^n)$$
$$= \phi a_0 + (\phi a_1)(\phi\beta) + \cdots + (\phi a_n)(\phi\beta^n)$$
$$= a_0 + a_1\beta^p + \cdots + a_n\beta^{pn}$$
$$= m_{\beta^p}(\beta^p)$$
$$= 0.$$

Injectivity of ϕ implies that β is a root of $m_{\beta^p}(x)$. It follows that $m_\beta(x)$ divides $m_{\beta^p}(x)$. Conversely $m_\beta(\beta^p) = \phi(m_\beta(\beta)) = 0$, and so $m_{\beta^p}(x)$ divides $m_\beta(x)$. Thus $m_\beta(x) = m_{\beta^p}(x)$. ∎

Continuing with the example, this lemma tells us that $m^1(x) = m^2(x) = m^4(x)$ and that $m^3(x) = m^6(x) = m^{12}(x) = m^{24}(x)$. Since $\alpha^{24} = \alpha^9$ we have $m^{24}(x) = m^9(x)$. It follows that α^3, α^6, α^{12}, *and* α^9 are all roots of $m^3(x)$. Thus $m^3(x)$ is the polynomial in $\mathbb{Z}_2[x]$ of least degree which has α^3, α^6, α^{12}, and α^9 as roots. Now

$$(x - \alpha^3)(x - \alpha^6)(x - \alpha^{12})(x - \alpha^9) = x^4 + x^3 + x^2 + x + 1.$$

Therefore $m^3(x) = x^4 + x^3 + x^2 + x + 1$.

The required generating polynomial for the BCH code is

$$g(x) = \operatorname{lcm}(m^1(x), m^2(x), m^3(x), m^4(x))$$
$$= m^1(x)m^3(x)$$
$$= (x^4 + x^3 + 1)(x^4 + x^3 + x^2 + x + 1)$$
$$= x^8 + x^4 + x^2 + x + 1.$$

Thus $g(x)$ generates a $(15, 7)$-code. A typical message word might be 1000100 and this would be encoded as 111001100000100.

The following result gives the relationship between the designated distance and minimum distance of a BCH code.

Theorem 3.4. *A BCH code C of designated distance d over $\mathbb{F} = \mathrm{GF}(q)$ has minimum distance $d_C \geqslant d$.*

Proof. Let α be a primitive element of $\mathrm{GF}(q^r)$ with $q^r - 1 \geqslant d$, and $g(x)$ the corresponding generator polynomial. Since $\mathbb{F}[x]$ is a unique factorization domain, the lowest common monic multiple of $m^1(x), \ldots, m^{d-1}(x)$, namely $g(x)$, is the monic polynomial in $\mathbb{F}[x]$ of least degree with roots $\alpha, \alpha^2, \ldots, \alpha^{d-1}$. Let $n = q^r - 1$. Since each α^i is a root of $x^n - 1$ (cf. Proposition 2.15), it follows that $g(x)$ divides $x^n - 1$ and so $\deg(g) \leqslant n$.

The minimum distance of a linear code is equal to the least weight of the non-zero codewords. (This is an exercise for the reader.) Thus $d_c \geqslant d$ if no non-zero codeword $c_0 + c_1 x + \cdots + c_{n-1} x^{n-1}$ has fewer than d non-zero coefficients c_i. That is, if no non-zero polynomial $c(x)$ in $\mathbb{F}[x]$ of degree less than n with roots $\alpha, \ldots, \alpha^{d-1}$ has fewer than d non-zero coefficients. Let us suppose the contrary, and let $c(x)$ be such a polynomial. So

$$c(x) = c_{n_1} x^{n_1} + \cdots + c_{n_{d-1}} x^{n_{d-1}}$$

where each c_{n_i} is an element of $\mathbb{F}$. Since $c(\alpha) = c(\alpha^2) = \cdots = c(\alpha^{d-1}) = 0$ we have the following homogeneous system of $d-1$ equations in the $d-1$ unknowns c_{n_i}:

$$
\begin{aligned}
c_{n_1} \alpha^{n_1} + \cdots + c_{n_{d-1}} \alpha^{n_{d-1}} &= 0 \\
c_{n_1} \alpha^{2n_1} + \cdots + c_{n_{d-1}} \alpha^{2n_{d-1}} &= 0 \\
\vdots \qquad\qquad \vdots \qquad\qquad &\vdots \\
c_{n_1} \alpha^{(d-1)n_1} + \cdots + c_{n_{d-1}} \alpha^{(d-1)n_{d-1}} &= 0.
\end{aligned}
$$

Without loss of generality we can assume that

$$n_1 > \ldots > n_{d-1} \geqslant 0$$

and that $n > n_1$ (why?). Since we are supposing the system to have a non-trivial solution, the following determinant must be zero:

$$\Delta = \begin{vmatrix} \alpha^{n_1} & \alpha^{n_2} & \ldots & \alpha^{n_{d-1}} \\ \alpha^{2n_1} & \alpha^{2n_2} & \ldots & \alpha^{2n_{d-1}} \\ \vdots & \vdots & & \vdots \\ \alpha^{(d-1)n_1} & \alpha^{(d-1)n_2} & \ldots & \alpha^{(d-1)n_{d-1}} \end{vmatrix}.$$

However, this is Vandermonde's determinant and reduces to

$$\Delta = (-1)^{d-1} \times (\alpha^{n_1}\alpha^{n_2} \ldots \alpha^{n_{d-1}}) \times \prod_{i>j} (\alpha^{n_i} - \alpha^{n_j}).$$

(This should at least be verified for $d = 5$.) It follows that Δ is non-zero since $n_j < n_i < n$. This contradiction proves the theorem.   ∎

In practice BCH codes are mainly used for error detection. One such code that has been used in European data communication systems is the binary (255, 231)-BCH code of designated distance 7. This code is formed over the field $\mathbb{F} = GF(2^8)$ which has a primitive element α of order 255. The encoding polynomial $g(x)$ has degree 24. The code guarantees error detection of up to six errors. Since the proportion of codewords is $2^{231}/2^{255} \simeq 1/(17 \times 10^6)$ of the total number of 255-bit words, if random errors were introduced into the error-detection circuitry, only about 1 in 17 million would be accepted. Extensive tests on actual European communications over a period of years did not turn up cases where errors caused by channels were not detected by the code.

If a BCH code is to be used for error detection then a method is needed for deciding whether or not a received word is a codeword. Suppose the generator polynomial $g(x)$ is constructed over $\mathbb{F} = GF(q)$ from the primitive element α in $GF(q^r)$. Then a polynomial $r(x)$ in $\mathbb{F}[x]$ of degree less than q^r is a codeword if and only if $g(x)$ divides $r(x)$. That is, if and only if $r(\alpha^i) = 0$ for $i = 1, 2, \ldots, d-1$. If $\mathbb{F}$ is of characteristic p then, by Lemma 3.3, we see that $r(x)$ is a codeword if and only if $r(\alpha^i) = 0$ for each i between 1 and $d-1$ which is not divisible by p.

As an illustration, consider the (15, 7)-BCH code over $\mathbb{F}_2$ which we have already constructed with generating polynomial $x^8 + x^4 + x^2 + x + 1$. We took a root α of $x^4 + x^3 + 1$ in $GF(2^4)$ as a primitive element. Hence a polynomial $r(x)$ in $\mathbb{Z}_2[x]$ of degree 15 or less is a codeword if and only if $r(\alpha^i) = 0$ for $i = 1, 3$.

The construction of BCH codes depends on the following two theorems.

Theorem 3.5.   *Every finite field $\mathbb{F}$ has a primitive element.*

Proof. Suppose $\mathbb{F}$ is the field of q elements. Recall that the order of a non-zero element a of $\mathbb{F}$ is the least positive integer t such that $a^t = 1$. Since necessarily $a^{q-1} = 1$ it follows that t divides $q - 1$. (To see this, note that there are integers s, r such that $q - 1 = st + r$ with $0 \leqslant r < t$. So $1 = a^{q-1} = (a^t)^s a^r = a^r$ and consequently $r = 0$.) Let e be the lowest common multiple of the orders of the non-zero elements of $\mathbb{F}$. Note that e must divide $q - 1$. Suppose that e has prime decomposition $e = p_1^{\varepsilon_1} \ldots p_n^{\varepsilon_n}$ where the p_i are distinct primes and $\varepsilon_i \geqslant 1$. Then, from the definition of e, $\mathbb{F}$ must contain elements b_i whose orders are divisible by $p_i^{\varepsilon_i}$. A suitable power a_i of b_i has order $p_i^{\varepsilon_i}$. Define

$$g = a_1 a_2 \ldots a_n.$$

We shall show that g has order e. For suppose $g^m = 1$ where $m \geqslant 1$. Then

$$a_i^m = a_1^{-m} \ldots a_{i-1}^{-m} a_{i+1}^{-m} \ldots a_n^{-m}.$$

Thus, if $w = p_1^{\varepsilon_1} \ldots p_{i-1}^{\varepsilon_{i-1}} p_{i+1}^{\varepsilon_{i+1}} \ldots p_n^{\varepsilon_n}$ then $a_i^{mw} = 1$. Hence $p_i^{\varepsilon_i}$ divides mw. But w and $p_i^{\varepsilon_i}$ are coprime, so $p_i^{\varepsilon_i}$ divides m. Hence e divides m. But $g^e = 1$. Hence g has order e.

We shall now show that $e = q - 1$, from which the reader should deduce that g is a primitive element. Since each of the $q - 1$ non-zero elements of $\mathbb{F}$ is a root of the equation $x^e - 1$, and since this equation has at most e roots, it follows that $e \geqslant q - 1$. But e divides $q - 1$ and so $e = q - 1$.

Theorem 3.6. *The field $\mathrm{GF}(p^n)$ contains precisely one copy of $\mathrm{GF}(p^m)$ as a subfield for each integer m which divides n. Moreover, these are the only subfields of $\mathrm{GF}(p^n)$.*

Proof. Suppose that m divides n, say $n = rm$. Then

$$p^n - 1 = (p^m - 1)(p^{m(r-1)} + p^{m(r-2)} + \cdots + 1).$$

Let $s = p^{m(r-1)} + p^{m(r-2)} + \cdots + 1$. Then

$$x^{p^n - 1} - 1 = (x^{p^m - 1} - 1)(x^{(p^m - 1)(s-1)} + x^{(p^m - 1)(s-2)} + \cdots + 1).$$

Hence $x^{p^m} - x$ divides $x^{p^n} - x$. Since we know that $\mathrm{GF}(p^n)$ is a splitting field for $x^{p^n} - x$ over $\mathbb{Z}_p$, it follows that $\mathrm{GF}(p^n)$ contains the splitting field $\mathrm{GF}(p^m)$ for $x^{p^m} - x$ over $\mathbb{Z}_p$. Since $x^{p^m} - x$ has only p^m roots the field $\mathrm{GF}(p^n)$ can only contain one copy of $\mathrm{GF}(p^m)$ as a subfield.

To prove the second assertion of the theorem, suppose that $GF(q)$ is an arbitrary subfield of $GF(p^n)$. Then $GF(p^n)$ is a vector space over $GF(q)$ of dimension r say. So $|GF(p^n)| = p^n = q^r$. Hence $q = p^m$ with m an integer such that $rm = n$.

■

Exercises

1. The third digit of the ISBN 0-38?-96576-9 is illegible. Determine this digit.

2. A binary code C is given as the null space of the matrix

$$H = \begin{pmatrix} 1 & 1 & 1 & 0 & 1 & 0 & 0 & 0 \\ 1 & 1 & 0 & 1 & 0 & 1 & 0 & 0 \\ 1 & 0 & 1 & 1 & 0 & 0 & 1 & 0 \\ 0 & 1 & 1 & 1 & 0 & 0 & 0 & 1 \end{pmatrix}.$$

   (i)   Determine the length, dimension, information rate, and minimum distance of C.
   (ii) Show that C is not perfect.
   (iii) Find a linear encoding function $\mathbb{F}^4 \to \mathbb{F}^8$ for C, where $\mathbb{F} = \mathbb{Z}_2$.
   (iv) Show that $\mathbf{r} = (1, 1, 0, 1, 0, 1, 0, 1)$ is not a codeword. Find a vector $\mathbf{e}$ of least weight such that $\mathbf{r} - \mathbf{e}$ is a codeword.
   (v)   If the code is used for error correction over a binary symmetric channel, with received words being decoded as the nearest codeword, show that the probability of correct transmission is $p^8 + 8p^7q + 7p^6q^2$.

3. Let $\mathbb{F} = \mathbb{Z}_2$, and let $E: \mathbb{F}^3 \to \mathbb{F}^6$ be the linear encoding function corresponding to left multiplication by the following matrix G (that is, $E(v) = Gv^t$):

$$G = \begin{pmatrix} 1 & 0 & 0 \\ 0 & 1 & 0 \\ 0 & 0 & 1 \\ 0 & 1 & 1 \\ 1 & 0 & 1 \\ 1 & 1 & 1 \end{pmatrix}.$$

   (i)   What is the probability that a message of six digits will be received and accepted as correct, when in fact at least one error has occurred and not been detected? (Assume a binary symmetric channel.)

(ii) Find a matrix H whose null space is the code in question.

4. Let H_r be the $r \times (2^r - 1)$ matrix over $\mathbb{Z}_2$ whose ith column is the binary number with value i. For instance

$$H_2 = \begin{pmatrix} 0 & 1 & 1 \\ 1 & 0 & 1 \end{pmatrix}.$$

The null-space of H_r is called the *binary Hamming code* of length $2^r - 1$.

(i) Show that binary Hamming codes are perfect codes with minimum distance 3.

(ii) If the $(7, 4)$-binary Hamming code is used, and if not more than one error occurs during transmission, what was the transmitted code word when

(a) $(0, 1, 1, 1, 1, 1, 0)$ is received?

(b) $(0, 1, 0, 0, 1, 1, 1)$ is received?

5. Show that $x^4 + x + 1$ is irreducible over $\mathbb{Z}_2$. Show that any root α of this polynomial in $GF(2^4)$ is primitive. Use α to find a generating polynomial for a 3-error-correcting binary BCH code of length 15. What is the minimum distance of this code?

6. Find a generator polynomial for a BCH code of length 8 and dimension 4 over $\mathbb{Z}_3$.

7. Let α be a primitive element of $GF(2^4)$ with minimum polynomial $x^4 + x + 1$ over $\mathbb{Z}_2$. Consider the BCH code of length 15 and designated distance 5 constructed from α. Show that the polynomial $x^{10} + x^9 + x^8 + x^6 + x^2 + x + 1$ is not in the code.

8. Find an irreducible polynomial over $\mathbb{Z}_3$ of degree 3 whose roots are primitive elements of $GF(27)$.

9. Determine all primitive elements of $GF(17)$ and $GF(9)$.

10. Let a, b be elements of $GF(2^n)$ with n odd. Show that $a^2 + ab + b^2 - 0$ implies $a = b = 0$.

11. Let L be a field all of whose non-zero elements are of the form α^i for some fixed α in L and integer i. Prove that L is finite.

4 Construction of primitive polynomials

In Chapters 2 and 3 we have seen how the existence and structure theorems for finite fields lead, at least in theory, to some interesting applications. However, to put the applications into practice we need to be able to construct 'concrete representations' of the field $GF(p^n)$ for given primes p and positive integers n. That is, we need to be able to find an irreducible polynomial $f(x)$ over $\mathbb{Z}_p$ of degree n, and to find a primitive element of $GF(p^n) \cong \mathbb{Z}_p[x]/(f(x))$. The present chapter is mainly devoted to this problem.

We shall say that a polynomial $f(x)$ in $\mathbb{Z}_p[x]$ is *primitive* if it is irreducible and if some root of it in $\mathbb{Z}_p[x]/(f(x))$ is a primitive element. Our problem is one of finding primitive polynomials.

Recall from Proposition 2.15 that the non-zero elements of $GF(q)$ are the roots of the polynomial $x^{q-1} - 1$. Consequently the theory of roots of unity is intimately tied up with finite fields. We shall develop this theory as a means to producing primitive polynomials. For our present purposes it is sufficient to consider roots of unity over finite fields. However, in Chapter 6 we shall give a proof of a theorem due to Wedderburn which depends on a result about roots of unity over the rational numbers; for this reason we keep our treatment fairly general.

Let n be a positive integer. The splitting field of $x^n - 1$ over a field K is called the *nth cyclotomic field* over K and is denoted by $K^{(n)}$. The roots of $x^n - 1$ in $K^{(n)}$ are the *nth roots of unity* over K.

The *order* of an nth root of unity α over K is the least positive integer m such that $\alpha^m = 1$. Note that the order of an nth root of unity must divide n. We say that α is a *primitive nth root of unity* if it has order n. If α is primitive then every other nth root of unity is of the form α^i for some integer i.

One special case of these definitions is when $K = \mathbb{Z}_p$ and $n = q$ is a prime power. In this case $K^{(q)} = GF(q)$ and the primitive qth roots of unity are the primitive elements of the field $GF(q)$.

Another special case is when $K = \mathbb{Q}$. Then $K^{(n)}$ is a subfield of the complex numbers and the nth roots of unity are represensted by the vertices of a regular polygon with n vertices on the unit circle in the complex plane. Explicitly, these vertices are $v_s = \exp(2s\pi\sqrt{-1}/n)$ for $s = 0, 1, \ldots, n-1$. The primitive nth roots of unity are the complex numbers v_s with s an integer coprime to n.

Theorem 4.1. *Let n be a positive integer and K a field of characteristic*
$p = 0$ *or p a prime. If $p = 0$ or if p does not divide n then there exists a*
primitive nth root of unity over K.

Proof. The case $n = 1$ is trivial, so suppose $n \geqslant 2$. Let e be the lowest
common multiple of the orders of the nth roots of unity. By copying the
proof of Theorem 3.5 an nth root of unity, say ξ, of order e can be
produced.

Since p does not divide n, the polynomial $x^n - 1$ and its non-zero
derivative nx^{n-1} have no common roots. There are therefore n distinct
nth roots of unity over K. Since each such root is a root of $x^e - 1$ we
must have $n \leqslant e$. However, e divides n. Thus $e = n$ and consequently ξ is
a primitive nth root of unity.   ∎

It is readily verified that if ξ is a primitive nth root of unity over K,
then the other primitive nth roots of unity are the powers ξ^s of ξ with s
coprime to n. Thus there are $\phi(n)$ different primitive nth roots of unity
over K, where $\phi(n)$, known as *Euler's function*, is the number of
integers s such that $1 \leqslant s \leqslant n$ and s is coprime to n.

Let K be a field of characteristic p and n an integer not divisible by p.
The polynomial $Q_n(x)$ whose roots are precisely the primitive nth roots
of unity over K is of great interest, and is called the *nth cyclotomic
polynomial* over K. More explicitly, if ξ is a primitive nth root of unity
over K then

$$Q_n(x) = \prod_{\substack{s=1 \\ \mathrm{hcf}(s,n)=1}}^{n} (x - \xi^s).$$

Clearly $Q_n(x)$ is independent of the choice of ξ.

To illustrate this definition let us determine the 8th cyclotomic
polynomial Q_8 over $\mathbb{Q}$. The primitive 8th roots of unity over $\mathbb{Q}$ are
$\xi = \exp(\pi\sqrt{-1}/4)$, $\xi^3 = \exp(3\pi\sqrt{-1}/4)$, $\xi^5 = \exp(5\pi\sqrt{-1}/4)$, and $\xi^7 = \exp(7\pi\sqrt{-1}/4)$. So

$$\begin{aligned}
Q_8(x) &= (x - \xi)(x - \xi^3)(x - \xi^5)(x - \xi^7) \\
&= x^4 - (\xi + \xi^3 + \xi^5 + \xi^7)x^3 + (\xi^4 + \xi^6 + 2\xi^8 + \xi^{10} + \xi^{12})x^2 \\
&\quad - (\xi^9 + \xi^{11} + \xi^{13} + \xi^{15})x + \xi^{16} \\
&= x^4 + 0x^3 + 0x^2 + 0x + 1 \\
&= x^4 + 1.
\end{aligned}$$

As a second illustration let us determine the 5th cyclotomic polynomial $Q_5(x)$ over $GF(4)$. The field $GF(4)$ is contained in the field $GF(16)$, and we know from Chapter 3 that any root in $GF(16)$ of the polynomial $x^4 + x^3 + 1$ is a primitive element. Let α be one such root. Since α is also a root of $x^{15} - 1$ it follows that $\xi = \alpha^3$ is a root of $x^5 - 1$. Moreover $\xi = \alpha^3$, $\xi^2 = \alpha^3 + \alpha^2 + \alpha + 1$, $\xi^3 = \alpha^2 + 1$, $\xi^4 = \alpha + 1$, and $\xi^5 = 1$ are the five distinct roots of $x^5 - 1$ in $GF(16)$. Hence the element $\xi = \alpha^3$ in $GF(16)$ is a primitive 5th root of unity over $GF(4)$. So

$$\begin{aligned}
Q_5(x) &= (x - \xi)(x - \xi^2)(x - \xi^3)(x - \xi^4) \\
&= x^4 - (\xi + \xi^2 + \xi^3 + \xi^4)x^3 + (\xi + \xi^2 + \xi^3 + \xi^4)x^2 \\
&\quad - (\xi + \xi^2 + \xi^3 + \xi^4)x + 1 \\
&= x^4 - 0x^3 + 0x^2 - 0x + 1 \\
&= x^4 + 1.
\end{aligned}$$

It is not just by chance that in our first example $Q_8(x)$ has coefficients in $\mathbb{Z}$, and in the second $Q_5(x)$ has coefficients in the prime subfield $\mathbb{Z}_2$. We will prove (Theorem 4.2) that cyclotomic polynomials over fields of characteristic 0 always have coefficients in $\mathbb{Z}$, and cyclotomic polynomials over fields of characteristic $p \geqslant 1$ always have coefficients in $\mathbb{Z}_p$. This result gives us one possible method of determining primitive polynomials of degree n over $\mathbb{Z}_p$. For let $q = p^n$. Then any root ξ of the $(q - 1)$th cyclotomic polynomial $Q_{q-1}(x)$ over $\mathbb{Z}_p$ is a primitive $(q - 1)$th root of unity and hence a primitive element of $GF(q)$. The minimum polynomial $m_\xi(x)$ of ξ over $\mathbb{Z}_p$ is thus a primitive polynomial of degree n. But $m_\xi(x)$ divides $Q_{q-1}(x)$ since $Q_{q-1}(\xi) = 0$. Thus $m_\xi(x)$ is an irreducible factor of $Q_{q-1}(x)$ in the ring $\mathbb{Z}_p[x]$. Moreover, any monic irreducible factor of $Q_{q-1}(x)$ is clearly the minimum polynomial of some primitive $(q - 1)$th root of unity and is therefore a primitive polynomial over $\mathbb{Z}_p$ of degree n. Thus to find the primitive polynomials of degree n over $\mathbb{Z}_p$ we might try factorizing $Q_{q-1}(x)$ into monic irreducible polynomials. Before we consider how such a factorization could be carried out, let us list in the following theorem some useful facts about cyclotomic polynomials. We use the product symbol $\prod_{d|n}$ to denote a product extended over all positive divisors d of a positive integer n.

Theorem 4.2 *Let K be a field of characteristic $p \geqslant 0$ and n an integer not divisible by p. Let $Q_n(x)$ be the nth cyclotomic polynomial over K. Then:*

(i) $x^n - 1 = \prod_{d|n} Q_d(x)$;

(ii)   *the coefficients of $Q_n(x)$ belong to the prime subfield $\mathbb{Z}_p$ of K if*
       $p \geq 2$, and to the ring $\mathbb{Z}$ if $p = 0$;

(iii) $Q_n(x) = \prod_{d|n} (x^{n/d} - 1)^{\mu(d)}$
       where

$$\mu(d) = \begin{cases} 1 & \text{if } d = 1, \\ (-1)^k & \text{if } d \text{ is the product of } k \text{ distinct primes,} \\ 0 & \text{if } d \text{ is divisible by the square of a prime.} \end{cases}$$

Proof.   (i) Let ξ be a primitive nth root of unity and ξ^s an arbitrary nth
root of unity over K. Then ξ^s has order $d = n/\mathrm{hcf}(s, n)$ (why?) and so is
a primitive dth root of unity. Since

$$x^n - 1 = \prod_{s=1}^{n} (x - \xi^s)$$

the formula in (i) is obtained by collecting together those factors
$(x - \xi^s)$ for which ξ^s is a primitive dth root of unity over K.
(ii) This is proved by induction on n. Note that $Q_n(x)$ is a monic
polynomial. For $n = 1$ we have $Q_1(x) = x - 1$ and the result obviously
holds. Suppose that the result is true for all $Q_d(x)$ with $1 \leq d < n$. Then
by (i) we have

$$Q_n(x) = (x^n - 1)/f(x)$$

with

$$f(x) = \prod_{d|n, \, d<n} Q_d(x).$$

The induction hypothesis implies that $f(x)$ is a polynomial with coef-
ficients in $\mathbb{Z}_p$ or $\mathbb{Z}$. It follows that, if we use the long division algorithm
to divide $x^n - 1$ by $f(x)$, the coefficients of the resulting polynomial
$Q_n(x)$ will belong to $\mathbb{Z}_p$ or $\mathbb{Z}$.
(iii) The function $\mu(d)$ is known as the *Möbius function* and, for all
$n \geq 1$, can be shown to satisfy the formula

$$\sum_{d|n} \mu(d) = \begin{cases} 1 & \text{if } n = 1, \\ 0 & \text{if } n > 1. \end{cases} \tag{4.1}$$

This formula clearly holds if $n = 1$. To prove it for $n > 1$ suppose that
$p_1, \ldots, p_k$ are the distinct prime divisors of n; then

$$\sum_{d|n} \mu(d) = \mu(1) + \sum_{i=1}^{k} \mu(p_i) + \sum_{1 \le i < j \le k} \mu(p_i p_j) + \cdots + \mu(p_1 p_2 \cdots p_k)$$

$$= 1 + \binom{k}{1}(-1) + \binom{k}{2}(-1)^2 + \cdots + \binom{k}{k}(-1)^k$$

$$= (1 + (-1))^k$$

$$= 0.$$

As a consequence of (4.1) we see that if we set $h(n) = Q_n(x)$ and $H(n) = x^n - 1$ then

$$\prod_{d|n}(x^{n/d} - 1)^{\mu(d)} = \prod_{d|n} H(n/d)^{\mu(d)}$$

$$= \prod_{d|n} \left\{ \prod_{c|(n/d)} h(c) \right\}^{\mu(d)} \qquad \text{by part (i)}$$

$$= \prod_{(d,c) \in A} h(c)^{\mu(d)}$$

where $A = \{(d, c) \in \mathbb{N} \times \mathbb{N} : d|n \text{ and } c|(n/d)\}$. Since the set A can also be described as $A = \{(d, c) \in \mathbb{N} \times \mathbb{N} : c|n \text{ and } d|(n/c)\}$ we have

$$\prod_{d|n}(x^{n/d} - 1)^{\mu(d)} = \prod_{c|n} \prod_{d|(n/c)} h(c)^{\mu(d)}$$

$$= \prod_{c|n} h(c)^{\sum_{d|(n/c)} \mu(d)}$$

$$= h(n) \qquad \text{by (4.1)}$$

$$= Q_n(x). \qquad \blacksquare$$

The following recalculation of the 8th cyclotomic polynomial $Q_8(x)$ over $\mathbb{Q}$ illustrates the formula in part (iii) of Theorem 4.2:

$$\begin{aligned}
Q_8(x) &= (x^8 - 1)^{\mu(1)}(x^4 - 1)^{\mu(2)}(x^2 - 1)^{\mu(4)}(x - 1)^{\mu(8)} \\
&= (x^8 - 1)(x^4 - 1)^{-1}(x^2 - 1)^0(x - 1)^0 \\
&= \frac{x^8 - 1}{x^4 - 1} \\
&= x^4 + 1.
\end{aligned}$$

Since we now have a method of computing cyclotomic polynomials, our problem of determining primitive polynomials is reduced to one of factorizing cyclotomic polynomials. Various algorithms exist for factorizing (arbitrary) polynomials over finite fields, and we shall study one due to Berlekamp. The various calculations involved in the algorithm will in general require computer assistance.

Let $f(x)$ be a monic polynomial in the ring $\mathrm{GF}(q)[x]$ of polynomials in the indeterminate x over the field $\mathrm{GF}(q)$. We need a method of factorizing $f(x)$ as

$$f(x) = f_1(x)^{\varepsilon_1} f_2(x)^{\varepsilon_2} \ldots f_k(x)^{\varepsilon_k}$$

where the $f_i(x)$ are distinct irreducible monic polynomials in $\mathrm{GF}(q)[x]$ and the ε_i are positive integers.

We shall first show how to reduce this factorization task to the case when $f(x)$ has no repeated factors, that is, when the exponents ε_i are all equal to 1. To this end, let

$$h(x) = \mathrm{hcf}(f(x), f'(x))$$

be the highest common monic factor of $f(x)$ and its formal derivative $f'(x)$. This polynomial $h(x)$ can be computed using the *Euclidean algorithm*, which is based on the fact that $\mathrm{GF}(q)[x]$ is a Euclidean domain and involves finding polynomials $q_1(x), \ldots, q_{s+1}(x)$ and $r_1(x), \ldots, r_s(x)$ in $\mathrm{GF}(q)[x]$ satisfying

$$\begin{aligned}
f(x) &= q_1(x)f'(x) + r_1(x) & \deg(r_1(x)) &< \deg(f'(x)) \\
f'(x) &= q_2(x)r_1(x) + r_2(x) & \deg(r_2(x)) &< \deg(r_1(x)) \\
r_1(x) &= q_3(x)r_2(x) + r_3(x) & \deg(r_3(x)) &< \deg(r_2(x)) \\
&\ \ \vdots & &\ \ \vdots \\
r_{s-2}(x) &= q_s(x)r_{s-1}(x) + r_s(x) & \deg(r_s(x)) &< \deg(r_{s-1}(x)) \\
r_{s-1}(x) &= q_{s+1}(x)r_s(x).
\end{aligned}$$

If a is the coefficient of the highest power of x in the last non-zero remainder $r_s(x)$, then it is an exercise to show that $h(x) = a^{-1}r_s(x)$. (Note that this algorithm does not depend on $f'(x)$ being the derivative of $f(x)$.)

We leave the following as an exercise for the reader: if $h(x) = 1$ then $f(x)$ can have no repeated factors.

When $h(x) = f(x)$ we must have $f'(x) = 0$; hence $f(x) = t(x)^p$ for some polynomial $t(x)$ in $GF(q)[x]$ and p the characteristic of $GF(q)$. In this case the factorization of $f(x)$ is reduced to the factorization of $t(x)$. If $t(x)$ has repeated factors then further reduction is necessary.

When $h(x) \neq 1$ and $h(x) \neq f(x)$ then the polynomial $f(x)/h(x)$ has no repeated factors since it can be verified that $h(x)$ is a multiple of

$$f_1(x)^{\varepsilon_1 - 1}f_2(x)^{\varepsilon_2 - 1} \dots f_k(x)^{\varepsilon_k - 1}.$$

In this case the factorization of $f(x)$ is reduced to the factorization of $h(x)$ and $f(x)/h(x)$. If $h(x)$ has repeated factors then it needs to be further reduced.

As an example suppose we want to factorize, in the ring $\mathbb{Z}_2[x]$, the polynomial

$$f(x) = x^{13} + x^{11} + x^{10} + x^9 + x^8 + x^7 + x^6 + x^5 + x^4 + x^3 + x^2 + 1.$$

So

$$f'(x) = x^{12} + x^{10} + x^8 + x^6 + x^4 + x^2$$

and the Euclidean algorithm yields

$$f(x) = xf'(x) + (x^{10} + x^8 + x^6 + x^4 + x^2 + 1)$$
$$f'(x) = x^2(x^{10} + x^8 + x^6 + x^4 + x^2 + 1).$$

Consequently the highest common factor of $f(x)$ and $f'(x)$ is

$$h(x) = x^{10} + x^8 + x^6 + x^4 + x^2 + 1.$$

We thus have

$$f(x) = (f(x)/h(x))h(x)$$
$$= (x^3 + 1)(x^{10} + x^8 + x^6 + x^4 + x^2 + 1),$$

with $x^3 + 1$ a product of distinct factors. We easily factorize $x^3 + 1$ to get

$$f(x) = (x + 1)(x^2 + x + 1)(x^{10} + x^8 + x^6 + x^4 + x^2 + 1).$$

We now need to factorize

$$g(x) = x^{10} + x^8 + x^6 + x^4 + x^2 + 1.$$

As $g'(x) = 0$ we must have $g(x) = t(x)^2$ for some $t(x)$. Clearly $t(x)$ must be a polynomial of degree 5; by 'observation' we find

$$t(x) = x^5 + x^4 + x^3 + x^2 + x + 1.$$

Now

$$t'(x) = x^4 + x^2 + 1$$

and the highest common factor of $t(x)$ and $t'(x)$ is $t'(x)$ itself since

$$t(x) = (x+1)(x^4 + x^2 + 1).$$

So we have shown that

$$f(x) = (x+1)^3(x^2 + x + 1)(x^4 + x^2 + 1)^2,$$

and it only remains to factorize $x^4 + x^2 + 1$. Considering the derivative we see that $x^4 + x^2 + 1$ must be the square of some polynomial of degree 2; it is an easy observation that

$$x^4 + x^2 + 1 = (x^2 + x + 1)^2.$$

Therefore we have shown that $f(x)$ factors as

$$f(x) = (x+1)^3(x^2 + x + 1)^5.$$

In this example we were lucky: $x^3 + 1$ was easy to factorize into irreducible factors, and $x^2 + x + 1$ is irreducible. The factorization of $f(x)$ is thus complete.

We now turn our attention to factorizing polynomials which have no repeated factors. The method we introduce is based on the following theorem.

Theorem 4.3. *Let $f(x)$ and $g(x)$ be polynomials in $\mathrm{GF}(q)[x]$ such that $f(x)$ is monic and $h(x)^q - h(x)$ is divisible by $f(x)$. Then*

$$f(x) = \prod_{c \in \mathrm{GF}(q)} \mathrm{hcf}(f(x), h(x) - c).$$

Proof. For each c in $\mathrm{GF}(q)$ the highest common factor of $f(x)$ and $h(x) - c$ divides $f(x)$. Since the polynomials $h(x) - c$ are pairwise coprime, so are their highest common factors with $f(x)$, and hence the product of these highest common factors divides $f(x)$. Conversely $f(x)$ divides

$$h(x)^q - h(x) = \prod_{c \in \mathrm{GF}(q)} (h(x) - c)$$

(this equation should be verified) and so $f(x)$ divides the monic polynomial

$$\prod_{c \in \mathrm{GF}(q)} \mathrm{hcf}(f(x), h(x) - c).$$

(Why?) This completes the proof.   ∎

Of course, Theorem 4.3 will not yield a useful factorization if for some $c \in \mathrm{GF}(q)$ the polynomial $h(x) - c$ is divisible by $f(x)$. For the theorem to be of use we need to be able to find a polynomial $h(x)$ such that $h(x)^q - h(x)$ is divisible by $f(x)$ and $0 < \deg(h(x)) < \deg(f(x))$; such a polynomial $h(x)$ is said to be $f(x)$-*reducing*. The existence of $f(x)$-reducing polynomials (see Theorem 4.5) is proved using the following result (in which the *congruence*

$$h(x) \equiv g_i(x) \qquad \text{modulo } f_i(x)$$

just means that $h(x) - g_i(x) = r(x)f_i(x)$ for some $r(x) \in K[x]$).

Proposition 4.4. (Chinese remainder theorem) *Let K be any field, let $f_1(x), \ldots, f_k(x)$ be non-zero polynomials in $K[x]$ that are pairwise coprime, and let $g_1(x), \ldots, g_k(x)$ be arbitrary polynomials in $K[x]$. Then there exists a polynomial $h(x)$ satisfying simultaneously the congruences*

$$h(x) \equiv g_1(x) \qquad \text{modulo } f_1(x),$$
$$h(x) \equiv g_2(x) \qquad \text{modulo } f_2(x),$$
$$\vdots$$
$$h(x) \equiv g_k(x) \qquad \text{modulo } f_k(x).$$

Moreover if $h(x)$ and $h'(x)$ are any two polynomials simultaneously satisfying the congruences then

$$h(x) \equiv h'(x) \qquad \text{modulo } f_1(x)f_2(x) \ldots f_k(x).$$

The proof of the Chinese remainder theorem is a special case of Exercise 6 at the end of this chapter.

Theorem 4.5. *Let $f(x)$ be a product of k distinct irreducible monic polynomials $f_i(x)$ in $\mathrm{GF}(q)[x]$. Then there are precisely q^k polynomials $h(x)$ in $\mathrm{GF}(q)[x]$ satisfying*

$$h(x)^q \equiv h(x) \qquad \text{modulo } f(x), \quad \deg(h(x)) < \deg(f(x)).$$

Proof. For each k-tuple $(c_1, \ldots, c_k)$ of elements of $\mathrm{GF}(q)$ the Chinese remainder theorem implies that there is a unique polynomial $h(x)$ in $\mathrm{GF}(q)[x]$ with $h(x) \equiv c_i$ modulo $f_i(x)$ for $1 \leq i \leq k$ and $\deg(h(x)) < \deg(f(x))$. Thus $h(x)$ satisfies

$$h(x)^q \equiv c_i^q = c_i \equiv h(x) \qquad \text{modulo } f_i(x) \text{ for } 1 \leq i \leq k.$$

Therefore

$$h(x)^q \equiv h(x) \qquad \text{modulo } f(x), \quad \deg(h(x)) < \deg(f(x)).$$

There are q^k k-tuples $(c_1, \ldots, c_k)$ and so there are at least q^k polynomials $h(x)$ satisfying the conditions of the theorem.

On the other hand, if $h(x)$ satisfies the conditions of the theorem, then, since $f(x)$ is a multiple of $h(x)^q - h(x)$, the identity

$$h(x)^q - h(x) = \prod_{c \in \mathrm{GF}(q)} (h(x) - c)$$

implies that every irreducible factor of $f(x)$ divides one of the polynomials $h(x) - c$. Hence $h(x) \equiv c_i$ modulo $f_i(x)$ for $1 \leq i \leq k$ and for some k-tuple $(c_1, \ldots, c_k)$. Consequently there are exactly q^k such polynomials $h(x)$. ∎

Given a polynomial $f(x)$ of degree n which is a product of k distinct irreducible monic polynomials in $\mathrm{GF}(q)[x]$, we find an $h(x)$ satisfying the conditions of Theorem 4.5 by first constructing an $n \times n$ matrix $B = (b_{ij})$ whose entries are in $\mathrm{GF}(q)$ and are determined by the equations

$$x^{iq} \equiv b_{i0} + b_{i1}x + b_{i2}x^2 + \cdots + b_{in-1}x^{n-1} \qquad \text{modulo } f(x).$$

The reader should verify that the following conditions on a polynomial

$$h(x) = a_0 + a_1 x + \cdots + a_{n-1} x^{n-1}$$

in $GF(q)[x]$ are equivalent:

(1) $h(x)^q \equiv h(x)$ modulo $f(x)$;

(2) $h(x^q) \equiv h(x)$ modulo $f(x)$;

(3) $a_0 + a_1 x^q + a_2 x^{2q} + \cdots + a_{n-1} x^{(n-1)q}$
$\equiv a_0 + a_1 x + \cdots + a_{n-1} x^{n-1}$ modulo $f(x)$;

(4) $(a_0, a_1, \ldots, a_{n-1}) B = (a_0, a_1, \ldots, a_{n-1})$;

(5) $(a_0, a_1, \ldots, a_{n-1}) (B - I) = (0, , 0, \ldots, 0)$ where I is the $n \times n$ identity matrix over $GF(q)$.

By Theorem 4.5 the system of equations in (5) has q^k solutions, where k is the number of distinct irreducible factors of $f(x)$. Thus the dimension of the null space of $B - I$ is k. The rank of $B - I$ is $n - k$.

If the rank of $B - I$ is $n - 1$, then $f(x)$ is irreducible.

If the rank of $B - I$ is $r < n - 1$, then $f(x)$ is reducible. The null space of $B - I$ has a basis of $k = n - r$ vectors in this case; these basis vectors correspond to polynomials $h_1(x), \ldots h_k(x)$ of degree $\leq n - 1$. (A vector $(a_0, \ldots, a_{n-1})$ corresponds to the polynomial $a_0 + a_1 x + \cdots + a_{n-1} x^{n-1}$.) Without loss of generality we can assume that $h_1(x) = 1$. Then $h_2(x), \ldots, h_k(x)$ are $f(x)$-reducing polynomials. As we shall see, Theorem 4.3 with $h(x) = h_2(x)$ produces a non-trivial factorization of $f(x)$. If this factorization does not succeed in splitting $f(x)$ into $k = n - r$ factors, then Theorem 4.3 with $h(x) = h_3(x)$ applied in turn to each factor of $f(x)$ will yield further factorization. If necessary Theorem 4.3 can then be applied to each of these further factorizations with $h(x) = h_4(x)$, and so on. This procedure is known as *Berlekamp's algorithm*.

Theorem 4.6. *If $f(x)$ is a product of k district irreducible monic polynomials in $GF(q)[x]$, then Berlekamp's algorithm eventually yields all of these k factors.*

Proof. Consider two distinct irreducible monic factors $f_1(x)$ and $f_2(x)$ of $f(x)$. By the argument of the second paragraph in the proof of Theorem 4.5, there exist elements c_{j1}, c_{j2} of $GF(q)$ such that $h_j(x) \equiv c_{j1}$ modulo $f_1(x)$, and $h_j(x) \equiv c_{j2}$ modulo $f_2(x)$ for $1 \leq j \leq k$. Suppose $c_{j1} = c_{j2}$ for $1 \leq j \leq k$. Then since any $f(x)$-reducing polynomial $h(x)$ is a linear combination of $h_1(x), \ldots, h_k(x)$, there would exist, for any such $h(x)$, an element c in $GF(q)$ with $h(x) \equiv c$ modulo $f_1(x)$ and $h(x) \equiv c$ modulo $f_2(x)$. But using the argument employed in the first part of the proof of Theorem 4.5 we see that, in particular, there is an $f(x)$-reducing polynomial $h(x)$ such that $h(x) \equiv 0$ modulo $f_1(x)$, and $h(x) \equiv 1$ modulo $f_2(x)$. This contradiction proves that $c_{j1} \ne c_{j2}$ for some j with $1 \le j \le k$. Thus $h_j(x) - c_{j1}$ will be divisible by $f_1(x)$, but not by $f_2(x)$. Hence any two irreducible factors of $f(x)$ will be separated by Berlekamp's algorithm. ∎

To illustrate Berlekamp's algorithm we shall factorize

$$f(x) = x^{10} + x^5 + 1$$

over $\mathbb{Z}_2[x]$. Since $f'(x) = x^4$ the polynomials $f(x)$ and $f'(x)$ are coprime and $f(x)$ has no repeated factors. The degree of $f(x)$ is $n = 10$, and so $B = (b_{ij})$ is the 10×10 matrix over $\mathbb{Z}_2$ with entries given by

$$x^{2i} \equiv \sum_{j=0}^{9} b_{ij} x^j \qquad \text{modulo } f(x).$$

That is

$$B = \begin{bmatrix} 1 & 0 & 0 & 0 & 0 & 0 & 0 & 0 & 0 & 0 \\ 0 & 0 & 1 & 0 & 0 & 0 & 0 & 0 & 0 & 0 \\ 0 & 0 & 0 & 0 & 1 & 0 & 0 & 0 & 0 & 0 \\ 0 & 0 & 0 & 0 & 0 & 0 & 1 & 0 & 0 & 0 \\ 0 & 0 & 0 & 0 & 0 & 0 & 0 & 0 & 1 & 0 \\ 1 & 0 & 0 & 0 & 0 & 1 & 0 & 0 & 0 & 0 \\ 0 & 0 & 1 & 0 & 0 & 0 & 0 & 1 & 0 & 0 \\ 0 & 0 & 0 & 0 & 1 & 0 & 0 & 0 & 0 & 1 \\ 0 & 1 & 0 & 0 & 0 & 0 & 0 & 0 & 0 & 0 \\ 0 & 0 & 0 & 1 & 0 & 0 & 0 & 0 & 0 & 0 \end{bmatrix}.$$

Using elementary row operations the transpose $(B - I)^t$ of the matrix $B - I$ can be reduced to

$$(B-I)^{tr} = \begin{bmatrix} 0 & 1 & 0 & 0 & 0 & 0 & 0 & 0 & 1 & 0 \\ 0 & 0 & 1 & 0 & 0 & 0 & 1 & 0 & 1 & 0 \\ 0 & 0 & 0 & 1 & 0 & 0 & 0 & 0 & 0 & 1 \\ 0 & 0 & 0 & 0 & 1 & 0 & 0 & 0 & 1 & 0 \\ 0 & 0 & 0 & 0 & 0 & 1 & 0 & 0 & 0 & 0 \\ 0 & 0 & 0 & 0 & 0 & 0 & 1 & 0 & 0 & 1 \\ 0 & 0 & 0 & 0 & 0 & 0 & 0 & 1 & 0 & 1 \\ 0 & 0 & 0 & 0 & 0 & 0 & 0 & 0 & 0 & 0 \\ 0 & 0 & 0 & 0 & 0 & 0 & 0 & 0 & 0 & 0 \\ 0 & 0 & 0 & 0 & 0 & 0 & 0 & 0 & 0 & 0 \end{bmatrix}.$$

Since for $\mathbf{a} = (a_0, \ldots, a_9)$ we have $\mathbf{a}(B-I) = 0$ if and only if $(B-I)^{tr}\mathbf{a}^t = 0$, it follows that the null space of $B-I$ has dimension 3 and hence $f(x)$ has precisely three distinct irreducible factors. Moreover, one basis for the null space is

$$\mathbf{a}_1 = (1, 0, 0, 0, 0, 0, 0, 0, 0, 0),$$
$$\mathbf{a}_2 = (0, 0, 1, 1, 0, 0, 1, 1, 0, 1),$$
$$\mathbf{a}_3 = (0, 1, 0, 1, 1, 0, 1, 1, 1, 1).$$

The polynomials $h_i(x)$ corresponding to these basis vectors are

$$h_1(x) = 1,$$
$$h_2(x) = x^2 + x^3 + x^6 + x^7 + x^9,$$
$$h_3(x) = x + x^3 + x^4 + x^6 + x^7 + x^8 + x^9.$$

By the Euclidean algorithm we find that

$$\text{hcf}(f(x), h_2(x)) = x^2 + x + 1,$$
$$\text{hcf}(f(x), h_2(x) - 1) = x^8 + x^7 + x^5 + x^4 + x^3 + x + 1,$$
$$\text{hcf}(x^8 + x^7 + x^5 + x^4 + x^3 + x + 1, h_3(x)) = x^4 + x^3 + 1,$$
$$\text{hcf}(x^8 + x^7 + x^5 + x^4 + x^3 + x + 1, h_3(x) - 1) = x^4 + x + 1.$$

Therefore the required factorization of $f(x)$ is

$$f(x) = (x^2 + x + 1)(x^4 + x^3 + 1)(x^4 + x + 1).$$

Berlekamp's algorithm together with Theorem 4.2 (iii) provides us, in theory, with a procedure for determining primitive polynomials. However, for even some quite small prime powers $q = p^n$ the $(q-1)$th cyclotomic polynomial $Q_{q-1}(x)$ turns out to have a high degree. So the application of Berlekamp's algorithm to $Q_{q-1}(x)$ is not practicable without the aid of a computer. Fortunately there are several computer software packages on the market (for instance, DERIVE, MACSYMA, MAPLE, and MATHEMATICA) which incorporate Berlekamp's algorithm. Even with the aid of one of these packages, a certain amount of ingenuity is usually required to break down the factorization of $Q_{q-1}(x)$ into manageable steps. This can be seen from the following example.

Let us set ourselves the task of determining a primitive polynomial of degree 8 over the field of three elements $\mathbb{Z}_3$ (cf. Exercise 18). Thus any root of such a polynomial is a primitive element in the field $GF(3^8)$ of 6561 elements.

The number $q-1=6560$ factorizes as

$$q-1=2^5.5.41.$$

The square-free divisors of $q-1$ are thus:

$$1, 2, 5, 41, 2.5, 2.41, 5.41, 2.5.41.$$

From Theorem 4.2 (iii) it follows that the $(q-1)$th cyclotomic polynomial over $\mathbb{Z}_3$ is

$$Q_{q-1}(x) = \frac{(x^{(2^5.5.41)}-1)(x^{(2^4.41)}-1)(x^{(2^4.5)}-1)(x^{(2^5)}-1)}{(x^{(2^4.5.41)}-1)(x^{(2^5.41)}-1)(x^{(2^5.5)}-1)(x^{(2^4)}-1)}$$

$$= \frac{(x^{(2^4.5.41)}+1)(x^{(2^4)}+1)}{(x^{(2^4.41)}+1)(x^{(2^4.5)}+1)}.$$

The degree of $Q_{q-1}(x)$ is $\phi(2^5.5.41)=2560$ (cf. Exercise 8), and consequently a direct application to $Q_{q-1}(x)$ of even a computerized version of Berlekamp's algorithm will not yield a factorization in reasonable time. However, by substituting

$$y=x^{16}$$

we find that

$$Q_{q-1}(x) = \frac{(y^{5.41}+1)(y+1)}{(y^{41}+1)(y^5+1)}$$

$$= \frac{(y^{41}+1)(y^{41.4}-y^{41.3}+y^{41.2}-y^{41}+1)(y+1)}{(y^{41}+1)(y+1)(y^4-y^3+y^2-y+1)}$$

$$= \frac{(y^{41.4}-y^{41.3}+y^{41.2}-y^{41}+1)}{(y^4-y^3+y^2-y+1)}$$

$$= y^{160}+y^{159}-y^{155}-y^{154}+y^{150}+y^{149}+\cdots+y+1.$$

This polynomial in y can be factorized using MACSYMA on a VAX mainframe computer, the result being

$$Q_{q-1}(x) = (y^8-y^5-y^4-y^3+y^2-y+1)$$
$$\times (y^8+y^5+y^2+y+1)(y^8+y^5+y^3+y+1)$$
$$\times (y^8+y^5+y^4-y^3-y+1)(y^8-y^6+y^5-y^4-y^3+y+1)$$
$$\times (y^8+y^6-y^5+y^4-y^3-y+1)$$
$$\times (y^8-y^7-y^5+y^4 \quad y^3+y^2+1)(y^8-y^7-y^5+y^4+y^3+1)$$
$$\times (y^8-y^7-y^6-y^5-y^4-y^3+y+1)$$
$$\times (y^8-y^7+y^6-y^5-y^4-y^3+1)$$
$$\times (y^8-y^7+y^6+y^5-y^3-y^2+y+1)(y^8+y^7-y^5+y^2+y+1)$$
$$\times (y^8+y^7-y^5-y^4-y^3-y^2-y+1)$$
$$\times (y^8+y^7-y^5-y^4+y^3-y^2+1)$$
$$\times (y^8+y^7-y^5+y^4+y^3+y+1)(y^8+y^7+y^5+y^3+1)$$
$$\times (y^8+y^7+y^5+y^4-y^3+y+1)$$
$$\times (y^8+y^7-y^6-y^5+y^3+y^2-y+1)(y^8+y^7+y^6-y^3+y+1)$$
$$\times (y^8+y^7+y^6+y^3+1).$$

Since we are searching for an arbitrary irreducible factor of $Q_{q-1}(x)$, we need only factorize any one of the above 20 factors of $Q_{q-1}(x)$. Using MACSYMA to factorize the second, we get

$$
\begin{aligned}
& y^8 + y^5 + y^2 + y + 1 \\
&= x^{128} + x^{80} + x^{32} + x^{16} + 1 \\
&= (x^8 - x^6 + x^4 - x^3 - x^2 + x - 1)(x^8 - x^6 + x^4 + x^3 - x^2 - x - 1) \\
&\times (x^8 - x^6 - x^5 + x^3 - 1) \\
&\times (x^8 - x^6 + x^5 - x^3 - 1)(x^8 - x^7 - x^5 + x^3 - 1) \\
&\times (x^8 - x^7 - x^5 + x^4 + x^3 - x^2 - 1) \\
&\times (x^8 - x^7 + x^5 - x^4 + x^3 - x - 1)(x^8 - x^7 - x^6 - x^4 - x^3 - x - 1) \\
&\times (x^8 - x^7 - x^6 - x^4 + x^3 + x^2 - 1) \\
&\times (x^8 - x^7 + x^6 + x^4 + x^2 - 1)(x^8 + x^7 - x^5 - x^4 - x^3 + x + 1) \\
&\times (x^8 + x^7 + x^5 - x^3 - 1) \\
&\times (x^8 + x^7 + x^5 + x^4 - x^3 - x^2 - 1)(x^8 + x^7 - x^6 - x^4 - x^3 + x^2 - 1) \\
&\times (x^8 + x^7 - x^6 - x^4 + x^3 + x - 1) \\
&\times (x^8 + x^7 + x^6 + x^4 + x^2 - 1).
\end{aligned}
$$

Thus any one of these 16 factors of $y^8 + y^5 + y^2 + y + 1$ is a primitive polynomial over $\mathbb{Z}_3$ of degree 8.

For the two MACSYMA calculations involved in this example, a VAX computer was left running (in interactive mode) for over one hour.

Exercises

1. Determine the 5th cyclotomic field over $\mathbb{Z}_2$.

2. Determine the cyclotomic polynomial $Q_{52}(x)$ over $\mathbb{Z}_3$.

3. For $n \geq 2$ let $\xi_1, \ldots, \xi_n$ be all the nth roots of unity over a field K. Prove that $\xi_1 + \xi_2^k + \cdots + \xi_n^k = 0$ for $k = 1, 2, \ldots, n-1$.

4. Find the highest common factor $h(x)$ of $f(x) = x^5 + 3x^3 + x^2 + 2x + 2$ and $g(x) = x^4 + 3x^3 + 3x^2 + x + 2$ in $\mathbb{Z}_5[x]$. Find polynomials $r(x)$, $s(x)$ in $\mathbb{Z}_5[x]$ such that $h(x) = r(x)f(x) + s(x)g(x)$.

5. Working in $\mathbb{Z}_2[x]$, find pairwise coprime monic polynomials $f_1(x), \ldots, f_k(x)$ such that $x^6 + 1 = f_1(x)^{\varepsilon_1} \ldots f_k(x)^{\varepsilon_k}$.

6. (Chinese remainder theorem) Let R be a commutative ring with identity, containing ideals $I_1, \ldots, I_k$ such that $R = I_i + I_j = \{a + b: a \in I_i, b \in I_j\}$ for each pair i, j. Show that for any elements $a_1, \ldots, a_k$ in R there exists an element x in R such that $x + I_i = a_i + I_i$ for $i = 1, \ldots, k$. Show moreover that if x' also satisfies $x' + I_i = a_i + I_i$ for $i = 1, \ldots, k$ then $x - x'$ lies in the ideal $\cap_{i=1}^{k} I_i$. (Hint: show that for each j there is an element b_j in $\cap_{i \neq j} I_i$ such that $b_j + I_j = 1 + I_j$; then set $x = \Sigma a_j b_j$.)

7. Interpret Exercise 6 for $R = K[x]$ with K a field, and also for $R = \mathbb{Z}$.

8. Let $\phi(n)$ be Euler's function. Show that
   (i) $\phi(p^s) = p^s - p^{s-1}$ for any prime p and integer s.
   (ii) $\phi(mn) = \phi(m)\phi(n)$ for any coprime integers m, n.

9. What is the degree of the 900th cyclotomic polynomial $Q_{900}(x)$ over $\mathbb{Q}$?

10. Use Berlekamp's algorithm to factorize $f(x) = x^8 + x^6 + x^4 + x^3 + 1$ over $\mathbb{Z}_2$.

11. Use Berlekamp's algorithm to factorize $f(x) = x^7 + x^6 + x^5 - x^3 + x^2 - x - 1$ over $\mathbb{Z}_3$.

12. Determine all of the primitive polynomials of degree 3 over $\mathbb{Z}_2$.

13. Use Berlekamp's algorithm to determine the number of distinct irreducible monic factors of $x^4 + 1$ over $\mathbb{Z}_p[x]$ for all odd primes p.

14. How many primitive polynomials over $\mathbb{Z}_3$ are there of degree 8?

15. Determine the splitting field of $x^8 + x^6 + x^5 + x^4 + x^3 + x^2 + 1$ over $\mathbb{Z}_2$.

16. Factorize a suitable cyclotomic polynomial to find an irreducible polynomial $f(x)$ in $GF(3)[x]$ of degree 4 such that any root θ of $f(x)$ has order 16 in $GF(81)$. Show that $GF(3)(\theta) = GF(81)$. Let $\alpha = \theta + \theta^2$. Show that α has order 5, and that $\alpha\theta$ has order 80. Determine a primitive polynomial of degree 4 over $GF(3)$ by finding the minimum polynomial of $\alpha\theta$ over $GF(3)$.

17. Prove that an irreducible polynomial in $GF(q)$ of degree n is irreducible in $GF(q^k)$ if and only if k and n are coprime.

18. Explain why, for any integer $n \geqslant 1$ and prime p, there exists a primitive polynomial of degree n over $\mathbb{Z}_p$.

5   Ruler and compass constructions

The last three chapters have been concerned primarily with finite fields. In this chapter we turn our attention to infinite fields and in particular to subfields of the real numbers $\mathbb{R}$. Our interest in such fields is derived from a construction problem in Euclidean geometry.

Many geometric constructions can be performed using only a pencil, compass, and unmarked ruler. For instance, suppose we wish to bisect an angle θ, as in Fig. 5.1. This can be done, using our limited tools, as follows. Firstly use the compass to draw a segment of a circle cutting the sides of the angle at points A and B say. Then draw two circles of equal radius centred at A and B; these two circles intersect at points C and D, say, as in Fig. 5.2. The line CD bisects θ.

Suppose however that we wish to trisect an angle θ. A little experimentation on the part of the reader will suggest that there is no obvious method using only a compass and unmarked ruler. This trisection problem was known to the Greeks, who expended considerable ingenuity in an unsuccessful search for a solution. We shall use the language of field extensions to explain the reason for the lack of success.

We first need to define precisely what is meant by a ruler and compass construction. Suppose that a set X of points in the Euclidean plane $\mathbb{R}^2$ is given, and consider the following two operations.

Operation 1 (ruler).   Draw a straight line through any pair of points in X.

Operation 2 (compass).   Draw a circle whose centre is some point in X and whose radius is equal to the distance between some pair of points in X.

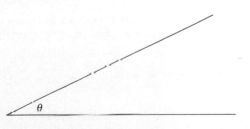

Fig. 5.1.

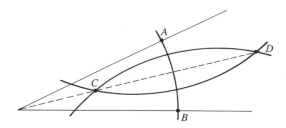

Fig. 5.2.

We shall say that a point A in $\mathbb{R}^2$ is *obtainable by ruler and compass in one step* from the set X if A is a point of intersection of: two distinct lines obtained using operation 1; or two distinct circles obtained using operation 2; or one such line and one such circle.

We shall say that a point A is *constructible (by ruler and compass)* if there is a finite sequence of points

$$A_1, A_2, A_3, \ldots, A_n = A$$

such that A_1 is obtainable by ruler and compass in one step from the two-point set $X_0 = \{(0,0), (1,0)\}$, and such that A_{i+1} is obtainable by ruler and compass in one step from the set

$$X_i = \{(0,0), (1,0), A_1, \ldots, A_i\}$$

for $i = 1, \ldots, n-1$.

For any point $A = (a, b)$ in $\mathbb{R}^2$ we shall denote by $|A|$ the distance $\sqrt{(a^2 + b^2)}$ from A to the origin. A real number α will be said to be *constructible (by ruler and compass)* if a constructible point A exists with $|A| = |\alpha|$. It is readily seen that α is constructible if and only if the point $(0, \alpha)$ is constructible.

Figure 5.3 shows that an angle $\theta \leqslant \pi/2$ can be trisected using ruler and compass if and only if the real number $\cos(\theta/3)$ is constructible. (The reader needs to verify that, using ruler and compass, it is possible to drop a perpendicular from a point A to a line.)

In order to further our analysis of this trisection problem we need a few general theorems on constructible real numbers.

Theorem 5.1.   *The set C of constructible real numbers is a subfield of $\mathbb{R}$.*

Proof.   Suppose that α and β are constructible real numbers. We must show that $\alpha - \beta$ is constructible, and that for $\beta \neq 0$ the product $\alpha\beta^{-1}$ is

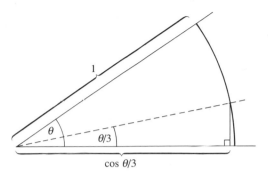

Fig. 5.3.

constructible. The proof (for $\alpha \geqslant \beta \geqslant 0$) follows from Fig. 5.4. (In fig. 5.4(b) the reader needs to verify that, using ruler and compass, it is possible to construct a line through a given point which is parallel to a given line.) ∎

It is possible to characterize the constructible real numbers in terms of arithmetic operations. Recall from Exercise 11 of Chapter 2 that for any subfield K of $\mathbb{R}$ and any real number α, the field $K(\alpha)$ is defined to be the intersection of all subfields of $\mathbb{R}$ containing K and the element α. Thus $K(\alpha)$ consists of all real numbers of the form

$$k_0 + k_1\alpha + k_2\alpha^2 + \cdots + k_n\alpha^n$$

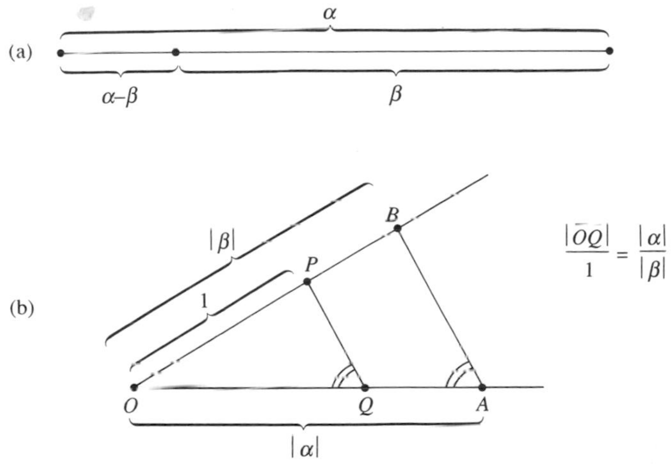

(a)

α

$\alpha-\beta$ β

(b)

$|\beta|$

B

P

1

O

Q

A

$|\alpha|$

$$\frac{|\overline{OQ}|}{1} = \frac{|\alpha|}{|\beta|}$$

Fig. 5.4.

with $k_i \in K$ and $n \geq 0$. (The reader may need to ponder this a little.)

For any finite sequence of real numbers $\alpha_1, \ldots, \alpha_n$ we define inductively the subfield $K(\alpha_1, \ldots, \alpha_n)$ of $\mathbb{R}$ by

$$K(\alpha_1, \ldots, \alpha_n) = K(\alpha_1, \ldots, \alpha_{n-1})(\alpha_n).$$

We shall say that a real number α is *obtainable from the rationals by taking square roots* if there exists a finite sequence of real numbers $\alpha_1, \alpha_2, \ldots, \alpha_n = \alpha$ such that: $\alpha_1 \in \mathbb{Q}(\sqrt{\beta_1})$ for some $\beta_1 \in \mathbb{Q}$; and $\alpha_i \in \mathbb{Q}(\sqrt{\beta_i})$ for some $\beta_i \in \mathbb{Q}(\alpha_1, \ldots, \alpha_{i-1})$ for $i = 2, 3, \ldots, n$.

For instance, the number

$$\alpha = \frac{\frac{1}{4} + \sqrt{5 + \sqrt{3 + \sqrt{2}}}}{\sqrt{7 + \sqrt{3}}}$$

is obtainable from the rationals by taking square roots. To see this it suffices to consider the following sequence of numbers:

$$\alpha_1 = \sqrt{2}, \quad \alpha_2 = \sqrt{3 + \sqrt{2}}, \quad \alpha_3 = \sqrt{5 + \sqrt{3 + \sqrt{2}}}, \quad \alpha_4 = \sqrt{3}, \quad \alpha.$$

Theorem 5.2. *A real number is constructible if and only if it is obtainable from the rationals by taking square roots.*

Proof. Let S be the set of real numbers obtainable from the rationals by taking square roots. Note that by definition S is a subfield of $\mathbb{R}$ which is closed under the operation of taking square roots (that is, $a \in S$ implies $\sqrt{a} \in S$).

Suppose that α is a constructible real number. Then there exists a sequence of points $A_1, \ldots, A_n$ in $\mathbb{R}^2$ with $|A_n| = |\alpha|$, such that A_i is obtainable by ruler and compass in one step from the set $\{(0, 0), A_0 = (1, 0), A_1, \ldots A_{i-1}\}$. Suppose that for some $0 \leq j < n$ the x- and y-coordinates of the points $A_0, \ldots, A_j$ are in S. (This is certainly the case for $j = 0$.) Then the point A_{j+1} is obtained in one of three possible ways.

One possibility is that A_j is the point of intersection of two distinct lines

$$ax + by + c = 0,$$

$$a'x + b'y + c' = 0,$$

where $a, a', b, b', c, c' \in S$. In this case the x- and y-coordinates of A_j are in S. (Why?)

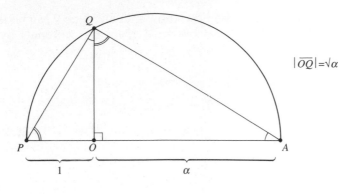

$$|\overline{OQ}|=\sqrt{\alpha}$$

Fig. 5.5.

The second possibility is that A_j is the point of intersection of a line

$$ax+by+c=0,$$

and a circle

$$x^2+y^2+dx+ey+f=0,$$

where $a,b,c,d,e,f \in S$. Solving these equations simultaneously leads to a quadratic equation. Since the roots of a quadratic equation can be given in terms of square roots of the coefficients of the equation, it follows that in this case also the x- and y-coordinates of A_j lie in S.

The third and final possibility is that A_j is the intersection of two distinct circles

$$x^2+y^2+dx+ey+f=0,$$
$$x^2+y^2+d'x+e'y+f'=0,$$

with $d,d',e,e',f,f' \in S$. Thus A_j is the intersection of the first circle with the line (the common chord)

$$(d-d')x+(e-e')y+f-f'=0.$$

Hence, in this case also, the x- and y-coordinates of A_j lie in S.

It follows by induction that the coordinates of A_n lie in S. Therefore $\alpha=|A_n|$ lies in S. In other words, any constructible real number α is obtainable from the rationals by taking square roots.

We now need to prove the converse: the set of constructible real numbers C contains S. This will complete the proof of the theorem. We know from Theorem 5.1 that C is a subfield of $\mathbb{R}$. It thus suffices to show that C is closed under the operation of taking square roots. (Why?) So suppose that $\alpha \in C$. Figure 5.5 shows that $\sqrt{\alpha}$ lies in C since the line OQ is of length $\sqrt{\alpha}$. ∎

In view of Theorem 5.2 we now know that an angle θ can be trisected if and only if $\cos(\frac{1}{3}\theta)$ can be obtained from the rationals by taking square roots. Note that

$$
\begin{aligned}
\cos(\theta) &= \cos(\tfrac{2}{3}\theta + \tfrac{1}{3}\theta) \\
&= \cos(\tfrac{2}{3}\theta)\cos(\tfrac{1}{3}\theta) - \sin(\tfrac{2}{3}\theta)\sin(\tfrac{1}{3}\theta) \\
&= (2\cos^2(\tfrac{1}{3}\theta) - 1)\cos(\tfrac{1}{3}\theta) - 2\sin(\tfrac{1}{3}\theta)\cos(\tfrac{1}{3}\theta)\sin(\tfrac{1}{3}\theta) \\
&= (2\cos^2(\tfrac{1}{3}\theta) - 1)\cos(\tfrac{1}{3}\theta) - 2\cos(\tfrac{1}{3}\theta)(1 - \cos^2(\tfrac{1}{3}\theta)) \\
&= 4\cos^3(\tfrac{1}{3}\theta) - 3\cos(\tfrac{1}{3}\theta).
\end{aligned}
$$

If, for instance, $\theta = \pi/3$, then $\cos(\theta) = \frac{1}{2}$, and $\cos(\frac{1}{3}\theta)$ is a root of the equation

$$4x^3 - 3x - \tfrac{1}{2} = 0,$$

or equivalently a root of the equation

$$8x^3 - 6x - 1 = 0.$$

Thus to show that the angle $\pi/3$ cannot be trisected using an unmarked ruler and compass alone, it would suffice to show that the root $\cos(\pi/9)$ of this last equation is not obtainable from the rationals by taking square roots. We shall show this. Our method is based on an analysis of the degree of the field extension $\mathbb{Q}(\beta): \mathbb{Q}$ where $\beta = \cos(\pi/9)$.

If the polynomial $f_\beta(x) = 8x^3 - 6x - 1$ were irreducible over $\mathbb{Q}$, then the polynomial $g(x) = \frac{1}{8}f_\beta(x)$ would be the minimum polynomial of β over $\mathbb{Q}$. Moreover, the quotient ring $\mathbb{Q}[x]/(g(x))$ would be a field, and the field extension $\mathbb{Q}[x]/(g(x)): \mathbb{Q}$ would be of degree 3 (see Theorems 2.6 and 2.7). We could then verify that there is a field isomorphism

$$\mathbb{Q}(\beta) \xrightarrow{\cong} \mathbb{Q}[x]/(g(x)),$$
$$k_0 + k_1\beta + \cdots + k_n\beta^n \mapsto (k_0 + k_1x + \cdots + k_nx^n) + I$$

where $I = (g(x))$. We would therefore have $[\mathbb{Q}(\beta): \mathbb{Q}] = 3$. The following three lemmas prove that $f_\beta(x)$ is irreducible over $\mathbb{Q}$.

Lemma 5.3. *The polynomial $f_\beta(x) = 8x^3 - 6x - 1$ is reducible over $\mathbb{Q}$ if and only if it is reducible over $\mathbb{Z}$.*

Proof. Certainly $f_\beta(x)$ is reducible over $\mathbb{Q}$ if it is reducible over $\mathbb{Z}$.

Suppose then that $f_\beta(x)$ is reducible over $\mathbb{Q}$; say

$$f_\beta(x) = (a_0 + a_1x + a_2x^2)(b_0 + b_1x),$$

with $a_i, b_i \in \mathbb{Q}$. Let d be the product of the denominators of the a_i and b_i. Then

$$df_\beta(x) = (a_0' + a_1'x + a_2'x^2)(b_0' + b_1'x) \tag{5.1}$$

where $a_i' = da_i \in \mathbb{Z}$, $b_i' = db_i \in \mathbb{Z}$. Let p be a prime divisor of d. Either p divides each a_i' or else p divides each b_i'. (For if not, then there must be smallest values i and j such that $p \nmid a_i'$ and $p \nmid b_j'$. However p divides the coefficient of x^{i+j} in $df_\beta(x)$, which is

$$a_0b_{i+j} + a_1b_{i+j-1} + \cdots + a_{i+j}b_0.$$

By the choice of i and j, p divides every term of this expression except perhaps a_ib_j. But p divides the whole expression, so $p | a_ib_j$. Hence $p | a_i$ or $p | b_j$, a contradiction.) We can thus divide both sides of (5.1) by p to obtain an equation

$$d'f_\beta(x) = (a_0'' + a_1''x + a_2''x^2)(b_0'' + b_1''x)$$

with $d', a_i'', b_i'' \in \mathbb{Z}$ and $d' < d$. Repeating this argument as many times as necessary, we see that $f_\beta(x)$ must factorize over $\mathbb{Z}$. ∎

Lemma 5.4. *The polynomial $f_\beta(x) = 8x^3 - 6x - 1$ is reducible over $\mathbb{Z}$ if and only if $f_\beta(x-1) = 8x^3 - 24x^2 + 18x - 3$ is reducible over $\mathbb{Z}$.*

Proof. For polynomials $g(x)$, $h(x)$ in $\mathbb{Z}[x]$ it is clear that $f_\beta(x) = g(x)h(x)$ if and only if $f_\beta(x-1) = g(x-1)h(x-1)$. This proves the lemma. ∎

Lemma 5.5. *The polynomial $f(x) = 8x^3 - 24x^2 + 18x - 3$ is irreducible over $\mathbb{Z}$.*

Proof. Suppose that $f(x)$ were reducible over $\mathbb{Z}$; say

$$f(x) = (a_0 + a_1x + a_2x^2)(b_0 + b_1x + b_2x^2),$$

with $a_i, b_i \in \mathbb{Z}$. (Clearly $a_2 = 0$ or $b_2 = 0$.) Let $q = 3$, and note that:

(1) $q \nmid 8$;

(2) $q | 3$, $q | 18$, $q | 24$;

(3) $q^2 \nmid 3$.

By (3), q cannot divide both a_0 and b_0 since $a_0 b_0 = 3$. But $q|3$. So without loss of generality suppose that $q|a_0$ and $q \nmid b_0$. If all coefficients a_i were divisible by q then (1) would be contradicted. Let a_{i_0} be the first a_i not divisible by q. Then the expression

$$a_{i_0} b_0 + a_{i_0-1} b_1 + \cdots + a_0 b_{i_0}$$

is equal to 24 or 18 or 3. Thus, by (2), q must divide b_0. This contradiction proves the lemma.   ∎

Lemmas 5.3, 5.4, and 5.5 show that $f_\beta(x)$ is irreducible over $\mathbb{Q}$, and hence that $[\mathbb{Q}(\beta): \mathbb{Q}] = 3$ for $\beta = \cos(\pi/9)$. The following theorem, in conjunction with Theorem 5.1, shows that for any constructible real number α the degree $[\mathbb{Q}(\alpha): \mathbb{Q}]$ must be a power of 2. Thus $\beta = \cos(\pi/9)$ is not constructible, and consequently there is no ruler and compass construction which trisects an arbitrary angle.

Theorem 5.6. *A real number α is obtainable from the rationals by taking square roots only if $[\mathbb{Q}(\alpha): \mathbb{Q}]$ is a power of 2.*

To prove Theorem 5.6 we need the following proposition.

Proposition 5.7. *If $M:L$ and $L:K$ are field extensions then the degree of $M:K$ is given by*

$$[M:K] = [M:L] \times [L:K].$$

Proof.   Let $\{e_i\}_{i \in I}$ be a basis for the vector space L over K, and let $\{f_j\}_{j \in J}$ be a basis of the vector space M over L. It is a routine exercise to show that the set $\{e_i f_j\}_{(i,j) \in I \times J}$ is a basis of the vector space M over K. (It has to be shown that the set is linearly independent, and that it generates L.) It follows that $[M:K] = |I \times J| = |I| \times |J| = [M:L] \times [L:K]$. Readers with some knowledge of cardinal arithmetic may like to note that this proof is valid if any of the extensions involved are of infinite degree.   ∎

Proof of Theorem 5.6.   Suppose that α is obtainable from the rationals by taking square roots. So there exists a finite sequence of real numbers $\alpha_1, \alpha_2, \ldots, \alpha_n = \alpha$ such that: $\alpha_1 \in \mathbb{Q}(\sqrt{\beta_1})$ for some $\beta_1 \in \mathbb{Q}$; and $\alpha_i \in \mathbb{Q}(\sqrt{\beta_i})$ for some $\beta_i \in \mathbb{Q}(\alpha_1, \ldots, \alpha_{i-1})$ for $i = 2, 3, \ldots, n$. The minimum polynomial of α_i over $\mathbb{Q}(\alpha_1, \ldots, \alpha_{i-1})$ is of degree 1 or 2. Hence $[\mathbb{Q}(\alpha_1, \ldots, \alpha_i): \mathbb{Q}(\alpha_1, \ldots, \alpha_{i-1})] = 1$ or 2. Using Proposition 5.7 we have

$$[\mathbb{Q}(\alpha_1, \ldots, \alpha_n): \mathbb{Q}] = [\mathbb{Q}(\alpha_1, \ldots, \alpha_n): \mathbb{Q}(\alpha_1, \ldots, \alpha_{n-1})]$$
$$\times [\mathbb{Q}(\alpha_1, \ldots, \alpha_{n-1}), \mathbb{Q}(\alpha_1, \ldots, \alpha_{n-2}]$$
$$\times \cdots \times [\mathbb{Q}(\alpha_1): \mathbb{Q}] = 2^r$$

for some r. It follows that $[\mathbb{Q}(\alpha_n): \mathbb{Q}] = [\mathbb{Q}(\alpha): \mathbb{Q}]$ is a power of 2. ∎

The question about trisecting angles is completely answered. For future reference it will be useful to have the following generalizations of Lemmas 5.3, 5.4, and 5.5. Their proofs are left as exercises.

Proposition 5.8. (Gauss) *A polynomial $f(x)$ in $\mathbb{Z}[x]$ is irreducible over $\mathbb{Q}$ if and only if it is irreducible over $\mathbb{Z}$.*

Proposition 5.9. *Let c be an element of a field K. A polynomial $f(x)$ in $K[x]$ is irreducible if and only if $f(x+c)$ is irreducible.*

Proposition 5.10. (Eisenstein's criterion) *Consider a polynomial*

$$f(x) = k_0 + k_1 x + \cdots + k_n x^n$$

in $\mathbb{Z}[x]$. Such a polynomial is irreducible over $\mathbb{Z}$ if there exists a prime q satisfying:

(i) $q \nmid k_n$;

(ii) $q | k_i$ *for* $i = 0, 1, \ldots, n-1$;

(iii) $q^2 \nmid k_0$.

Exercises

1. Prove Propositions 5.8, 5.9, and 5.10.

2. Decide which of the following polynomials is irreducible:
   $x^7 + 11x^3 - 33x + 22$ over $\mathbb{Q}$;
   $x^3 - 7x^2 + 3x + 3$ over $\mathbb{Q}$;
   $x^4 + 1$ over $\mathbb{Q}$;
   $x^q + 1$ over $\mathbb{Q}$ for any $q = 2^n$;
   $1 + x + x^2$ over $\mathbb{Q}$;
   $1 + x + x^2 + \cdots + x^{p-1}$ over $\mathbb{Q}$ for any prime p.

3. Let n be an even integer which is not divisible by 4. Prove that $\sqrt[m]{n}$ is irrational for $m = 2, 3, 4, \ldots$. Generalize this result.

4. What is the degree of the extension $\mathbb{Q}(\sqrt{2},\sqrt[3]{3},\sqrt[5]{5},\sqrt[7]{7})$?

5. Prove that the side of a cube of 2 units volume is not constructible by unmarked ruler and compass alone. (In other words, a cube cannot be doubled in volume.)

6. Prove that a square of area π units cannot be constructed using unmarked ruler and compass alone. Assume the result of Lindemann, proved in 1882, which states that π is *transcendental*, i.e. that π is not the root of any polynomial over $\mathbb{Q}$ of finite degree. (In other words, the circle cannot be squared.)

7. Show that it is impossible to construct a regular 9-gon using unmarked ruler and compass alone.

8. Suppose that $L:K$ is a field extension of prime degree $[L:K]$. Prove that there exists an element α in L such that $L = K(\alpha)$.

9. Let $L:K$ be a finite field extension and $f(x)$ an irreducible polynomial over K. Prove that if $\deg(f(x))$ and $[L:K]$ are coprime then $f(x)$ has no zeros in L.

6 Pappus' theorem and Desargues' theorem

In Chapter 2 we saw that any field K gives rise to a projective plane $PG(2, K)$. One very natural question to ask is: do all projective planes arise from a field in this way? In the present chapter we show that the answer is no. We do this by first proving that a classical theorem of Euclidean geometry, namely Pappus' theorem, holds in the projective plane $PG(2, K)$ for all fields K, and then by exhibiting a projective plane in which Pappus' theorem does not hold.

Another theorem of Euclidean geometry which may or may not hold in a given projective plane is Desargues' theorem. A famous result of projective geometry states that in any finite projective plane Pappus' theorem is implied by Desargues' theorem. (The finiteness condition here is essential: we shall exhibit an infinite projective plane in which Desargues' theorem holds and Pappus' theorem is false.) We outline a proof of this famous geometric result. The proof, which is the only known proof, is remarkable in that it relies on a deep algebraic theorem about rings due to J. H. M. Wedderburn. We give a full proof of Wedderburn's theorem.

We call a projective plane of the form $PG(2, K)$, where K is a field, a *projective field plane*. One possibility for obtaining a projective plane π which is not a projective field plane consists of two steps: (1) try to construct a projective plane $\pi = PG(2, R)$ from some ring R which is not a field; (2) show that $PG(2, R)$ does not possess some geometric property possessed by all projective field planes. (Note that step (1) alone is not enough.)

A careful analysis of the construction of the projective field plane $PG(2, K)$ shows that (in common with much of the elementary linear algebra) it does not rely on the field axiom requiring multiplication in K to be commutative. This means that the construction generalizes to yield projective planes $PG(2, D)$ for D any ring satisfying all the axioms of a field except (possibly) the axiom requiring commutative multiplication. We call such a ring D a *division ring*. Thus a division ring is a ring with identity in which every non-zero element has a multiplicative inverse. Any field is of course a division ring. If we are to show that there exists a projective plane $PG(2, D)$ which is not a field plane, then we first need to give at least one example of a division ring which is not a field.

The division ring we exhibit is due to the Irish mathematician W. R. Hamilton. Around 1837 Hamilton noted that complex numbers $a + ib$ (where $a, b \in \mathbb{R}$) could be considered abstractly as pairs of real numbers (a, b) with addition $(a, b) + (a', b') = (a + a', b + b')$, and multiplication $(a, b)(a', b') = (aa' - bb', ab' + a'b)$. He looked for an analogous multiplication of vectors in $\mathbb{R}^3$: the multiplication had to be distributive,

$$u(v + w) = uv + uw,$$

and be such that the length of the product of two vectors is the product of the lengths of the two vectors,

$$|uv| = |u||v|.$$

After six unsuccessful years of trying to multiply vectors of the form $a + b\mathbf{i} + c\mathbf{j}$ (where $\mathbf{1}, \mathbf{i}, \mathbf{j}$ are mutually perpendicular vectors in $\mathbb{R}^3$) he realized on 16 October 1843 that what was needed was a new imaginary symbol $\mathbf{k}$ which is 'perpendicular' to the other three elements $\mathbf{1}, \mathbf{i}, \mathbf{j}$. In modern parlance, Hamilton showed that the four-dimensional real vector space $\mathbb{D}$ with basis $\mathbf{1}, \mathbf{i}, \mathbf{j}, \mathbf{k}$ is endowed with a multiplication giving it the structure of a division ring; this division ring $\mathbb{D}$ is known as the *ring of quaternions*.

More precisely, $\mathbb{D}$ consists of all 4-tuples of real numbers (a, b, c, d). Addition in $\mathbb{D}$ is given by

$$(a, b, c, d) + (a', b', c', d') = (a + a', b + b', c + c', d + d').$$

Four elements of $\mathbb{D}$ are renamed as follows:

$$\mathbf{1} = (1, 0, 0, 0) \qquad \mathbf{i} = (0, 1, 0, 0)$$
$$\mathbf{j} = (0, 0, 1, 0) \qquad \mathbf{k} = (0, 0, 0, 1).$$

Furthermore, for $a, b, c, d \in \mathbb{R}$ we let

$$a = (a, 0, 0, 0) \qquad b\mathbf{i} = (0, b, 0, 0)$$
$$c\mathbf{j} = (0, 0, c, 0) \qquad d\mathbf{k} = (0, 0, 0, d),$$

and thus

$$(a, b, c, d) = a + b\mathbf{i} + c\mathbf{j} + d\mathbf{k}.$$

The multiplication in $\mathbb{D}$ is given by defining

$$1x = x1 = x \qquad \text{for all } x \in \mathbb{D},$$
$$\mathbf{i}^2 = \mathbf{j}^2 = \mathbf{k}^2 = -1,$$
$$\mathbf{ij} = \mathbf{k}, \quad \mathbf{jk} = \mathbf{i}, \quad \mathbf{ki} = \mathbf{j}, \quad \mathbf{ji} = -\mathbf{k}, \quad \mathbf{kj} = -\mathbf{i}, \quad \mathbf{ik} = -\mathbf{j}.$$

These definitions extend uniquely to a non-commutative ring multiplication on the quaternions $\mathbb{D}$:

$$(a + b\mathbf{i} + c\mathbf{j} + d\mathbf{k})(a' + b'\mathbf{i} + c'\mathbf{j} + d'\mathbf{k})$$
$$= (au' - bb' - cc' - dd') + (ab' + ba' + cd' - dc')\mathbf{i}$$
$$+ (ac' + ca' + db' - bd')\mathbf{j} + (ad' + da' + bc' - cb')\mathbf{k}.$$

This multiplication satisfies the axioms of a division ring.

We can use the quaternions $\mathbb{D}$ to construct a projective plane $PG(2, \mathbb{D})$. (See Chapter 2 for the definition of $PG(2, K)$.) It is not immediately obvious that $PG(2, \mathbb{D})$ is not 'equal to' a projective field plane; we have to prove this.

Two projective planes π, π' are said to be *isomorphic* if there is a bijection $P \mapsto P'$ between the points of π and the points of π', and a bijection $L \mapsto L'$ between the lines of π and the lines of π' such that a point P in π is incident with a line L in π if and only if the corresponding point P' and line L' in π' are incident. Such a pair of bijections is called an *isomorphism* of projective planes. (An isomorphism is essentially just a relabelling of lines and points.)

One way to show that $PG(2, \mathbb{D})$ is not isomorphic to a projective field plane is to show that $PG(2, \mathbb{D})$ does not possess some property common to all projective field planes, this propety being preserved by isomorphisms. A suitable geometric property is the following 'theorem' due to Pappus. This is a theorem of Euclidean geometry, but may or may not hold in any given projective plane.

Pappus' theorem. *Let L_1 and L_2 be two distinct lines incident with a point P. Let P_1, P_2, P_3 be three distinct points incident with L_1, and Q_1, Q_2, Q_3 three distinct points incident with L_2 such that none of the P_i or Q_i is the point P.*

Let R_1 be the point incident with the lines P_2Q_3 and Q_2P_3.
Let R_2 be the point incident with the lines P_1Q_3 and Q_1P_3.
Let R_3 be the point incident with the lines P_1Q_2 and Q_1P_2.

Then R_1, R_2, R_3 are collinear.

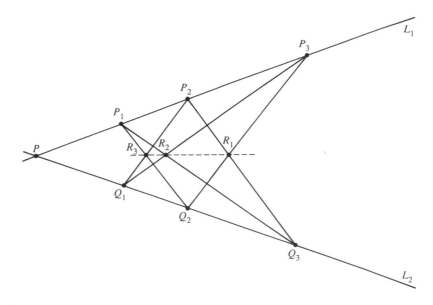

Fig. 6.1.

The relevant picture for Pappus' theorem is shown in Fig. 6.1.

It can be seen from a careful inspection of the pictorial representation of PG(2, $\mathbb{Z}_3$) given in Chapter 2 that Pappus' theorem holds in this projective plane. Also, Pappus' theorem holds (by default) in PG(2, $\mathbb{Z}_2$) since no line contains four distinct points. These observations generalize to the following theorem.

Theorem 6.1. *Let D be a division ring. Pappus' theorem holds in the projective plane* PG(2, D) *if and only if D is a field.*

In order to prove Theorem 6.1 we need to understand how the structure of the plane PG(2, D) is related to the multiplication in D. To this end we construct a binary operation μ on the points of any line in a given projective plane.

Let π be an arbitrary projective plane. Choose a line L in π and three distinct points P_0, P_1, P_∞ on L. Choose also three lines L_0, L_1, L_∞ distinct from L which pass through P_0, P_1, and P_∞, respectively, and such that the common point of L_0 and L_1 is not on L_∞. Such a choice of points P_i and lines L, L_i is called a (*multiplicative*) *coordinate system* for π. Let Q be the point common to L_0 and L_1, and let R be the point common to L_∞ and L_1. The appropriate picture is shown in Fig. 6.2.

Let P_a, P_b be two points other than P_∞ on the line L. The line P_aQ meets the line L_∞ at the point A, say, and the line P_bR meets L_0 at the point B, say. Let P_{ab} be the common point of the lines AB and L. We thus have a binary operation μ on the points of L distinct from P_∞, defined by

$$\mu(P_a, P_b) = P_{ab}.$$

This binary operation is of course dependent on the choice of coordinate system. The appropriate picture is shown in Fig. 6.3.

The proof of the following lemma is left as a (substantial) exercise. The comments following the lemma will help with its proof.

Lemma 6.2. *Let a, b be two elements of a division ring D. In $PG(2, D)$ let L be the line represented by the equation $x_2 = 0$, and label certain points of L as follows:*

$$P_0 = [0, 1, 0], \qquad P_1 = [1, 1, 0], \qquad P_\infty = [1, 0, 0]$$
$$P_a = [a, 1, 0], \qquad P_b = [b, 1, 0].$$

Let L_0, L_∞ be any lines which, together with L and the points P_i, form a multiplicative coordinate system. Then the binary operation μ satisfies

$$\mu(P_a, P_b) = [ab, 1, 0].$$

Before we can prove Theorem 6.1 we need some further notation and a lemma. Recall that for elements x_0, x_1, x_2 in D, at least one of which is non-zero, we let $[x_0, x_1, x_2]$ denote the set of triples $\{(ax_0, ax_1, ax_2): a \in D\}$. Now D^3 can be considered as a vector space

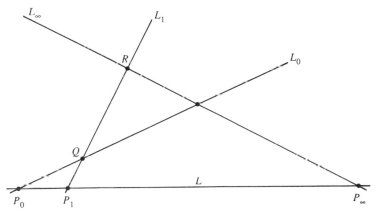

Fig. 6.2.

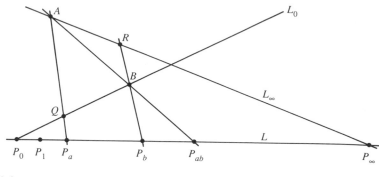

Fig. 6.3.

over D (the definition of a vector space over a field K extends to one over a division ring D). Since multiplication in D is not necessarily commutative we keep to the convention that scalar multiplication of a vector (x_0, x_1, x_2) in D^3 by a scalar a in D is always given by left multiplication:

$$a(x_0, x_1, x_2) = (ax_0, ax_1, ax_2).$$

In vector space terminology the set $[x_0, x_1, x_2]$ is just the subspace of D^3 generated by the vector (x_0, x_1, x_2). We extend this notation by using $[\mathbf{v}]$ to denote the subspace of D^3 generated by a non-zero vector $\mathbf{v}$ in D^3. Recall that for any two subspaces W, W' in D^3 their *sum* is

$$W + W' = \{w + w': w \in W, w' \in W'\}.$$

So if $[\mathbf{v}]$ and $[\mathbf{v}']$ are two points in PG$(2, K)$ then the line joining these points is the subspace $[\mathbf{v}] + [\mathbf{v}']$ of D^3. With this new notation we can prove the following technical lemma.

Lemma 6.3. *Let D be a division ring, and let A_1, A_2, A_3, B be four points in PG$(2, D)$, no three of which are collinear. Then there exists a basis $\mathbf{e}_1$, $\mathbf{e}_2$, $\mathbf{e}_3$ of D^3 such that $A_i = [\mathbf{e}_i]$ for $i = 1, 2, 3$ and $B = [\mathbf{e}_1 + \mathbf{e}_2 + \mathbf{e}_3]$.*

Proof. Let $\mathbf{f}_1$, $\mathbf{f}_2$, $\mathbf{f}_3$, $\mathbf{g}$ be any vectors such that $A_i = [\mathbf{f}_i]$ for $i = 1, 2, 3$ and $B = [\mathbf{g}]$. Since $D^3 = A_1 + A_2 + A_3$ it follows that the three vectors $\mathbf{f}_i$ generate D^3 and (since D^3 is of dimension 3) are thus a basis of D^3. Therefore

$$\mathbf{g} = a_1\mathbf{f}_1 + a_2\mathbf{f}_2 + a_3\mathbf{f}_3$$

for some a_i in D. Since the subspace B is not contained in the subspace $A_i + A_j$ for any pair $1 \leq i, j \leq 3$ it follows that the elements a_1, a_2, a_3 are all non-zero. Thus we can set $\mathbf{e} = a\mathbf{f}$ for $i = 1, 2, 3$. ∎

We are now in a position to prove Theorem 6.1. Let a, b be arbitrary elements of a division ring D. We need to show that $ab = ba$ if and only if Pappus' theorem holds in $PG(2, D)$. For convenience we may assume that $a \neq b$, $a \neq 1$ or 0, and $b \neq 1$ or 0. Using the notation of Lemma 6.2 let Q be the intersection of lines L_0 and L_1; let R be the intersection of lines L_∞ and L_1; let A, B' be the points of intersection of the line L_∞ with the lines P_aQ, P_bQ; let A', B be the points of intersection of L_0 with P_aR, P_bR. Let $P_{ab} = \mu(P_a, P_b)$ and let $P_{ba} = \mu(P_b, P_a)$. By Lemma 6.2 we have $P_{ab} = [ab, 1, 0]$ and $P_{ba} = [ba, 1, 0]$. Figure 6.4 summarizes the situation.

Suppose that Pappus' theorem holds in $PG(2, D)$. Then, applying it to the points A, Q, P_a and P_b, R, B we see that the points A', B', P_{ab} are collinear, as shown in Fig. 6.5.

Hence $P_{ba} = P_{ab}$. It follows that $ba = ab$, and consequently that D must be a field.

Conversely, suppose that D is a field. Then $ab = ba$ and so the points A', B', P_{ab} are collinear. Now let P_1, P_2, P_3 and Q_1, Q_2, Q_3 be any six points in $PG(2, D)$ satisfying the hypothesis of Pappus' theorem. By Lemma 6.3 there is a basis $\mathbf{e}_1, \mathbf{e}_2, \mathbf{e}_3$ of D^3 such that $P_a = [\mathbf{e}_1]$, $Q = [\mathbf{e}_2]$, $P_b = [\mathbf{e}_3]$, $B = [\mathbf{e}_1 + \mathbf{e}_2 + \mathbf{e}_3]$. There is also a basis $\mathbf{f}_1, \mathbf{f}_2, \mathbf{f}_3$ of D^3 such that $P_1 = [\mathbf{f}_1]$, $P_2 = [\mathbf{f}_2]$, $Q_1 = [\mathbf{f}_3]$, $Q_2 = [\mathbf{f}_1 + \mathbf{f}_2 + \mathbf{f}_3]$. Let $\phi : D^3 \to D^3$ be the

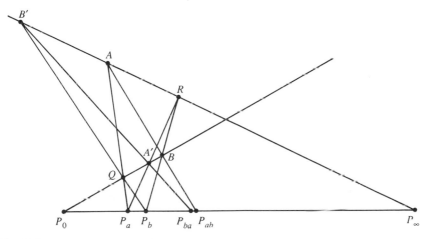

Fig. 6.4.

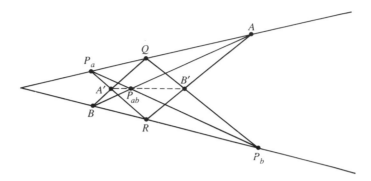

Fig. 6.5.

linear isomorphism defined by

$$\phi(\lambda_1\mathbf{e}_1 + \lambda_2\mathbf{e}_2 + \lambda_3\mathbf{e}_3) = \lambda_1\mathbf{f}_1 + \lambda_2\mathbf{f}_2 + \lambda_3\mathbf{f}_3$$

for $\lambda_i \in D$. The reader can check that ϕ induces an isomorphism $\bar{\phi}$ from $PG(2, D)$ to itself; on points $[\mathbf{v}]$ and lines $[\mathbf{v}] + [\mathbf{w}]$ the isomorphism $\bar{\phi}$ is defined by

$$[\mathbf{v}] \mapsto [\phi\mathbf{v}]$$
$$[\mathbf{v}] + [\mathbf{w}] \mapsto [\phi\mathbf{v}] + [\phi\mathbf{w}].$$

In particular

$$\bar{\phi}P_a = P_1,$$
$$\bar{\phi}Q = P_2,$$
$$\bar{\phi}P_b = Q_1,$$
$$\bar{\phi}B = Q_2.$$

By a judicious choice of the line L_∞ in Lemma 6.2 we can also assume that

$$\bar{\phi}A = P_3,$$
$$\bar{\phi}R = Q_3.$$

(The reader should attempt to verify this claim.) Since the points A, Q, P_a and B, R, P_b satisfy Pappus' theorem, it follows that so too do the points P_1, P_2, P_3 and Q_1, Q_2, Q_3. This completes the proof of Theorem 6.1. ∎

At this point a very natural question to ask is: are all projective planes of the form PG(2, *D*) for some division ring *D*? The answer is no. We shall not concern ourselves with a proof of this. Rather, we shall explain how the projective planes of the form PG(2, *D*) can be characterized by the following theorem of Euclidean geometry.

Desargues' theorem.   *Let A_1, A_2, B_1, B_2, C_1, C_2 be points such that the three lines A_1A_2, B_1B_2, and C_1C_2 are incident with a common point O. Let C_3 be the point of intersection of the lines A_1B_1 and A_2B_2. Let A_3 be the point of intersection of the lines B_1C_1 and B_2C_2. Let B_3 be the point of intersection of the lines A_1C_1 and A_2C_2.*

Then the points A_3, B_3, and C_3 are collinear.

The appropriate picture for Desargues' theorem is shown in Fig. 6.6. We shall outline a proof of the following result.

Theorem 6.4.   *Desargues' theorem holds in a projective plane π if and only if π is isomorphic to PG(2, D) for some division ring D.*

The idea behind the proof of Theorem 6.4 is derived from Lemma 6.2 and an analogous lemma giving a geometric description of addition in *D*. To state this analogous lemma let π be an arbitrary projective plane. Let *L* be a line in π and P_∞ a point on *L*. Let P_0 be a point on *L*

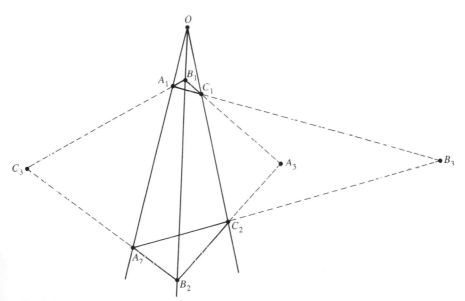

Fig. 6.6.

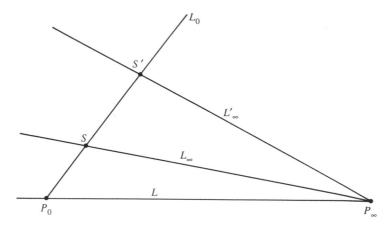

Fig. 6.7.

distinct from P_∞, and let L_∞, L'_∞ be two lines through P_∞ which are distinct from each other and L. Let L_0 be any line through P_0 distinct from L. Such a choice of points P_i and lines L, L_i, L'_∞ is called an (*additive*) *coordinate system*. Let S and S' be the points of intersection of the line L_0 with L_∞ and L'_∞. The appropriate picture is shown in Fig. 6.7.

Let P_a, P_b be any two points on L distinct from P_∞. The line SP_a intersects L'_∞ at a point A, and the line $S'P_b$ intersects L_∞ at a point B, say. Let P_{a+b} be the point on L in common with the line AB. The appropriate picture is shown in Fig. 6.8.

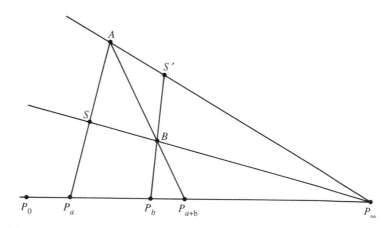

Fig. 6.8.

We define a binary operation σ on the points of L distinct from P_∞ by setting $\sigma(P_a, P_b) = P_{a+b}$. The proof of the following lemma is left as an exercise.

Lemma 6.5. *Let a, b be two elements of a division ring D. In* PG$(2, D)$ *let L be the line represented by the equation $x_2 = 0$, and label certain points of L as follows:*

$$P_0 = [0, 1, 0], \qquad P_\infty = [1, 0, 0]$$
$$P_a = [a, 1, 0], \qquad P_b = [b, 1, 0].$$

Let L_0, L_∞, L'_∞ be any lines which, together with L and the points P_0, P_∞, form an additive coordinate system. Then the binary operation σ satisfies

$$\sigma(P_a, P_b) = [a + b, 1, 0].$$

The outline proof of Theorem 6.4 is as follows. The binary operations σ and μ are defined for any projective plane π. For any line L in π, and point P_∞ on L, let D be the set of points on L distinct from P_∞. A series of difficult verifications shows that the addition and multiplication on D yielded by σ and μ satisfy the axioms of a division ring if and only if Desargues' theorem holds in π. It can also be verified that if D is a division ring then π is isomorphic to PG$(2, D)$.

We end this chapter by using Theorem 6.4 to prove the following deep result.

Theorem 6.6. *If Desargues' theorem holds in a finite projective plane π then Pappus' theorem holds in π.*

The finiteness condition in Theorem 6.6 is essential since, by Theorem 6.4, the quaternions $\mathbb{D}$ yield a projective plane PG$(2, \mathbb{D})$ in which Desargues' theorem holds, but in which, by Theorem 6.1, Pappus' theorem does not hold. The division ring $\mathbb{D}$ is infinite, and hence PG$(2, D)$ is infinite.

The only known proof of Theorem 6.6 uses Theorem 6.2 to show that any finite projective plane in which Desargues' theorem holds is of the form PG$(2, D)$ with D a finite division ring. The proof is completd by combining Theorem 6.1 with the following algebraic result originally proved by J. H. M. Wedderburn in 1909.

Theorem 6.7. (Wedderburn) *Any finite division ring is a field.*

Proof. Let D be a finite division ring. Let $D^* = D \backslash \{0\}$ be the set of non-zero elements of D. For each element a in D^* we define the *conjugacy class* of a to be the set

$$\langle a \rangle = \{x \in D^*: x = yay^{-1} \text{ for some } y \text{ in } D^*\}.$$

The verification of the following claim is left to the reader.

Claim 1. *For any two elements a, b in D^* either $\langle a \rangle = \langle b \rangle$ or $\langle a \rangle \cap \langle b \rangle = \emptyset$. (In other words the conjugacy classes form a partition of D^*.)*

Let $S = \{s_1, \ldots, s_k\}$ be any subset of D^* with the property that

$$D^* = \bigcup_{i=1}^{k} \langle s_i \rangle \qquad \text{and} \qquad \langle s_i \rangle \cap \langle s_j \rangle = \emptyset \text{ for } i \neq j.$$

Certainly such a set S can be found. The proof of the theorem consists of a close analysis of the equation

$$|D^*| = \sum_{i=1}^{k} |\langle s_i \rangle| \tag{6.1}$$

in which $|\ \ |$ denotes the number of elements in a set.

To carry out this analysis we define the *centre* of D to be the set

$$Z = \{z \in D: zx = xz \text{ for all } x \text{ in } D\},$$

and we let $Z^* = Z \backslash \{0\}$. The proof of the following claim is left to the reader.

Claim 2. *The set Z is a field.*

Since Z is a finite field we must have $Z = \mathrm{GF}(q)$ for some prime power q. The division ring D can be considered as a vector space over Z. As D is finite it must be of finite dimension n over Z. Therefore $|D| = q^n$ for some integer n. We shall obtain the theorem by showing that $D = Z$, or equivalently that $n = 1$. To do this we use proof by contradiction. So suppose that $n > 1$.

For any element a in D we define the *centralizer* of a to be the set

$$C(a) = \{x \in D: xa = ax\},$$

and we let $C(a)^* = C(a) \backslash \{0\}$. We leave the proof of the following claim to the reader.

Claim 3. *For any a in D the set $C(a)$ is a division ring.*

Since clearly for any a the centralizer $C(a)$ contains Z, we can consider $C(a)$ as a vector space over $Z = \mathrm{GF}(q)$ of finite dimension r. Hence $|C(a)| = q^r$ for some integer r.

Claim 4. *r divides n.*

To prove this, note that $|C(a)^*| = q^r - 1$ and $|D^*| = q^n - 1$. For each x in D^* let

$$xC(a)^* = \{xy : y \in C(a)^*\}.$$

It is readily shown that for x, x' in D^* either $xC(a)^* = x'C(a)^*$ or $xC(a)^* \cap x'C(a)^* = \emptyset$. It follows that D^* can be expressed as a union of disjoint sets of the form $xC(a)^*$, each disjoint set having $|C(a)^*|$ elements. Therefore $|C(a)^*| = q^r - 1$ divides $|D^*| = q^n - 1$. Suppose that

$$n = mr + t \qquad \text{with } 0 \leqslant t < r.$$

Then

$$q^n - 1 = q^{mr}q^t - 1 = q^t(q^{mr} - 1) + (q^t - 1).$$

Now $q^r - 1$ divides $q^{mr} - 1$ since

$$q^{mr} - 1 = (q^r - 1)(q^{r(m-1)} + q^{r(m-2)} + \cdots + 1).$$

But $q^r - 1$ also divides $q^n - 1$, and hence $q^r - 1$ divides $q^t - 1$. But $q^r - 1$ is greater than $q^t - 1$, implying that $t = 0$. This proves Claim 4.

We now come back to the equation (6.1). Since the conjugacy class of any element z in the centre Z is clearly the singleton $\langle z \rangle = \{z\}$, it follows that the set S contains the set Z. Let $S' = S \backslash Z$. Then equation (6.1) can be rewritten as

$$|D^*| = |Z| + \sum_{s \in S'} |\langle s \rangle|. \tag{6.2}$$

We leave as a very worthwhile exercise for the reader the proof that, if $C(s)$ is of dimension $r(s)$ over Z, then

$$|\langle s \rangle| = \frac{|D^*|}{|C(s)^*|} = \frac{q^n - 1}{q^{r(s)} - 1}.$$

In view of this formula for the order of $\langle s \rangle$, and in view of Claim 4, equation (6.2) becomes:

$$q^n - 1 = q - 1 + \sum_{s \in S'} \frac{q^n - 1}{q^{r(s)} - 1} \qquad (6.3)$$

where, for each $s \in S'$, the integer $r(s)$ divides n and $1 \leq r(s) < n$.

Let $Q_n(x)$ be the nth cyclotomic polynomial over $\mathbb{Q}$. We have proved in Chapter 4 that the coefficients of $Q_n(x)$ are integers. Therefore $Q_n(q)$ is an integer.

Another fact that we have proved about the polynomial $Q_n(x)$ is that it divides $x^n - 1$. If d is any integer such that d divides n and $1 \leq d < n$, then the polynomial $x^d - 1$ and $Q_n(x)$ have no common root in $\mathbb{C}$ (each root of $Q_n(x)$ and no root of $x^d - 1$ is a primitive nth root of unity), and so

$$\mathrm{hcf}(Q_n(x), x^d - 1) = 1.$$

Since $Q_n(x)$ divides

$$x^n - 1 = (x^d - 1) \frac{x^n - 1}{x^d - 1}$$

we see that $Q_n(x)$ must divide the polynomial

$$\frac{x^n - 1}{x^d - 1}.$$

It follows from all this that the integer $Q_n(q)$ divides the integers

$$q^n - 1, \qquad \frac{q^n - 1}{q^{r(s)} - 1}$$

for each $s \in S'$.

The following claim is now an immediate consequence of equation (6.3).

Claim 5. $Q_n(q)$ *divides* $q-1$.

Claim 5 leads to a contradiction. For let ξ be a primitive nth root of unity over $\mathbb{Q}$. Then

$$|Q_n(q)| = \left| \prod_{\substack{i=1 \\ \text{hcf}(i,n)=1}}^{n} (q-\xi^i) \right|$$

$$= \prod_{\substack{i=1 \\ \text{hcf}(i,n)=1}}^{n} |q-\xi^i|$$

$$> \prod_{\substack{i=1 \\ \text{hcf}(i,n)=1}}^{n} (q-1) \qquad \text{(This is clear geometrically since } n>1.)$$

$$\geqslant q-1. \qquad \text{(Since } q \geqslant 2.)$$

But $|Q_n(q)| > q-1$ contradicts Claim 5. Hence our supposition that $n>1$ is false. So $n=1$ and Wedderburn's theorem is proved. ∎

Exercises

Let V be a vector space of dimension $n \geqslant 3$ over a division ring D. Let $\mathscr{P}(V)$ denote the collection of all subspaces of V. We say that a subspace U is *incident* with a subspace W if either U contains W or W contains U. A subspace of dimension 1 is called a *point*, and a subspace of dimension 2 is called a *line*. We call $\mathscr{P}(V)$ a *projective space* of dimension $n-1$.

1. Show that there is a unique line through any pair of distinct points.

2. Let L and L' be distinct lines. Show that either L and L' meet in a unique point, or else they have no point in common.

3. Let A, B, C be three distinct points which are not collinear. Let π be the following collection of points and lines. The points of π are the one-dimensional subspaces of the vector space $A+B+C$; the lines in π are the two-dimensional subspaces of $A+B+C$. Show that π is a projective plane. Show moreover that π is isomorphic to PG(2, D).

4. Show that Desargues' theorem holds in π. (Hint: choose points S_1, S_2 in $\mathscr{P}(V)$ outside the plane π and collinear with O. Show that the

lines S_1A_1 and S_2A_2 are coplanar and hence intersect at a point A. Similarly S_1B_1 and S_2B_2 intersect at a point B, and S_1C_1 intersects S_2C_2 at a point C. Let π' be the plane determined by the points A, B, C. Lines AC and A_1C_1 (resp. AC and A_2C_2) meet at a point B' (resp. B''); lines BC and B_1C_1 (resp. BC and B_2C_2) meet at A' (resp. A''); and lines AB and A_1B_1 (resp. AB and A_2B_2) meet at C' (resp. C''). Show that A', B', C', A'', B'', and C'' are all collinear. Deduce that $A' = A'' = A_3$, and $B' = B'' = B_3$, and $C' = C'' = C_3$.)

7 Solution of polynomials by radicals: Galois groups

In this chapter we consider the problem of finding formulae for the roots of polynomials over $\mathbb{Q}$. Nice formulae, involving only the four field operations $+$, $-$, $\times$, $/$ and the extraction of nth roots, exist for all such polynomials of degree 4 or less. For instance, the two roots γ_1, γ_2 of an arbitrary quadratic polynomial

$$x^2 + bx + c$$

with coefficients b, $c \in \mathbb{Q}$, are given by

$$\gamma_1 = \tfrac{1}{2}(-b + \sqrt{b^2 - 4c}), \qquad \gamma_2 = \tfrac{1}{2}(-b - \sqrt{b^2 - 4c}).$$

This quadratic result was in use as far back as AD 100. By the year 1545 analogous expressions for the roots of cubic and quartic polynomials had also been discovered. Much fruitless effort was subsequently spent in the search for a formula for the roots of an arbitrary quintic equation. Early in the nineteenth century, however, the Norwegian mathematician Niels Abel succeeded in showing that no 'nice' general formula exists in the quintic case. Only for certain quintic polynomials (such as a product of a quadratic and a cubic) do 'nice' expressions for the roots exist. Abel's result raised the question of finding a method for deciding exactly which polynomials allow 'nice' expressions for their roots. Abel was working on this when he died in 1829. The answer was found by Evariste Galois, a French mathematician. Galois, who was killed in a duel in 1832 at the age of 21, submitted three memoirs on his work to the Academy of Sciences in Paris; all three were rejected! Fortunately their contents were later appreciated and publicized by Joseph Liouville. Galois' work, which we describe in part in this and the next chapter, has all the hallmarks of a great piece of mathematics: it solved a long-standing problem; it relied on revolutionary yet simple new mathematical ideas; and it lead to the establishment of a major branch of mathematics now known as Galois theory.

The above expressions for the roots of a quadratic polynomial are easily verified by checking the identity

$$(x + \tfrac{1}{2}(b + \sqrt{b^2 - 4c}))(x + \tfrac{1}{2}(b - \sqrt{b^2 - 4c})) = x^2 + bx + c.$$

Consider now an arbitrary cubic polynomial

$$x^3 + bx^2 + cx + d \tag{7.1}$$

with $b, c, d \in \mathbb{Q}$. On substituting $u = x + \frac{1}{3}b$ this cubic becomes

$$u^3 + su + t \tag{7.2}$$

where

$$s = c - \tfrac{1}{3}b^2 \quad \text{and} \quad t = \tfrac{2}{27}b^3 - \tfrac{1}{3}bc + d.$$

If $\gamma_1, \gamma_2, \gamma_3$ are the roots of (7.2) then the roots (7.1) are just

$$\gamma_1 - \tfrac{1}{3}b, \qquad \gamma_2 - \tfrac{1}{3}b, \qquad \gamma_3 - \tfrac{1}{3}b.$$

To find $\gamma_1, \gamma_2, \gamma_3$ we introduce the complex number

$$\omega = \exp(\tfrac{2}{3}\pi\sqrt{-1})$$

(ω is a cube root of unity) and consider

$$y = \gamma_1 + \omega\gamma_2 + \omega^2\gamma_3,$$
$$z = \gamma_1 + \omega^2\gamma_2 + \omega\gamma_3.$$

Using the identity $\omega^3 = 1$ and the fact that the γ_i are roots of (7.2) it can (and should!) be shown that

$$y^3 + z^3 = -27t,$$
$$y^3z^3 = -27s^3.$$

These two identities yield the factorization:

$$(x - y^3)(x - z^3) = x^2 + 27tx - 27s^3.$$

In other words, y^3 and z^3 are the roots of the quadratic polynomial $x^2 + 27tx - 27s^3$. By considering $0 + y + z$, $0 + \omega y + z$, and $0 + y + \omega z$ and using the identities $0 = \gamma_1 + \gamma_2 + \gamma_3$ and $1 + \omega + \omega^2 = 0$, the reader should show that

$$\gamma_1 = \tfrac{1}{3}(y + z),$$
$$\gamma_2 = \tfrac{1}{3}(\omega^2 y + \omega z),$$
$$\gamma_3 = \tfrac{1}{3}(\omega y + \omega^2 z).$$

In conclusion then, we have a formula for the roots of the polynomial $x^3 + bx^2 + cx + d$ involving only the four field operations and the extraction of square and cube roots. For instance, one of the roots is:

$$\gamma_1 = \tfrac{1}{3}(\sqrt[3]{\tfrac{1}{2}(-27t + \sqrt{(27t)^2 + 108s^3})} + \sqrt[3]{\tfrac{1}{2}(-27t - \sqrt{(27t)^2 + 108s^3})} - b)$$

where $s = c - \tfrac{1}{3}b^2$ and $t = \tfrac{2}{27}b^3 - \tfrac{1}{3}bc + d$.

Consider now an arbitrary quartic polynomial

$$x^4 + bx^3 + cx^2 + dx + e$$

with $b, c, d, e \in \mathbb{Q}$. On substituting $u = x + \tfrac{1}{4}b$ this quartic reduces to the form

$$u^4 + ru^2 + su + t$$

with $r, s, t \in \mathbb{Q}$. The roots of the first quartic are easily deduced from those of the second. Let $\gamma_1, \gamma_2, \gamma_3, \gamma_4$ be the roots of the second, and consider

$$y_1 = (\gamma_1 + \gamma_2)(\gamma_3 + \gamma_4),$$
$$y_2 = (\gamma_1 + \gamma_3)(\gamma_2 + \gamma_4),$$
$$y_3 = (\gamma_1 + \gamma_4)(\gamma_2 + \gamma_3).$$

With some effort it can be verified that

$$y_1 + y_2 + y_3 = 2r,$$
$$y_1 y_2 + y_1 y_3 + y_2 y_3 = r^2 - 4t,$$
$$y_1 y_2 y_3 = -s^2.$$

Consequently y_1, y_2, y_3 are the roots of the cubic polynomial

$$x^3 - 2rx^2 + (r^2 - 4t)x + s^2.$$

We call this cubic polynomial the *cubic resolvant* of our original quartic polynomial. The roots of the cubic resolvant determine $\gamma_1, \gamma_2, \gamma_3, \gamma_4$ as follows:

$$\gamma_1 = \tfrac{1}{2}(\sqrt{-y_1} + \sqrt{-y_2} + \sqrt{-y_3}),$$
$$\gamma_2 = \tfrac{1}{2}(\sqrt{-y_1} - \sqrt{-y_2} - \sqrt{-y_3}),$$
$$\gamma_3 = \tfrac{1}{2}(-\sqrt{-y_1} + \sqrt{-y_2} - \sqrt{-y_3}),$$
$$\gamma_4 = \tfrac{1}{2}(\sqrt{-y_1} - \sqrt{-y_2} + \sqrt{-y_3}),$$

the square roots being chosen so that $(\sqrt{-y_1})\,(\sqrt{-y_2})\,(\sqrt{-y_3}) = -t$. Since the y_i can be expressed using the formula for the roots of a cubic, it follows that there exists an (albeit rather complicated) formula for the roots of an arbitrary quartic polynomial over $\mathbb{Q}$ involving only the four field operations and the extraction of square and cube roots.

The remainder of this chapter and the next is mainly devoted to proving the impossibility of finding a formula for the roots of an arbitrary quintic polynomial over $\mathbb{Q}$ involving only the four field operations and the extraction of nth roots.

Before any such proof can be started, the phrase 'formula for the roots involving only the four field operations and the extraction of nth roots' needs to be replaced by something more mathematically precise. We do this by defining a *radical extension* of $\mathbb{Q}$ to be a field extension $L:\mathbb{Q}$ for which there exists a sequence of complex numbers α_1, $\alpha_2, \ldots, \alpha_m \in \mathbb{C}$ such that $L = \mathbb{Q}\,(\alpha_1, \ldots, \alpha_m)$ and such that for each $i = 1, \ldots, m$ there exists an integer $n(i) \ge 2$ for which

$$\alpha_i^{n(i)} \in \mathbb{Q}(\alpha_1, \ldots, \alpha_{i-1}).$$

Intuitively then, a root α of some polynomial over $\mathbb{Q}$ can be expressed in terms of a formula involving only the four field operations and the extraction of nth roots if and only if α lies in some radical extension L of $\mathbb{Q}$.

For instance, all the roots of the polynomial $x^3 + sx + t$ over $\mathbb{Q}$ lie in the radical extension $\mathbb{Q}\,(\alpha_1, \alpha_2)$ of $\mathbb{Q}$ with

$$\alpha_1 = \sqrt{(27t)^2 + 108s^3}, \qquad \alpha_2 = \sqrt[3]{\tfrac{1}{2}(-27t - \sqrt{(27t)^2 + 108s^3})}.$$

We shall say that a polynomial $p(x)$ over $\mathbb{Q}$ is *soluble by radicals* if there exists a radical extension $L:\mathbb{Q}$ such that all of the roots of $p(x)$ are contained in L (that is, L must contain a splitting field for $p(x)$ over $\mathbb{Q}$). Our main aim in this chapter and the next is to explain why the quintic polynomial $x^5 - 4x + 2$ is not soluble by radicals.

Suppose that Σ is a splitting field for some polynomial $p(x)$ over $\mathbb{Q}$, ans suppose that experimentation leads us to conjecture that $p(x)$ is not soluble by radicals. How should we then set about proving our conjecture? The answer, according to Evariste Galois, is that we should investigate the set of all field isomorphisms $\phi : \Sigma \to \Sigma$ satisfying

$$\phi(a) = a \qquad \text{for all } a \in \mathbb{Q};$$

such an isomorphism is called a $\mathbb{Q}$-*automorphism* of Σ. In other words, a $\mathbb{Q}$-automorphism is an isomorphism which *fixes* each element in $\mathbb{Q}$. We denote the set of all $\mathbb{Q}$-automorphisms of Σ by $\Gamma(\Sigma:\mathbb{Q})$.

For convenience, throughout the remainder of the chapter we shall assume that any splitting field Σ of a polynomial $p(x)$ over $\mathbb{Q}$ is always chosen to be a subfield of $\mathbb{C}$. By the fundamental theorem of algebra (which states that any polynomial splits over $\mathbb{C}$) such a splitting field exists. We thus talk of 'the' splitting field of a polynomial.

To illustrate the definition of $\Gamma(\Sigma:\mathbb{Q})$ consider the case when $\Sigma = \mathbb{Q}(\sqrt{2})$. Thus Σ is the splitting field for the polynomial x^2-2 over $\mathbb{Q}$, and each element of Σ can be uniquely expressed in the form $a+b\sqrt{2}$ with $a, b \in \mathbb{Q}$. Any $\mathbb{Q}$-automorphism $\phi:\Sigma\to\Sigma$ must satisfy

$$\phi(a+b\sqrt{2}) = (\phi a) + (\phi b)(\phi\sqrt{2})$$
$$= a + b(\phi\sqrt{2}).$$

It follows that the $\mathbb{Q}$-automorphism ϕ is completely determined by the value of $\phi(\sqrt{2})$. Since

$$(\phi\sqrt{2})^2 = \phi(2)$$
$$= 2$$

there are only two possible $\mathbb{Q}$-automorphisms:

$$\phi_1:\Sigma\to\Sigma, \quad a+b\sqrt{2}\mapsto a+b\sqrt{2},$$
$$\phi_1:\Sigma\to\Sigma, \quad a+b\sqrt{2}\mapsto a-b\sqrt{2}.$$

As ϕ_1 is just the identity map, it is certainly a $\mathbb{Q}$-automorphism. To see that ϕ_2 is a $\mathbb{Q}$-automorphism it suffices to note that

$$\phi_2((a+b\sqrt{2}) + (c+d\sqrt{2})) = \phi_2((a+c) + (b+d)\sqrt{2})$$
$$= (a+c) - (b+d)\sqrt{2}$$
$$= (a-b\sqrt{2}) + (c-d\sqrt{2})$$
$$= \phi_2(a+b\sqrt{2}) + \phi_2(c+d\sqrt{2}),$$

and

$$\phi_2((a+b\sqrt{2})(c+d\sqrt{2})) = \phi_2((ac+2bd) + (bc+ad)\sqrt{2})$$
$$= (ac+2bd) - (bc+ad)\sqrt{2}$$
$$= (a-b\sqrt{2})(c-d\sqrt{2})$$
$$= (\phi_2(a+b\sqrt{2}))(\phi_2(c+d\sqrt{2}))$$

for all $a, b, c, d \in \mathbb{Q}$. Therefore, in this example, the set $\Gamma(\Sigma : \mathbb{Q})$ consists of just two $\mathbb{Q}$-automorphisms: $\Gamma(\Sigma : \mathbb{Q}) = \{\phi_1, \phi_2\}$.

In general the computation of the set $\Gamma(\Sigma : \mathbb{Q})$ is very difficult. If we are to use this set to explain why a particular polynomial $p(x)$ is not soluble by radicals, then we will at least have to be able to compute it for the case when Σ is the splitting field of the given polynomial $p(x)$. Thus for the moment we shall leave the problem of solubility by radicals, and direct our attention to the problem of computing $\Gamma(\Sigma : \mathbb{Q})$.

Theorem 7.1. *Let $p(x)$ be a polynomial over $\mathbb{Q}$ of degree $\geq n$ with distinct roots $\gamma_1, \ldots, \gamma_n$. Let Σ be the splitting field of $p(x)$ over $\mathbb{Q}$.*

(i) *Suppose ϕ, ψ are $\mathbb{Q}$-automorphisms of Σ. Then $\phi(\gamma_i) = \psi(\gamma_i)$ for $i = 1, \ldots, n$ if, and only if, ϕ is identical to ψ.*

(ii) *For any $\mathbb{Q}$-automorphism ϕ of Σ there exists a permutation σ: $\{1, \ldots, n\} \rightarrow \{1, \ldots, n\}$ such that*

$$\phi(\gamma_i) = \gamma_{\sigma(i)}$$

for $i = 1, \ldots, n$.

(iii) *Suppose that $p(x)$ is irreducible. Then for any i, i' such that $1 \leq i, i' \leq n$, there exists a $\mathbb{Q}$-automorphism ϕ of Σ satisfying:*

$$\phi(\gamma_i) = \gamma_{i'}.$$

(iv) *The composite $\phi \circ \psi$ of two $\mathbb{Q}$-automorphisms ϕ, ψ is a $\mathbb{Q}$-automorphism.*

Proof of (i). Any element α in Σ can be expressed (not necessarily uniquely) in the form

$$\alpha = a_1 \delta_1 + a_2 \delta_2 + \cdots + a_k \delta_k$$

with each $a_i \in \mathbb{Q}$ and with each δ_i a product of roots; this is because $\Sigma = \mathbb{Q}(\gamma_1, \ldots, \gamma_n)$ (cf. Exercise 11 of Chapter 2). If $\phi(\gamma_i) = \psi(\gamma_i)$ for $i = 1, \ldots, n$ then $\phi(\delta_i) = \psi(\delta_i)$ for $i = 1, \ldots, k$ and consequently

$$\begin{aligned}
\phi(\alpha) &= \phi(a_1 \delta_1 + a_2 \delta_2 + \cdots + a_k \delta_k) \\
&= a_1(\phi\delta_1) + a_2(\phi\delta_2) + \cdots + a_k(\phi\delta_k) \\
&= a_1(\psi\delta_1) + a_2(\psi\delta_2) + \cdots + a_n(\psi\delta_n) \\
&= \psi(\alpha).
\end{aligned}$$

Conversely, if $\phi = \psi$ then clearly $\phi(\gamma_i) = \psi(\gamma_i)$ for $i = 1, \ldots, n$. ∎

Proof of (ii). Let $\phi: \Sigma \to \Sigma$ be a $\mathbb{Q}$-automorphism of Σ. For any root γ_i of $p(x)$ we have

$$p(\phi \gamma_i) = \phi(p(\gamma_i))$$
$$= \phi(0)$$
$$= 0.$$

Hence $\phi(\gamma_i)$ is a root of $p(x)$, say $\phi(\gamma_i) = \gamma_{\sigma(i)}$. Since ϕ is by definition injective, it follows that $\sigma: \{1, \ldots, n\} \to \{1, \ldots, n\}$ is also injective, and hence a permutation. ∎

Proof of (iii). Suppose that $p(x)$ is irreducible over $\mathbb{Q}$, and suppose we are given two of its roots γ_i, $\gamma_{i'}$. Consider the two subfields $\mathbb{Q}(\gamma_i)$ and $\mathbb{Q}(\gamma_{i'})$ of Σ. Consider also the field $\mathbb{Q}[\beta]/(p(\beta))$ obtained from the ring $\mathbb{Q}[\beta]$ of polynomials in the indeterminate β by factoring the ideal $I = (p(\beta))$. We have three inclusions $\mathbb{Q} \hookrightarrow \mathbb{Q}(\gamma_i)$, $\mathbb{Q} \hookrightarrow \mathbb{Q}(\gamma_{i'})$, $\mathbb{Q} \hookrightarrow \mathbb{Q}[\beta]/(p(\beta))$ and two field isomorphisms

$$\psi: \mathbb{Q}[\beta]/(p(\beta)) \to \mathbb{Q}(\gamma_i), \qquad f(\beta) + I \mapsto f(\gamma_i),$$
$$\psi': \mathbb{Q}[\beta]/(p(\beta)) \to \mathbb{Q}(\gamma_{i'}), \qquad f(\beta) + I \mapsto f(\gamma_{i'}).$$

Both ψ and ψ' restrict to the identity on $\mathbb{Q}$. Let Σ' be a splitting field for $p(x)$ over $\mathbb{Q}[\beta]/(p(\beta))$. The following diagram summarizes our data.

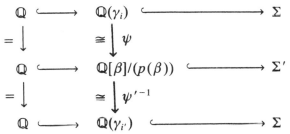

Note that Σ is the splitting field for $p(x)$ over $\mathbb{Q}(\gamma_i)$, and also the splitting field for $p(x)$ over $\mathbb{Q}(\gamma_{i'})$. Using Proposition 2.16 we have isomorphisms

$$\overline{\psi}: \Sigma \to \Sigma' \qquad \text{and} \qquad \overline{\psi'^{-1}}: \Sigma' \to \Sigma$$

which restrict to ψ and ψ'^{-1}, and in particular restrict to the identity on $\mathbb{Q}$. The composite isomorphism

$$\overline{\psi'^{-1}} \circ \overline{\psi}: \Sigma \to \Sigma' \to \Sigma$$

is a $\mathbb{Q}$-automorphism of Σ which sends γ_i to $\gamma_{i'}$.   ∎

Proof of (iv)   This is left as an exercise for the reader.   ∎

Part (iv) of Theorem 7.1 tells us that $\Gamma(\Sigma:\mathbb{Q})$ is a set with an algebraic structure: any two elements ϕ, ψ can be composed to form an element $\phi \circ \psi$. For arbitrary ϕ, ψ, η in $\Gamma(\Sigma:\mathbb{Q})$ the reader can check the following.

1. Composition is associative:

$$(\phi \circ \psi) \circ \eta = \phi \circ (\psi \circ \eta).$$

2. The identity $\mathbb{Q}$-automorphism, which we denote by $1 : \Sigma \to \Sigma$, satisfies

$$\phi \circ 1 = 1 \circ \phi = \phi.$$

3. There is an inverse ϕ^{-1} satisfying

$$\phi^{-1} \circ \phi = \phi \circ \phi^{-1} = 1.$$

In order to emphasize this structure we refer to $\Gamma(\Sigma:\mathbb{Q})$ as the *Galois group* of the extension $\Sigma:\mathbb{Q}$, or the *Galois group* of the polynomial $p(x)$ for which Σ is a splitting field. (Any set with a composition $\circ$ satisfying (i), (ii), and (iii) is called a *group*. Chapter 8 contains a brief introduction to the theory of groups.)

Let Σ be the splitting field of an arbitrary polynomial $p(x)$ over $\mathbb{Q}$, and let $\gamma_1, \ldots, \gamma_n$ be the distinct roots of $p(x)$ in Σ. From parts (i) and (ii) of Theorem 7.1 it follows that any $\mathbb{Q}$-automorphism of Σ is completely determined by a permutation of the roots

$$\gamma_i \mapsto \gamma_{\sigma(i)}, \qquad i = 1, \ldots, n$$

or equivalently by the corresponding permutation

$$\sigma : \{1, \ldots, n\} \to \{1, \ldots, n\}.$$

Since there are precisely $n!$ such permutations, there can be at most $n!$ $\mathbb{Q}$-automorphisms of Σ. (We have no reason to expect every permutation of $\{1, \ldots, n\}$ to determine a $\mathbb{Q}$-automorphism.) We shall often represent a $\mathbb{Q}$-automorphism by its corresponding permutation σ.

For instance, in the case when Σ is the splitting field of $x^2 - 2$ over $\mathbb{Q}$, we have seen that $\Gamma(\Sigma:\mathbb{Q})$ consists of two $\mathbb{Q}$-automorphisms ϕ_1, $\phi_2 : \Sigma \to \Sigma$. The roots of $x^2 - 2$ are $\gamma_1 = \sqrt{2}$ and $\gamma_2 = -\sqrt{2}$. The identity automorphism ϕ_1 is represented by the permutation σ_1: $\{1, 2\} \rightarrow \{1, 2\}$ defined by $\sigma_1(1) = 1$, $\sigma_1(2) = 1$. The $\mathbb{Q}$-automorphism ϕ_2 is represented by the permutation σ_2: $\{1, 2\} \rightarrow \{1, 2\}$ defined by $\sigma_2(1) = 2$, $\sigma_2(2) = 1$.

We should always bear in mind that the representation of $\mathbb{Q}$-automorphisms by permutations depends on the way in which we order the roots!

As we are going to have to study permutations in some depth, it will be useful to establish a little notation. We let S_n denote the set consisting of all of the $n!$ permutations of $\{1, \ldots, n\}$. (The letter S stands for *symmetry*.) A permutation σ in S_n will be said to be of *degree* n. Given m distinct integers $i_1, i_2, \ldots, i_m \in \{1, \ldots, n\}$ we write

$$\sigma = (i_1 \quad i_2 \quad \ldots \quad i_m)$$

to denote the permutation σ of degree n described by

$$\sigma(i_1) = i_2$$

$$\sigma(i_2) = i_3$$

$$\vdots$$

$$\sigma(i_{m-1}) = i_m$$

$$\sigma(i_m) = i_1$$

and

$$\sigma(i) = i \qquad \text{for } i \in \{1, \ldots, n\} \backslash \{i_1, \ldots, i_m\}.$$

If σ and τ are two permutations of degree n, then we write $\sigma\tau$ to denote the *composite* permutation of degree n defined by

$$\sigma\tau(i) = \sigma(\tau(i)) \qquad \text{for } i = 1, \ldots, n.$$

This composition on the set S_n satisfies the following for all ρ, σ, τ in S_n:

(1) composition is associative:

$$(\rho\sigma)\tau = \rho(\sigma\tau);$$

(2) the identity permutation 1 satisfies

$$\rho 1 = 1\rho = \rho;$$

(3) there is an inverse permutation ρ^{-1} satisfying

$$\rho^{-1}\rho = \rho\rho^{-1} = 1.$$

Since composition is associative we usually write $\rho\sigma\tau$ instead of $\rho(\sigma\tau)$ or $(\rho\sigma)\tau$.

As an example, consider the permutations ρ, σ, τ of degree 5 represented by $\rho = (1 \quad 5 \quad 4 \quad 3)$, $\sigma = (1 \quad 5 \quad 3)$, $\tau = (3 \quad 4)$. Explicitly, ρ, σ, and τ are given by

$$\rho(1) = 5 \qquad \sigma(1) = 5 \qquad \tau(1) = 1$$
$$\rho(2) = 2 \qquad \sigma(2) = 2 \qquad \tau(2) = 2$$
$$\rho(3) = 1 \qquad \sigma(3) = 1 \qquad \tau(3) = 4$$
$$\rho(4) = 3 \qquad \sigma(4) = 4 \qquad \tau(4) = 3$$
$$\rho(5) = 4 \qquad \sigma(5) = 3 \qquad \tau(5) = 5.$$

The composite permutation $\nu = \rho\sigma\tau = (1 \quad 5 \quad 4 \quad 3)(1 \quad 5 \quad 3)(3 \quad 4)$ is described explicitly by

$$\nu(1) = 4$$
$$\nu(2) = 2$$
$$\nu(3) = 3$$
$$\nu(4) = 5$$
$$\nu(5) = 1.$$

The inverse ρ^{-1} is described explicitly by

$$\rho^{-1}(1) = 3$$
$$\rho^{-1}(2) = 2$$
$$\rho^{-1}(3) = 4$$
$$\rho^{-1}(4) = 5$$
$$\rho^{-1}(5) = 1.$$

As already indicated, a formal introduction to the theory of groups will be given in Chapter 8. For the moment, any non-empty subset G of S_n which is closed under composition (that is, $\sigma, \tau \in G$ implies $\sigma\tau \in G$) will be called a *group of degree n*, or simply a *group*. A subset H of a group G is called a *subgroup* if H is itself a group.

The following set V of four permutations, in which 1 stands for the identity, is an example of a group of degree 4:

$$V = \{1, \quad (1\ \ 2)(3\ \ 4), \quad (1\ \ 3)(2\ \ 4), \quad (1\ \ 4)(2\ \ 3)\}.$$

To show that V is closed under composition, it suffices to write out all of the 16 possible compositions in tabular form:

	1	(1 2)(3 4)	(1 3)(2 4)	(1 4)(2 3)
1	1	(1 2)(3 4)	(1 3)(2 4)	(1 4)(2 3)
(1 2)(3 4)	(1 2)(3 4)	1	(1 4)(2 3)	(1 3)(2 4)
(1 3)(2 4)	(1 3)(2 4)	(1 4)(2 3)	1	(1 2)(3 4)
(1 4)(2 3)	(1 4)(2 3)	(1 3)(2 4)	(1 2)(3 4)	1

In this table the composite $((1\ \ 2)(3\ \ 4))(1\ \ 3)(2\ \ 4))$, for instance, is found as the common entry in the row headed by $(1\ \ 2)(3\ \ 4)$ and column headed by $(1\ \ 3)(2\ \ 4)$.

To illustrate the utility of Theorem 7.1 and the above notation on permutations, we shall now compute $\Gamma(\Sigma:\mathbb{Q})$ for the case where Σ is the splitting field of $x^3 - 2$ over $\mathbb{Q}$. The roots of this polynomial are

$$\gamma_1 = \sqrt[3]{2},$$
$$\gamma_2 = \sqrt[3]{2}\,\exp(\tfrac{2}{3}\pi\sqrt{-1}),$$
$$\gamma_3 = \sqrt[3]{2}\,\exp(\tfrac{4}{3}\pi\sqrt{-1}).$$

Thus $\Sigma = \mathbb{Q}(\gamma_1, \gamma_2, \gamma_3)$. The isomorphism $\mathbb{C} \to \mathbb{C}$ given by complex conjugation

$$a + b\sqrt{-1} \mapsto a - b\sqrt{-1} \qquad a, b \in \mathbb{R},$$

restricts to a $\mathbb{Q}$-automorphism $\Sigma \to \Sigma$ which sends

$$\gamma_1 \mapsto \gamma_1$$
$$\gamma_2 \mapsto \gamma_3$$
$$\gamma_3 \mapsto \gamma_2$$

and which is thus represented by the permutation $(2\ \ 3)$. Since $x^3 - 2$ is irreducible over $\mathbb{Q}$ it follows from Theorem 7.1 (iii) that at least one of the two permutations $(1\ \ 3)$ or $(1\ \ 3\ \ 2)$ represents a $\mathbb{Q}$-automorphism. If the permutation $(1\ \ 3)$ represents a $\mathbb{Q}$-automorphism then, since $\Gamma(\Sigma:\mathbb{Q})$ is closed under composition, so does the permutation

$$(2 \quad 3)(1 \quad 3)(2 \quad 3)(1 \quad 3) = (1 \quad 3 \quad 2).$$

We can conclude that both $(2 \quad 3)$ and $(1 \quad 3 \quad 2)$ represent $\mathbb{Q}$-automorphisms of Σ. Consequently each of the following six permutations represents a $\mathbb{Q}$-automorphism:

$(2 \quad 3)$, $(1 \quad 3) = (1 \quad 3 \quad 2)(2 \quad 3)$,

$(1 \quad 3 \quad 2)$, $(1 \quad 2 \quad 3) = (1 \quad 3 \quad 2)(1 \quad 3 \quad 2)$,

$(1 \quad 2) = (2 \quad 3)(1 \quad 3 \quad 2)$, $\quad 1$.

There are only $3! = 6$ permutations in S_3. Hence $\Gamma(\Sigma : \mathbb{Q}) = S_3$.

This example generalizes to the following theorem.

Theorem 7.2. *Let $p(x)$ be any irreducible polynomial of degree 3 over $\mathbb{Q}$ which has two non-real roots. Let Σ be the splitting field of $p(x)$ over $\mathbb{Q}$. Then $\Gamma(\Sigma : \mathbb{Q}) = S_3$.*

Proof Let γ_1, γ_2, γ_3 be the roots, and suppose that γ_2, γ_3 are not real. As the degree of $p(x)$ is odd, one of the roots, namely γ_1, must be real. Since complex conjugation yields a $\mathbb{Q}$-automorphism of Σ which permutes the complex roots, it follows that γ_2 and γ_3 are complex conjugates. The proof can now be completed using the same arguments as in the preceding example.   ∎

So far we have two examples illustrating the computation of the Galois group $\Gamma(\Sigma : \mathbb{Q})$; in the first $\Gamma(\Sigma : \mathbb{Q}) = S_2$, and in the second $\Gamma(\Sigma : \mathbb{Q}) = S_3$. There are however plenty of examples (see below) where $\Gamma(\Sigma : \mathbb{Q}) \subsetneq S_n$. In computing the group $\Gamma(\Sigma : \mathbb{Q})$ it is important to be able to determine the number $|\Gamma(\Sigma : \mathbb{Q})|$ of $\mathbb{Q}$-automorphisms. The following theorem is a result in this direction.

Theorem 7.3. *Let Σ be the splitting field of some polynomial over $\mathbb{Q}$ with no repeated roots. Then the number of $\mathbb{Q}$-automorphisms is equal to the degree of the extension $\Sigma : \mathbb{Q}$,*

$$|\Gamma(\Sigma : \mathbb{Q})| = [\Sigma : \mathbb{Q}].$$

Proof. We shall use induction on $[\Sigma : \mathbb{Q}]$. It will be helpful to have as our inductive hypothesis a slightly more general version of the theorem. Let K b any subfield of $\mathbb{C}$ and let Σ' be the splitting field of some polynomial $p(x)$ over K. Suppose that $p(x)$ has no repeated

roots. An isomorphism $\Sigma' \to \Sigma'$ which fixes K is called a
K-*automorphism*; the group of K-automorphisms is denoted by
$\Gamma(\Sigma':K)$.

Inductive hypothesis. $|\Gamma(\Sigma':K)|=[\Sigma':K]$.

The inductive hypothesis is certainly true if $[\Sigma':K]=1$, for in this case
$\Sigma'=K$. Let us assume it is true whenever $[\Sigma':K]<k$. Suppose now that
$[\Sigma':K]=k$. Choose any root γ of $p(x)$ such that $\gamma \in \Sigma'/K$, and let $m(x)$
be the minimum polynomial of γ over K. Then the field $K(\gamma)$ is
isomorphic to $K[x]/m(x))$ and so, by Theorem 2.6, $[K(\gamma):K]=$
$\deg(m(x))=d$, say. From Proposition 5.7 we deduce that $[\Sigma':K(\gamma)]=$
$k/d=s$, say. By the inductive hypothesis we thus have

$$|\Gamma(\Sigma':K(\gamma))|=s.$$

The roots $\gamma_1,\ldots,\gamma_d$ of $m(x)$ are distinct (since $m(x)$ is a factor of
$p(x)$), and therefore using Theorem 7.1 (iii) we can choose d distinct
K-automorphisms $\tau_1,\ldots,\tau_d$ of Σ' such that $\tau_i(\gamma)=\gamma_i$. We have precisely s distinct $K(\gamma)$-automorphisms $\rho_1,\ldots,\rho_s$ of Σ'. We thus have
$k=sd$ distinct K-automorphisms

$$\phi_{ij}=\tau_j\rho_i \qquad i=1,\ldots,s, \quad j=1,\ldots,d.$$

(The reader should verify $\phi_{ij}\neq\phi_{kl}$ for $(i,j)\neq(k,l)$.)

It remains to show that the ϕ_{ij} exhaust the possible K-automorphisms
of Σ'. Let $\tau:\Sigma'\to\Sigma'$ be any K-automorphism. Then $\tau(\gamma)$ is a root of
$m(x)$, so that $\tau(\gamma)-\gamma_j$ for some j. The map $\phi=\tau_j^{-1}\tau$ is a
$K(\gamma)$-automorphism of Σ' since $\phi(\gamma)=\gamma$. So by induction $\phi=\rho_i$ for
some i. Hence $\tau=\tau_j\phi=\phi_{ij}$. Consequently $|\Gamma(\Sigma':K)|=[\Sigma':K]$. The
theorem (in fact a slightly generalized version of the theorem) follows
by induction. ∎

As an illustration of the utility of Theorem 7.3 we shall now compute
the Galois group $\Gamma(\Sigma:\mathbb{Q})$ for Σ the splitting field of x^4-2 over $\mathbb{Q}$. Let
$\xi=\sqrt[4]{2}$ and $i=\sqrt{-1}$. Then

$$x^2-2=(x-\xi)(x+\xi)(x-i\xi)(x+i\xi)$$

and $\Sigma=\mathbb{Q}(i,\xi)$. From Proposition 5.7 we have

$$[\Sigma:\mathbb{Q}]-[\mathbb{Q}(i,\xi):\mathbb{Q}(\xi)][\mathbb{Q}(\xi):\mathbb{Q}].$$

Since by Eisenstein's criterion (Proposition 5.10) the polynomial x^4-2
is irreducible over $\mathbb{Q}$, this polynomial must be the minimum polynomial
of ξ over $\mathbb{Q}$. Hence

$$[\mathbb{Q}(\xi):\mathbb{Q}] = \deg(x^4 - 2) = 4.$$

The minimum polynomial of i over $\mathbb{Q}(\xi)$ is $x^2 + 1$, and hence

$$[\mathbb{Q}(i, \xi):\mathbb{Q}(\xi)] = \deg(x^2 + 1) = 2.$$

Consequently $[\Sigma:\mathbb{Q}] = 8$. Theorem 7.3 therefore implies that

$$|\Gamma(\Sigma:\mathbb{Q})| = 8.$$

To complete the computation we need to give explicit descriptions of the eight $\mathbb{Q}$-automorphisms of Σ. Let us set $\gamma_1 = \xi$, $\gamma_2 = -\xi$, $\gamma_3 = i\xi$, $\gamma_4 = -i\xi$. By a direct check, or by several applications of Theorem 7.1 (iii), we see that there are $\mathbb{Q}$-automorphisms ϕ, $\psi:\Sigma \to \Sigma$ defined by

$$\phi(\gamma_1) = \gamma_3$$
$$\phi(\gamma_2) = \gamma_4$$
$$\phi(\gamma_3) = \gamma_2$$
$$\phi(\gamma_4) = \gamma_1,$$

and

$$\psi(\gamma_1) = \gamma_1$$
$$\psi(\gamma_2) = \gamma_2$$
$$\psi(\gamma_3) = \gamma_4$$
$$\psi(\gamma_4) = \gamma_3.$$

It follows, using the fact that the Galois group is closed under composition (and using our permutation notation to denote $\mathbb{Q}$-automorphisms), that the eight $\mathbb{Q}$-automorphisms are:

$(1\ \ 3\ \ 2\ \ 4),$

$(3\ \ 4),$

$(1\ \ 3)(2\ \ 4) = (1\ \ 3\ \ 2\ \ 4)(3\ \ 4),$

$(1\ \ 4)(2\ \ 3) = (3\ \ 4)(1\ \ 3\ \ 2\ \ 4),$

$1 = (3\ \ 4)(3\ \ 4),$

$(1\ \ 2)(3\ \ 4) = (1\ \ 3\ \ 2\ \ 4)(1\ \ 3\ \ 2\ \ 4),$

$(1\ \ 4\ \ 2\ \ 3) = (1\ \ 3\ \ 2\ \ 4)(1\ \ 3\ \ 2\ \ 4)(1\ \ 3\ \ 2\ \ 4),$

$(1\ \ 2) = (1\ \ 3\ \ 2\ \ 4)(1\ \ 3\ \ 2\ \ 4)(3\ \ 4).$

This group of eight elements is usually denoted by D_4, and referred to as the *dihedral* group of order 8.

We now have a reasonable understanding of $\mathbb{Q}$-automorphisms, and at this stage we could try to compute the Galois group $\Gamma(\Sigma:\mathbb{Q})$ in the single case that really interests us, namely when Σ is the splitting field of $x^5 - 4x + 2$. In view, however, of the intrinsic interest in the computation of $\mathbb{Q}$-automorphisms, we shall indulge ourselves a little by first computing $\Gamma(\Sigma:\mathbb{Q})$ when: (1) Σ is the splitting field of $x^4 + 4x + 2$ and; (2) Σ is the splitting field of $x^4 + 8x + 12$. The following general result will help us in this.

Theorem 7.4. *Let $p(x)$ be an irreducible polynomial of degree 4 over $\mathbb{Q}$ $\mathbb{Q}$ whose cubic resolvant is also irreducible over $\mathbb{Q}$. Let Σ be the splitting field for $p(x)$ over $\mathbb{Q}$. Then either*

$$\Gamma(\Sigma:\mathbb{Q}) = S_4 \quad \text{or} \quad |\Gamma(\Sigma:\mathbb{Q})| = 12.$$

Proof. We must first show that the four roots $\gamma_1, \gamma_2, \gamma_3, \gamma_4$ of $p(x)$ are distinct. To see this, suppose it were the case that $\gamma_1 = \gamma_2$. Then by Theorem 2.12 the root γ_1 would also be a root of the derivative $p'(x) = d/dx(p(x))$. Thus the minimum polynomial of γ over $\mathbb{Q}$, which (since $p(x)$ is irreducible) is a scalar multiple of $p(x)$ and hence of the same degree as $p(x)$, would divide the derivative $p'(x)$ which is of a lower degree. This clearly can't happen and so the four roots of $p(x)$ are distinct. Note that $\Gamma(\Sigma:\mathbb{Q}) \subseteq S_4$ implies $|\Gamma(\Sigma:\mathbb{Q})| \leq 4! = 24$.

We can show that 4 divides $|\Gamma(\Sigma:\mathbb{Q})|$. It suffices to note that $[\Sigma:\mathbb{Q}] = [\Sigma:\mathbb{Q}(\gamma_1)][\mathbb{Q}(\gamma_1):\mathbb{Q}]$, and that $[\mathbb{Q}(\gamma_1):\mathbb{Q}] = \deg(p(x)) = 4$.

We can also show that 3 divides $|\Gamma(\Sigma:\mathbb{Q})|$, from which we conclude that $|\Gamma(\Sigma:\mathbb{Q})| = 12$ or 24, and hence conclude the theorem. To show that 3 divides $|\Gamma(\Sigma:\mathbb{Q})|$ we can assume the coefficient of x^3 in $p(x)$ is zero and that

$$\gamma_1 = \tfrac{1}{2}(\sqrt{-y_1} + \sqrt{-y_2} + \sqrt{-y_3}),$$
$$\gamma_2 = \tfrac{1}{2}(\sqrt{-y_1} - \sqrt{-y_2} - \sqrt{-y_3}),$$
$$\gamma_3 = \tfrac{1}{2}(-\sqrt{-y_1} + \sqrt{-y_2} - \sqrt{-y_3}),$$
$$\gamma_4 = \tfrac{1}{2}(-\sqrt{-y_1} - \sqrt{-y_2} + \sqrt{-y_3}),$$

where y_1, y_2, y_3 are the roots of the cubic resolvant $g(x)$ and where the square roots $\sqrt{-y_1}, \sqrt{-y_2}, \sqrt{-y_3}$ are suitably chosen. Clearly

$$\Sigma = \mathbb{Q}(\gamma_1, \gamma_2, \gamma_3, \gamma_4) \subseteq \mathbb{Q}(\sqrt{-y_1}, \sqrt{-y_2}, \sqrt{-y_3}).$$

But

$$\sqrt{-y_1} = \gamma_1 + \gamma_2$$
$$\sqrt{-y_2} = \gamma_1 + \gamma_3$$
$$\sqrt{-y_3} = -(\gamma_3 + \gamma_2)$$

implies that $\mathbb{Q}(\gamma_1, \gamma_2, \gamma_3, \gamma_4) \supseteq \mathbb{Q}(\sqrt{-y_1}, \sqrt{-y_2}, \sqrt{-y_3})$. Consequently

$$\Sigma = \mathbb{Q}(\sqrt{-y_1}, \sqrt{-y_2}, \sqrt{-y_3}).$$

We can thus break up the field extension $\Sigma : \mathbb{Q}$ into two field extensions $\Sigma : L$ and $L : \mathbb{Q}$, where $L = \mathbb{Q}(y_1, y_2, y_3)$ is a splitting field for the cubic resolvant $g(x)$ over $\mathbb{Q}$. Since $g(x)$ is irreducible over $\mathbb{Q}$ it follows that 3 divides $[L : \mathbb{Q}]$. But then 3 divides $[\Sigma : \mathbb{Q}] = [\Sigma : L][L : \mathbb{Q}]$.   ∎

Consider for the moment $p(x) = x^4 + 4x + 2$. This polynomial is irreducible over $\mathbb{Q}$ by Eisenstein's criterion with $q = 2$. The cubic resolvant in this case is $g(x) = x^3 - 8x - 16$. Again using Eisenstein's criterion with $q = 2$, we see that the polynomial $\frac{1}{8}g(2x) = x^3 - 2x - 2$ is irreducible over $\mathbb{Q}$. Therefore $g(x)$ is irreducible over $\mathbb{Q}$. Thus for Σ the splitting field of $p(x)$ we have either $|\Gamma(\Sigma : \mathbb{Q})| = 12$ or $|\Gamma(\Sigma : \mathbb{Q})| = 24$. In order to decide which of these two possibilities is the case, we need to introduce and study the 'discriminant' of $p(x)$.

Let $p(x)$ be a polynomial over $\mathbb{Q}$ with roots $\gamma_1, \ldots, \gamma_n$, and splitting field $\Sigma = \mathbb{Q}(\gamma_1, \ldots, \gamma_n)$. Thus

$$p(x) = (x - \gamma_1)(x - \gamma_2) \ldots (x - \gamma_n).$$

Put

$$\delta = \prod_{1 \leq i < j \leq n} (\gamma_i - \gamma_j);$$

thus δ is an element in Σ. If $p(x)$ has a repeated root then $\delta = 0$; otherwise $\delta \neq 0$. In the following discussion leading up to Theorem 7.6 we suppose that $p(x)$ has no repeated roots. Any $\mathbb{Q}$-automorphism $\phi : \Sigma \to \Sigma$ permutes the roots γ_i, and so

$$\phi(\delta) = \text{sign}(\phi) \times \delta \qquad \text{with } \text{sign}(\phi) = \pm 1.$$

This notion of the *sign* of a $\mathbb{Q}$-automorphism extends to an arbitrary permutation $\sigma \in S_n$ (which need not necessarily represent a $\mathbb{Q}$-automorphism), for we can define

$$\sigma(\delta) = \prod_{1 \le i < j \le n} (\gamma_{\sigma(i)} - \gamma_{\sigma(j)});$$

clearly

$$\sigma(\delta) = \mathrm{sign}(\sigma) \times \delta \qquad \text{with } \mathrm{sign}(\sigma) = \pm 1.$$

We shall follow convention and let A_n denote the subset of S_n consisting of all those permutations having sign $= +1$ (A stands for *alternating*); it is left to the reader to show that A_n is a subgroup. As an illustration, the group A_4 consists of the following 12 permutations:

1,	(1 2 3),	(1 2 4),
(1 4 3),	(2 3 4),	(2 4 3),
(1 3 2),	(1 3 4),	(1 4 2),
(1 2)(3 4),	(1 3)(2 4),	(1 4)(2 3).

Returning to the general case of A_n, if it should happen that our element δ lies in $\mathbb{Q}$, then every $\mathbb{Q}$-automorphism ϕ must fix δ (in other words $\phi(\delta) = \delta$) and consequently $\Gamma(\Sigma : \mathbb{Q}) \subseteq A_n$.

A subgroup G of S_n is *transitive* if for all $1 \le i,\ i' \le n$ there exists a permutation σ in G such that $\sigma(i) = i'$. By theorem 7.1 (iii) the Galois group of an irreducible polynomial is transitive. It will be shown, as a consequence of Theorem 8.4, that A_4 is the only transitive subgroup of S_4 with precisely 12 elements. So the element δ can be used to help us decide which of the two possibilities in Theorem 7.4 is the case: if $\delta \in \mathbb{Q}$ then $\Gamma(\Sigma : \mathbb{Q}) = A_4$ since every element of $\Gamma(\Sigma : \mathbb{Q})$ fixes δ and so has sign $= +1$; if $\delta \notin \mathbb{Q}$ then there is at least one $\mathbb{Q}$-automorphism which does not fix δ (see Lemma 7.5 below) and so $\Gamma(\Sigma : \mathbb{Q}) = S_4$. For computational reasons it is preferable to consider δ^2 instead of δ.

The number

$$\Delta = \delta^2$$

is called the *discriminant* of the polynomial $p(x)$. For any $\mathbb{Q}$-automorphism $\phi : \Sigma \to \Sigma$ we have

$$\phi(\Delta) = (\phi(\delta))(\phi(\delta)) = \mathrm{sign}(\phi)^2 \times \Delta = \Delta.$$

This, together with the following Lemma 7.5, shows that the discriminant Δ always lies in $\mathbb{Q}$. If $\delta = \sqrt{\Delta}$ lies in $\mathbb{Q}$ then, as we have already noted, $\Gamma(\Sigma:\mathbb{Q})\subseteq A_n$. If $\sqrt{\Delta}\notin\mathbb{Q}$ then Lemma 7.5 implies the existence of a $\mathbb{Q}$-automorphism ϕ such that $\phi(\delta)\neq\delta$, and consequently $\Gamma(\Sigma:\mathbb{Q})$ is not contained in A_n. The situation is summarized by Theorem 7.6.

Lemma 7.5. *If α is an element in the splitting field Σ of $p(x)$ over $\mathbb{Q}$ satisfying $\phi(\alpha)=\alpha$ for all $\mathbb{Q}$-automorphisms ϕ in $\Gamma(\Sigma:\mathbb{Q})$, then α lies in $\mathbb{Q}$.*

Proof. Suppose that $\alpha\in\Sigma\backslash\mathbb{Q}$. Let $m(x)$ be the minimum polynomial of α over $\mathbb{Q}$, and let Σ' be the splitting field of $m(x)$ over $\mathbb{Q}$. Since $m(x)$ is irreducible of degree ≥ 2 and thus has at least two distinct roots there is, by Theorem 7.1 (iii), a $\mathbb{Q}$-automorphism $\phi:\Sigma'\to\Sigma'$ such that $\phi(\alpha)\neq\alpha$. Since Σ is the splitting field of $p(x)$ over Σ' we can use Proposition 2.16 to extend ϕ to a $\mathbb{Q}$-automorphism of Σ.   ∎

Theorem 7.6. *Let Σ be the splitting field of $p(x)$ over $\mathbb{Q}$, and let Δ be the discriminant of $p(x)$.*

(i) *If $\Delta=0$ then $p(x)$ has a repeated root.*

(ii) *If $\Delta\neq 0$ and $\sqrt{\Delta}\in\mathbb{Q}$ then $\Gamma(\Sigma:\mathbb{Q})$ is contained in A_n.*

(iii) *If $\Delta\neq 0$ and $\sqrt{\Delta}\notin\mathbb{Q}$ then $\Gamma(\Sigma:\mathbb{Q})$ is not contained in A_n.*

(iv) *If $p(x)$ is irreducible of degree 4 with an irreducible cubic resolvant, then:*

$$\Gamma(\Sigma:\mathbb{Q})=S_4 \quad \text{if} \quad \sqrt{\Delta}\notin\mathbb{Q},$$
$$\Gamma(\Sigma:\mathbb{Q})=A_4 \quad \text{if} \quad \sqrt{\Delta}\in\mathbb{Q}.$$

For Theorem 7.6 to be of any use we need to be able to compute the discriminant Δ.

It is not difficult to compute the discriminant Δ of a quadratic polynomial $p(x)=x^2+bx+c$. For, suppose the roots of $p(x)$ are γ_1,γ_2, so that

$$p(x)=(x-\gamma_1)(x-\gamma_2).$$

Then $b=-(\gamma_1+\gamma_2)$ and $c=\gamma_1\gamma_2$, and we have

$$\begin{aligned}\Delta &= (\gamma_1-\gamma_2)^2\\ &= \gamma_1^2+\gamma_2^2-2\gamma_1\gamma_2\\ &= (\gamma_1+\gamma_2)^2-4\gamma_1\gamma_2\\ &= b^2-4c.\end{aligned}$$

Note that Theorem 7.6 completely determines the Galois group Γ of the quadratic polynomial $p(x)$: if $\sqrt{b^2-4c}\in\mathbb{Q}$ then $\Gamma=\{1\}$; if $\sqrt{b^2-4c}\notin\mathbb{Q}$ then $\Gamma=S_2=\{1,(1,2)\}$.

Similar computations can be done for polynomials of higher degree but are extremely lengthy and intricate. For instance, a quartic polynomial $p(x)=x^4+bx^3+cx^2+dx+e$ can (with considerable effort) be shown to have discriminant

$$\Delta=(\gamma_1-\gamma_2)^2(\gamma_1-\gamma_3)^2(\gamma_1-\gamma_4)^2(\gamma_2-\gamma_3)^2(\gamma_2-\gamma_4)^2(\gamma_3-\gamma_4)^2$$
$$=256(I^3-27J^2)$$

where

$$I=e-\frac{bd}{4}+\frac{c^2}{12},\qquad J=\frac{ce}{6}-\frac{d^2}{16}-\frac{b^2e}{16}+\frac{bcd}{48}-\frac{c^3}{216}.$$

For example, the discriminant of x^4+4x+2 is $\Delta=256(-19)$, and the discriminant of $x^4+8x+12$ is $\Delta=256(1296)$. We have already shown that x^4+4x+2 and its cubic resolvent are irreducible over $\mathbb{Q}$. We leave the following as an exercise for the reader: the polynomial $x^4+8x+12$ and its cubic resolvent are also irreducible over $\mathbb{Q}$. If Σ is the splitting field for x^4+4x+2 over $\mathbb{Q}$ then, since $\sqrt{256(-19)}\notin\mathbb{Q}$, Theorem 7.6 (iv) implies that $\Gamma(\Sigma:\mathbb{Q})=S_4$. If Σ is the splitting field for $x^4+8x+12$ over $\mathbb{Q}$ then, since $\sqrt{256(1296)}=576\in\mathbb{Q}$, Theorem 7.6 (iv) implies that $\Gamma(\Sigma.\mathbb{Q})=A_4$.

We now return to the computation of the Galois group $\Gamma(\Sigma:\mathbb{Q})$ in the case that most interests us, namely when Σ is the splitting field of $p(x)=x^5-4x+2$ over $\mathbb{Q}$. By Eisentein's criterion with $q=2$ this polynomial is irreducible over $\mathbb{Q}$. Since $p(-2)<0$, $p(0)>0$, $p(1)<0$, and $p(2)>0$, the intermediate value theorem in calculus implies that $p(x)$ has at least one real root in each of the three intervals $[-2,0]$, $[0,1]$, and $[1,2]$. The derivative $p'(x)=5x^4-4$ has only two real roots. Therefore Rolle's theorem implies that $p(x)$ has at most three real roots. We can conclude that $p(x)$ has exactly three real roots, and therefore two non-real roots. The computation $\Gamma(\Sigma:\mathbb{Q})=S_5$ is a special case of the following generalization of Theorem 7.2.

Theorem 7.7. *Let $p(x)$ be any irreducible polynomial of degree n over $\mathbb{Q}$, n a prime, which has exactly two non-real roots. Let Σ be the splitting field of $p(x)$ over $\mathbb{Q}$. Then $\Gamma(\Sigma:\mathbb{Q})=S_n$.*

Proof.   Using arguments as in the proof of Theorem 7.4 we see that
$p(x)$ has n distinct roots, and therefore $\Gamma(\Sigma:\mathbb{Q})$ is a subgroup of S_n. Let
the two non-real roots be γ_1 and γ_2. Then complex conjugation gives us
the $\mathbb{Q}$-automorphism

$$(1 \quad 2) \in \Gamma(\Sigma:\mathbb{Q}).$$

Now $[\mathbb{Q}(\gamma_1):\mathbb{Q}] = \deg(p(x)) = n$, and $[\Sigma:\mathbb{Q}] = [\Sigma:\mathbb{Q}(\gamma_1)][\mathbb{Q}(\gamma_1):\mathbb{Q}]$. So
n divides $|\Gamma(\Sigma:\mathbb{Q})|$. Since n is prime it follows from Theorem 8.3 that
there exists a $\mathbb{Q}$-automorphism σ satisfying

$$\sigma^n = \sigma\sigma \ldots \sigma = 1$$

and

$$\sigma^i \neq 1 \qquad \text{for any } 1 \leq i \leq n-1;$$

we say that σ has *order* n. The only such permutations σ in S_n are of the
form

$$\sigma = (i_1 \quad i_2 \quad \ldots \quad i_n).$$

We leave the following as a tough exercise: the only subgroup of S_n
containing $(1 \quad 2)$ and such a σ is the group S_n itself. (See any
introductory book on group theory for a proof.) Hence $\Gamma(\Sigma:\mathbb{Q}) = S_n$.
∎

We now have to tackle the difficult question: how does the Galois
group of a polynomial yield information on the solubility of the
polynomial by radicals? More precisely, what property is possessed
by all Galois groups of polynomials that are soluble by radicals,
but not possessed by the Galois group $\Gamma(\Sigma:\mathbb{Q}) = S_5$ of the polynomial
$x^5 - 4x + 2$?

Suppose that a polynomial $p(x)$ is soluble by radicals. Then
its splitting field Σ is contained in a radical extension L of $\mathbb{Q}$. In other
words there are numbers $\alpha_1, \ldots, \alpha_m$ in $\mathbb{C}$ and integers $n(i) \geq 2$ such
that $L = \mathbb{Q}(\alpha_1, \ldots, \alpha_m)$ and $\alpha_i^{n(i)} \in \mathbb{Q}(\alpha_1, \ldots, \alpha_{i-1})$.

We can define a bigger radical extension M of $\mathbb{Q}$ as follows. Let M_1
be the splitting field of $x^{n(1)} - 1$ over $\mathbb{Q}$. Let M_2 be the splitting field of
$x^{n(2)} - 1$ over $M_1(\alpha_1)$. Let M_3 be the splitting field of $x^{n(3)} - 1$ over
$M_2(\alpha_2)$. Continue defining extensions M_i in this way, ending with M_m
the splitting field of $x^{n(m)} - 1$ over $M_{m-1}(\alpha_{m-1})$. Then set $M = M_m(\alpha_m)$.
Clearly M is a radical extension of $\mathbb{Q}$ containing Σ.

Our analysis of $\Gamma(\Sigma:\mathbb{Q})$ will run as follows. We shall first show that
the Galois group $\Gamma(M:\mathbb{Q})$ has a certain property not possessed by the

group S_5. Then we will show that $\Gamma(\Sigma:\mathbb{Q})$ is a subgroup of $\Gamma(M:\mathbb{Q})$ possessing this property. Consequently the polynomial $x^5 - 4x + 2$, whose Galois group is S_5, cannot be solved by radicals. A fair amount of the work in the analysis will be left to the reader.

One property of a group that we need to consider is whether or not its composition is commutative. A group G will be said to be *Abelian* or *commutative* if

$$\sigma\tau = \tau\sigma$$

for all σ, τ in G. (The term 'Abelian' is after the mathematician Niels Abel.) As an example consider the subset

$$C_4 = \{1, \ (1 \ \ 2 \ \ 3 \ \ 4), \ (1 \ \ 3)(2 \ \ 4), \ (1 \ \ 4 \ \ 3 \ \ 2)\}$$

of S_4. It is readily checked that C_4 is an abelian subgroup. (The letter C stands for *cyclic*.) By contrast, neither of the subgroups A_4 or D_4 are abelian.

Lemma 7.8. *The Galois group $\Gamma(M_i : M_{i-1}(\alpha_{i-1}))$ is Abelian for $i = 1, \ldots, m$ and $M_0(\sigma_0) = \mathbb{Q}$.*

Proof For convenience let $n = n(i)$ and $K = M_{i-1}(\alpha_{i-1})$. By Theorem 4.1 some root γ of $x^n - 1$ has the property that each of the other roots is some power of γ. Therefore $M_i = K(\gamma)$, and hence any K-automorphism of M_i, is determined by its effect on γ. Further, K-automorphisms permute the roots of $x^n - 1$. Hence any K-automorphism of M_i is of the form

$$\phi_j : \gamma \mapsto \gamma^j.$$

But $\phi_j\phi_k$ and $\phi_k\phi_j$ both send γ to γ^{jk}, and so the Galois group is Abelian. ∎

Lemma 7.9. *The Galois group $\Gamma(M_i(\alpha_i) : M_i)$ is Abelian for $i = 1, \ldots, m$.*

Proof. For convenience let $n = n(i)$ and $a = \alpha_i^{n(i)} \in M_i$. Then any root of the polynomial $x^n - a$ is of the form $\alpha_i\gamma$ with γ an appropriate root of $x^n - 1$ in M_i. We can thus think of $M_i(\alpha_i)$ as a splitting field for $x^n - a$ over M_i. Any M_i-automorphism of $M_i(\alpha_i)$ therefore permutes the roots of $x^n - a$, and is determined by its effect on α_i. Given two such M_i-automorphisms

$$\phi : \alpha_i \mapsto \gamma \alpha_i$$

$$\psi : \alpha_i \mapsto \gamma' \alpha_i$$

with γ, γ' roots of unity in M_i, we have

$$\phi\psi(\alpha_i) = \gamma'\gamma\alpha_i$$

$$= \gamma\gamma'\alpha_i$$

$$= \psi\phi(\alpha_i).$$

Hence the Galois group is Abelian.   ∎

In view of Lemmas 7.8 and 7.9 we see that the Galois group $\Gamma(M:\mathbb{Q})$ is, in some sense, built up of Abelian groups. We need to make this vague observation precise.

Consider for the moment the two field extensions $M_{i+1}:M_i(\alpha_i)$ and $M_i(\alpha_i):M_i$. Since any $M_i(\alpha_i)$-automorphism of M_{i+1} is also an M_i-automorphism of M_{i+1}, the Galois group $\Gamma(M_{i+1}:M_i(\alpha_i))$ is a subgroup (that is, a subset which is closed under composition) of the Galois group $\Gamma(M_{i+1}:M_i)$. Moreover, for any ϕ in the subgroup $\Gamma(M_{i+1}:M_i(\alpha_i))$ and any ψ in the 'big' group $\Gamma(M_{i+1}:M_i)$ the reader can check that the composite automorphism

$$\psi\phi\psi^{-1}$$

lies in the subgroup $\Gamma(M_{i+1}:M_i(\alpha_i))$. (First show that if $\beta \in M_i(\alpha_i)$ then $\psi^{-1}(\beta) \in M_i(\alpha_i)$.) In view of this we make the following definition.

A subgroup N of a group G is said to be a *normal subgroup* if, for any $\phi \in N$ and any $\psi \in G$ the element $\psi\phi\psi^{-1}$ lies in N.

For example, the subgroup A_n of permutations in S_n having sign $= +1$ is a normal subgroup since for any permutations σ, τ we have

$$\text{sign}(\sigma\tau\sigma^{-1}) = \text{sign}(\tau).$$

(We leave this equality as an exercise.) As another example, it is easily checked that the four-element group V is a normal subgroup of A_4. (Note however, that V is not a normal subgroup of S_4.)

Roughly speaking, a normal subgroup does for a group what an ideal does for a ring. In particular, by considering 'cosets' of a normal subgroup N of G we arrive at the notion of a quotient group G/N. By a *coset* of N in G we mean a set of the form

$$\sigma N = \{\sigma\tau : \tau \in N\},$$

where $\sigma \in N$. As with rings, it can be checked that two cosets are either equal or disjoint, and thus form a partition of G. Cosets can be composed by defining

$$(\sigma N) \circ (\sigma' N) = \sigma\sigma' N.$$

The reader should check that this composition is well defined since N is normal.

As an illustration, let us consider the quotient group A_4/V. The cosets of V in A_4 are:

$$I = 1V = \{1, \quad (1\ \ 2)(3\ \ 4), \quad (1\ \ 3)(2\ \ 4), \quad (1\ \ 4)(2\ \ 3)\}$$
$$X = (1\ \ 2\ \ 3)V = \{(1\ \ 2\ \ 3), \quad (1\ \ 3\ \ 4), \quad (2\ \ 4\ \ 3), \quad (1\ \ 4\ \ 2)\}$$
$$Y = (1\ \ 2\ \ 4)V = \{(1\ \ 2\ \ 4), \quad (1\ \ 4\ \ 3), \quad (1\ \ 3\ \ 2), \quad (2\ \ 3\ \ 4)\}.$$

Note that for example $(1\ \ 2\ \ 3)V = (1\ \ 3\ \ 4)V = (2\ \ 4\ \ 3)V$. The composition of the cosets I, X, Y is described by the following multiplication table:

	I	X	Y
I	I	X	Y
X	X	Y	I
Y	Y	I	X.

The following multiplication table for the subgroup

$$C_3 = \{1, \quad (1\ \ 2\ \ 3), \quad (1\ \ 3\ \ 2)\}$$

of S_4 corresponds to the multiplication table of A_4/V under the substitution $1 = I$, $(1\ \ 2\ \ 3) = X$, $(1\ \ 3\ \ 2)$:

	1	(1 2 3)	(1 3 2)
1	1	(1 2 3)	(1 3 2)
(1 2 3)	(1 2 3)	(1 3 2)	1
(1 3 2)	(1 3 2)	1	(1 2 3).

In an obvious sense the quotient group A_4/V has the same algebraic 'shape' as C_3; we say that A_4/V is *isomorphic* to C_3 and write $A_4/V \cong C_3$.

In general we say that two groups G and G' are *isomorphic* if there is a bijective function $\phi : G \to G'$ satisfying $\phi(\sigma\tau) = (\phi\sigma)(\phi\tau)$ for all σ, τ in G.

Let us now return to the normal subgroup $\Gamma(M_{i+1}:M_i(\alpha_i))$ of $\Gamma(M_{i+1}:M_i)$. For convenience set $N=\Gamma(M_{i+1}:M_i(\alpha_i))$ and $G=\Gamma(M_{i+1}:M_i)$. Using arguments as in the proof of Theorem 7.3 the reader should show that every automorphism ρ in G is of the form

$$\rho=\nu\tau$$

with $\nu\in N$ and $\tau\in\Gamma(M_i(\alpha_i):M_i)$. We leave as an exercise for the reader the fairly intricate verification that there is a well-defined isomorphism

$$G/N\to\Gamma(M_i(\alpha_i):M_i),\qquad \rho N\mapsto\tau.$$

Since $\Gamma(M_i(\alpha_i):M_i)$ is Abelian (and isomorphisms clearly preserve the property of being Abelian) it follows that

$$G/N=\Gamma(M_{i+1}:M_i)/\Gamma(M_{i+1}:M_i(\alpha_i))$$

is Abelian. A similar argument shows that the quotient group

$$\Gamma(M_{i+1}(\alpha_{i+1}):M_i)/\Gamma(M_{i+1}(\alpha_{i+1}):M_i(\alpha_i))$$

is also Abelian. The following theorem summarizes the situation.

Theorem 7.10. *Let M be the above radical extension of $\mathbb{Q}$, and let G be the Galois group of the extension $M:\mathbb{Q}$. Then there exists a family of subgroups N_i, $i=0,\ldots,m$, of G such that:*

(i) $\{1\}=N_0\subseteq N_1\subseteq\ldots\subseteq N_m=G$;

(ii) N_i *is a normal subgroup of N_{i+1} for $i=0,\ldots,m-1$;*

(iii) *the quotient group N_{i+1}/N_i is Abelian for $i=0,\ldots,m-1$.*

Any group G possessing a family of subgroups N_i satisfying properties (i), (ii), and (iii) of Theorem 7.10 is called a *soluble group*.

One example of a soluble group is S_4. It has subgroups $\{1\}\subseteq V\subseteq A_4\subseteq S_4$ with A_4 a normal subgroup of S_4, V a normal subgroup of A_4, and clearly $\{1\}$ a normal subgroup of V. The group $V\cong V/\{1\}$ is Abelian. We have already shown that $C_3\cong A_4/V$, and C_3 is Abelian. It is readily checked that S_4/A_4 consists of just two cosets and is Abelian.

The following three theorems complete our proof that x^5-4x+2 is not soluble by radicals. Theorems 7.12 and 7.13 are proved in the next chapter.

Theorem 7.11.   *Let* Σ *be the splitting field of a polynomial over* $\mathbb{Q}$ *which is soluble by radicals. Let* $M:\mathbb{Q}$ *be the radical extension constructed above. Then* $\Gamma(M:\Sigma)$ *is a normal subgroup of* $\Gamma(M:\mathbb{Q})$ *and there is an isomorphism* $\Gamma(M:\mathbb{Q})/\Gamma(M:\Sigma)\cong\Gamma(\Sigma:\mathbb{Q})$.

Proof.   It should be clear that $\Gamma(M:\Sigma)$ is a normal subgroup of $\Gamma(M:\mathbb{Q})$. Now M is the splitting field of the polynomial

$$f(x)=(x^{n(1)}-a_1)(x^{n(1)}-1)\ldots(x^{n(m)}-a_m)(x^{n(m)}-1)$$

over $\mathbb{Q}$, where $a_i=\alpha_i^{n(i)}$. Using arguments as in the proof of Theorem 7.3 we see that every automorphism ϕ in $\Gamma(M:\mathbb{Q})$ is of the form

$$\phi=\rho\tau$$

with $\rho\in\Gamma(M:\Sigma)$ and $\tau\in\Gamma(\Sigma:\mathbb{Q})$. With some effort it can be checked that there is an isomorphism $\Gamma(M:\mathbb{Q})/\Gamma(M:\Sigma)\cong\Gamma(\Sigma:\mathbb{Q})$.   ∎

Theorem 7.12.   *If* N *is a normal subgroup of a soluble group* G *then the quotient group* G/N *is soluble. Hence any group isomorphic to* G/N *is soluble.*

Theoream 7.13.   *The group* S_5 *is not soluble.*

Exercises

1. Solve by radicals the following polynomials over $\mathbb{Q}$:
   - (i) x^3-7x+5;
   - (ii) x^3-7x+6;
   - (iii) x^4+5x^3-2x-1;
   - (iv) x^4+4x+2.

2. Compute the Galois group of the followng polynomials over $\mathbb{Q}$:
   - (i) $(x^3-2)^2$;
   - (ii) x^3-x^2+x-1;
   - (iii) x^3+x+1;
   - (iv) x^4+1;
   - (v) $x^4+x^3+x^2+x+1$;
   - (vi) x^4-3x^3+4;
   - (vii) $(x^2-2)(x^3-3)$.

3. Suppose that $p(x)$ is a polynomial over $\mathbb{Q}$ with roots $\gamma_1,\ldots,\gamma_n$ in some splitting field. Let $D=\mathrm{d}/\mathrm{d}x$. Show that the discriminant of $p(x)$ is

$$\Delta = \eta_n \prod_{i=1}^{n} Dp(\alpha_i)$$

where $\eta_n = 1$ if $n = 0$ or 1 modulo 4, and $\eta_n = -1$ otherwise.

4. Use Exercise 3 to find the discriminant of the following polynomials over $\mathbb{Q}$:
   (i) $x^3 + sx + t$;
   (ii) $x^5 + sx + t$.

5. Show that the Galois group of the polynomial $x^5 + 20x + 16$ over $\mathbb{Q}$ is a subgroup of A_5. (In fact the Galois group is equal to A_5.)

6. Define the Galois group of an arbitrary field extension $L:K$. Compute the Galois group of the finite field extension $GF(p^n):GF(p)$. More generally compute the Galois group of the extension $GF(p^n):GF(p^m)$ whenever m divides n.

7. (i) List all of the subgroups of S_3.
   (ii) Let Σ be the splitting field of $x^3 - 2$ over $\mathbb{Q}$. For each subgroup G of S_3 find a subfield L of Σ such that $\Gamma(\Sigma:L) = G$.

8 Introduction to groups

In this chapter we give a brief introduction to the theory of groups. Each of the results presented has for its movtivation some aspect of our account of Galois groups given in Chapter 7. The chapter can, however, be read totally independently of Chapter 7. To achieve this independence some material from Chapter 7 is repeated.

A *group* is a set G with a binary operation $\circ$ (called *multiplication*) satisfying the following axioms.

1. There is an *identity* element 1 in G satisfying

$$1 \circ x = x \circ 1 = x \qquad \text{for all } x \text{ in } G.$$

2. For each element x in G there is an *inverse* x^{-1} in G satisfying

$$x \circ x^{-1} = x^{-1} \circ x = 1.$$

3. The multiplication is associative:

$$(x \circ y) \circ z = x \circ (y \circ z) \qquad \text{for all } x, y, z \text{ in } G.$$

As with rings, the product $x \circ y$ of two elements will usually be written as xy.

One example of a group is the set S_n of all $n!$ permutations

$$\sigma : \{1, \ldots, n\} \to \{1, \ldots, n\}$$

of the set $\{1, \ldots, n\}$. The multiplication of two such permutations σ and σ' is defined by

$$\sigma\sigma' : \{1, \ldots, n\} \to \{1, \ldots, n\}, \qquad i \mapsto \sigma(\sigma'(i)).$$

An element of S_n is called a permutation of *degree n*. We call S_n the *symmetric group* of degree n.

Given m distinct integers $i_1, \ldots, i_m$ in $\{1, \ldots, n\}$ we write

$$\sigma = (i_1 \quad i_2 \quad \ldots \quad i_m)$$

to denote the permutation of degree n defined by

$$\sigma(i_1) = i_2$$
$$\sigma(i_2) = i_3$$
$$\vdots$$
$$\sigma(i_m) = i_1$$

and

$$\sigma(i) = i \qquad \text{for } i \notin \{i_1, \ldots, i_m\};$$

this type of permutation is called a *cycle*.

As an illustration let us consider the symmetric group of degree 3. The group S_3 consists of six permutations and can be completely described by the following multiplication table.

	1	(1 2)	(1 3)	(2 3)	(1 3 2)	(1 2 3)
1	1	(1 2)	(1 3)	(2 3)	(1 3 2)	(1 2 3)
(1 2)	(1 2)	1	(1 3 2)	(1 2 3)	(1 3)	(2 3)
(1 3)	(1 3)	(1 2 3)	1	(1 3 2)	(2 3)	(1 2)
(2 3)	(2 3)	(1 3 2)	(1 2 3)	1	(1 2)	(1 3)
(1 2 3)	(1 2 3)	(1 3)	(2 3)	(1 2)	1	(1 3 2)
(1 3 2)	(1 3 2)	(2 3)	(1 2)	(1 3)	(1 2 3)	1

In this table the product (1 3)(1 3 2), for instance, is found as the common entry in the row headed by (1 3) and the column headed by (1 3 2).

Certain group theoretic properties are reflected in this table.

1. The action of the identity element corresponds to the fact that the first row and the first column of the inner square consist of the group elements in their original order.

2. The existence of an inverse for each element, and indeed its value, is made plain because precisely one element in each row and each column of the inner square is equal to 1.

3. Associativity of the multiplication is a bit more difficult to see. Let a_{ij} be the entry in the ith row and jth column of the inner square. For any integers i, j, k such that $1 \le i, j, k \le 6$ we can consider the "rectangle" in the inner square shown in Fig. 8.1. Note that

$$a_{ij}a_{jk} = (xy^{-1})(y(x^{-1}a_{ik}))$$
$$= (x(yy^{-1})x^{-1})a_{ik}$$
$$= a_{ik}$$

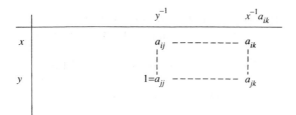

Fig. 8.1.

The equality $a_{ik} = a_{ij}a_{jk}$ for all i, j, k is equivalent to associativity of multiplication.

4. Each row in the inner square contains every element of S_3, and so does each column.

The group theoretic properties 3 and 4 lead to an alternative, visual characterization of finite groups, as we shall now explain. Any square table in which each row and column consists of the same elements in some order is called a *Latin square*. The multiplication table of any finite group is an example of a Latin square. The converse is not however true: the Latin square

	1	a	b	c	d
1	1	a	b	c	d
a	a	1	d	b	c
b	b	c	1	d	a
c	c	d	a	1	b
d	d	b	c	a	1

cannot be interpreted as the multiplication table of a group since $(ab)c = dc = a$, whilst $a(bc) = ad = c$. We leave the following as an exercise: any $n \times n$ Latin square in which each diagonal entry is equal to 1 can be interpreted as the multiplication table of a group if and only if the equation

$$a_{ij}a_{jk} = a_{ik}$$

holds for all i, j, k. (Here a_{ij} represents the entry in the ith row and jth column of the Latin square.)

Other examples of groups can be obtained from a ring R with identity: the set R^* of units in R (that is, elements x in R which possess a multiplicative inverse x^{-1}) is a group in which the multiplication is the ring multiplication. This gives us examples of infinite groups such as

$$\mathbb{Q}^*, \qquad \mathbb{R}^*, \qquad M_n(\mathbb{Z})^*, \qquad M_n(\mathbb{Q})^*,$$

as well as examples of finite groups such as

$$\mathbb{Z}_m^*, \qquad M_n(\mathbb{Z}_m)^*, \qquad M_n(\mathrm{GF}(q))^*.$$

Given a ring R with identity, the group $M_n(R)^*$ of invertible $n \times n$ matrices over R is called the *general linear group of degree n* over R, and denoted by $\mathrm{GL}_n(R)$.

Let G be a group. Any non-empty subset S of G which is itself a group under the multiplication in G is called a *subgroup* of G. Equivalently, a non-empty subset S of G is a subgroup if for all x, y in S the element xy^{-1} lies in S. The reader should verify this equivalence.

Consider the general linear group $\mathrm{GL}_n(\mathbb{C})$ of degree n over $\mathbb{C}$. The reader should verify that the following are all subgroups of $\mathrm{GL}_n(\mathbb{C})$:

(1) the general linear group $\mathrm{GL}_n(\mathbb{R})$ of degree n over $\mathbb{R}$;

(2) the general linear group $\mathrm{GL}_n(\mathbb{Z})$ of degree n over $\mathbb{Z}$;

(3) the *special linear group* $\mathrm{SL}_n(\mathbb{C})$ of degree n over $\mathbb{C}$ consisting of all $n \times n$ complex matrices with determinant equal to 1;

(4) the *orthogonal group* $\mathrm{O}_n(\mathbb{C})$ of degree n over $\mathbb{C}$ consisting of all $n \times n$ complex matrices which are orthogonal;

(5) the *unimodular group* $\mathrm{UM}_n(\mathbb{Z})$ of degree n consisting of all $n \times n$ matrices over $\mathbb{Z}$ with determinant equal to ± 1;

(6) the general linear group $\mathrm{GL}_{n-1}(\mathbb{C})$ of degree $n-1$ over $\mathbb{C}$, provided $n \geq 2$ and we identify an $(n-1) \times (n-1)$ matrix A with the $n \times n$ matrix

$$\left(\begin{array}{ccc|c} & & & 0 \\ & A & & \vdots \\ & & & 0 \\ \hline 0 & \cdots & 0 & 1 \end{array} \right)$$

The reader should verify that subgroups of a finite group G are just those non-empty subsets S which are closed under multiplication. (This is not true for infinite groups: consider the additive group of the integers and the subset of positive integers.) Consequently a subgroup S can be detected from the multiplication table of G, ordered so that the first row begins with

1, by deleting those rows and columns beginning with elements in $G\backslash S$: the set S is a subgroup if and only if no element of $G\backslash S$ occurs in any of the remaining rows. Thus for instance the subset $\{1, \quad (1 \quad 2 \quad 3), \quad (1 \quad 3 \quad 2)\}$ is a subgroup of S_3:

	1	–	–	–	(1 3 2)	(1 2 3)
1	1	–	–	–	(1 3 2)	(1 2 3)
–	–	–	–	–	–	–
–	–	–	–	–	–	–
–	–	–	–	–	–	–
(1 2 3)	(1 2 3)	–	–	1		(1 3 2)
(1 3 2)	(1 3 2)	–	–	–	(1 2 3)	1

The complete collection of subgroups of S_3 is represented by the *subgroup lattice* shown in Fig. 8.2. We shall explain the hyphens in this lattice.

If S is a subgroup of a group G then for any x in G the subset

$$xSx^{-1} = \{xyx^{-1} : y \in S\}$$

is also a subgroup. (This needs to be verified.) We say that the subgroup xSx^{-1} is *conjugate* to S, and represent this fact in the subgroup lattice of G by placing hyphens between the subgroups S and xSx^{-1}. In the subgroup lattice of S_3, for instance, the subgroups $\{1 \quad (1 \quad 2)\}$ and $\{1, \quad (1 \quad 3)\}$ are conjugate since

$$\{1, \quad (1 \quad 2)\} = (1 \quad 3 \quad 2)\{1, \quad (1 \quad 2)\}(1 \quad 2 \quad 3).$$

The reader should prove that 'being conjugate' is an equivalence relation. Every subgroup of a group G is clearly conjugate to itself; a subgroup that

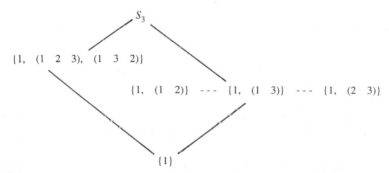

Fig. 8.2.

is not conjugate to any other subgroup is said to be *normal* in G. It is immediate from the subgroup lattice of S_3 that the subgroup

$$\{1, \quad (1 \quad 2 \quad 3), \quad (1 \quad 3 \quad 2)\}$$

is normal in S_3; so too are the identity group $\{1\}$ and the whole group S_3.

Given a subgroup S of a group G, we define the *cosets* of S in G to be the sets

$$xS = \{xy : y \in S\}.$$

The reader can verify that two cosets xS and $x'S$ are either identical or else have no elements in common. The cosets of S thus form a partition of G. A subset T of G is called a *transversal* of S if it satisfies two properties:

(1) $tS \neq t'S$ for all distinct elements t and t' in T;

(2) $G = \underset{t \in T}{\cup} \, tS$.

For a finite group G, the fact that any two cosets of S contain the same number of elements implies that

$$|G| = |T| \times |S|.$$

The number $|T|$ of elements in T is called the *index* of S in G, and we write

$$[G:S] = |T|.$$

We thus have the following theorem of Lagrange, which is a generalization of the version given in Chapter 0. The *order* of a group is the number of elements in the group.

Theorem 8.1. (Lagrange) *Let G be a finite group. The order of any subgroup of G divides the order of G.*

Our analysis of the subgroup lattice of S_3 agrees with Lagrange's theorem. The order of S_3 is 6 and the orders of its subgroups are 1, 2, 3, and 6. It should perhaps be emphasized that it is not the case that for each divisor of the order of a group there exists a subgroup of that order; there are however results in this direction (see Theorem 8.3 below).

Given a subset X of a group G we let $\langle X \rangle$ denote the intersection of all those subgroups of G containing X. It is easily verified that $\langle X \rangle$ is a subgroup; we say that $\langle X \rangle$ is the subgroup *generated* by X. For instance, in S_3 we have

$$\langle (1 \quad 2 \quad 3) \rangle = \{1, \ (1 \quad 2 \quad 3), \ (1 \quad 3 \quad 2)\},$$
$$\langle (1 \quad 2) \rangle = \{1, \ (1 \quad 2)\},$$
$$\langle (1 \quad 2), \ (1 \quad 2 \quad 3) \rangle = S_3.$$

A group C is said to be *cyclic* if it is generated by a single element x, that is, if $C = \langle x \rangle$. The *order* of any element x in a group G is defined to be the order of the cyclic subgroup $\langle x \rangle$. For instance, in S_3 the order of $(1 \quad 2 \quad 3)$ is three, and the order of $(1 \quad 2)$ is 2.

An interesting, and in general very difficult problem, is to decide how many 'different' groups G there are of a given order. If the order is a prime p then this problem is easily solved: by Lagrange's theorem any element in G has to have order dividing p; we can thus find an element x in G such that the cyclic group $\langle x \rangle$ has order p; thus $G = \langle x \rangle$ is cyclic. There is essentially just one cyclic group of order p (cf. the definition of "isomorphism" below). If the order is not a prime the situation is more complicated. To appreciate this, the reader may like to verify that there are essentially just two different groups of order 6.

We say that a group G is *Abelian* or *commutative* if

$$xy = yx$$

for all $x, y \in G$. We define the *exponent* $\exp(G)$ of a finite Abelian group G to be the lowest common multiple of the orders of the elements of G. We have actually met this notion before; the number e used in the proof of Theorem 3.5 is the exponent of the group $\mathbb{F}^*$ of non-zero elements of a finite field $\mathbb{F}$. Indeed, Theorem 3.5 easily generalizes to the following result.

Theorem 8.2. *Let G be a finite Abelian group of exponent* $\exp(G)$. *There exists an element in G whose order is* $\exp(G)$.

As a consequence of Theorem 8.2 we have the following result: if a prime p divides the order of an Abelian group G then G contains an element of order p. (To see this, let x be an element of order $\exp(G)$. The prime p must divide $\exp(G)$, say $\exp(G) = pm$. So x^m has order p.) This result generalizes to non-Abelian groups, as we shall now show (Theorem 8.3).

We say that two elements x and y in G are *conjugate* if there exists an element z in G such that

$$x = zyz^{-1}.$$

The reader can verify that conjugacy is an equivalence relation on G. The set of all elements in G that are conjugate to x is called the *conjugacy class* of x, and denoted by $[x]$. Since conjugacy is an equivalence relation, the conjugacy classes form a partition of G. We let $\|[x]\|$ denote the number of elements in the conjugacy class $[x]$. For some elements x in G, such as the identity element, the conjugacy class $[x]$ consists of just the one element x. The set of all such elements x with $\|[x]\| = 1$ is called the *centre* of G and denoted $Z(G)$; that is

$$Z(G) = \{x \in G : xy = yx \text{ for all } y \in G\}.$$

Suppose that G is finite and let X denote a subset of G consisting of one element from each distinct conjugacy class $[x]$ with $\|[x]\| \geq 2$. Then we have the numerical equation

$$|G| = |Z(G)| + \sum_{x \in X} \|[x]\|. \tag{8.1}$$

For each element x of an arbitrary group G the *centralizer* of x is the subgroup

$$C(x) = \{z \in G : xz = zx\}.$$

The reader can verify that the cosets of $C(x)$ in G are in one-to-one correspondence with the elements in the conjugacy class $[x]$; the correspondence being

$$\theta : yC(x) \mapsto yxy^{-1}.$$

It needs to be verified that θ is well defined and one-to-one. For finite G this correspondence implies

$$\|[x]\| = [G : C(x)].$$

The above equation (8.1) can therefore be rewritten as

$$|G| = |Z(G)| + \sum_{x \in X} [G : C(x)]. \tag{8.2}$$

This equation (8.2) is known as the *class equation*. We have actually met it before in the proof of Wedderburn's theorem given in Chapter 6. The class equation enables us to prove the following result due to Cauchy.

Theorem 8.3. (Cauchy) *If a prime p divides the order of a finite group then there is an element of order p in the group.*

Proof. We know the result is true for Abelian groups. Let G be an arbitrary finite group whose order is pn. We shall use induction on n. If $n = 1$ then, as we have already shown, the group G must be cyclic and the theorem is true. Suppose then that the theorem is true for all groups of order $< pn$. We must show it is true for our group G of order pn. Let X denote a subset of G consisting of one element from each distinct conjugacy class $[x]$ with $\|[x]\| \geq 2$. If for some $x \in X$ the prime p divides the order of the subgroup $C(x)$ we are done since $C(x)$ is a proper subgroup. So suppose that p does not divide $|C(x)|$ for all x in X. Since $|G| = [G : C(x)] \times |C(x)|$ it follows that p divides $[G : C(x)]$ for all x in X. The class equation thus implies that p divides $|Z(G)|$. But $Z(G)$ is Abelian; we know the theorem is true for Abelian groups, and therefore G contains an element of order p. ∎

As an illustration of Cauchy's theorem, recall from Chapter 0 that the order of the general linear group of degree 3 over $\mathbb{Z}_5$ is 1 488 000;

$$|GL_3(\mathbb{Z}_5)| = 2^7 \times 3 \times 5^3 \times 31.$$

Therefore there exist 3×3 matrices over $\mathbb{Z}_5$ of orders 2,3,5, and 31. The reader may like to try to find such matrices!

The groups that are of particular relevance to our account of Galois theory in Chapter 7 are permutation groups (that is, subgroups of S_n). Especially important are those permutation groups G of degree n with the property that for any $i, i' \in \{1, \dots, n\}$ there exists a permutation σ in G satisfying

$$\sigma(i) = i';$$

such groups G are said to be *transitive* of degree n. For example, the transitive groups of degree 3 are S_3 and the cyclic subgroup $\{1, (1 \ 2 \ 3), (1 \ 3 \ 2)\}$ of S_3. For any permutation group G we defined the *stabilizer* of 1 to be the set

$$G_1 = \{\sigma \in G : \sigma(1) = 1\}.$$

It is readily seen that G_1 is a subgroup of G. The stabilizer can be used to give an alternative characterization of transitive groups.

Theorem 8.4. *A permutation group G of degree n is transitive if and only if the stabilizer G_1 is of index n in G.*

Proof. Suppose G is transitive. Then G contains permutations

$$\sigma_{11}, \sigma_{12}, \ldots, \sigma_{1n},$$

which transform 1 into $1, 2, \ldots, n$, respectively. The cosets

$$\sigma_{11}G_1, \sigma_{12}G_1, \ldots, \sigma_{1n}G_1 \tag{8.3}$$

are distinct, because all elements in $\sigma_{1i}G_1$ transform 1 into i. We need need to show that (8.3) is a complete list of cosets. Let τ be any element of G and suppose that $\tau(1) = x$. Then $\sigma_{1x}^{-1}\tau$ leaves 1 unchanged, and so $\sigma_{1x}^{-1}\tau$ lies in G_1. Thus $\tau \in \sigma_{1x}G_1$. It follows that $[G:G_1] = n$.

Conversely, suppose that G_1 is of index n and let

$$T = \{\tau_1, \ldots, \tau_n\}$$

be a transversal of G_1 in G. For $i \neq j$ we have $\tau_i(1) \neq \tau_j(1)$. (To see why, consider $\tau_i\tau_j^{-1} \in G_1$.) Therefore, by rearranging T we have

$$T = \{\rho_{11}, \rho_{12}, \ldots, \rho_{1n}\}$$

where $\rho_{1i}(1) = i$. For any x, $y \in \{1, \ldots, n\}$ we have $\rho_{1y}\rho_{1x}^{-1}(x) = y$; consequently G is transitive. ■

We can use Theorem 8.4 to show that there is exactly one transitive group G of order 12 and degree 4. (This result was used in Chapter 7). If such a group G exists, then

$$[G:G_1] = 4.$$

Since $|G| = 12$, we must have $|G_1| = 3$. Thus G_1 is cyclic of order 3; more precisely

$$G_1 = \{1, \ (2 \ 3 \ 4), \ (2 \ 4 \ 3)\}.$$

The same argument shows that, for G_i $(1 \leq i \leq 4)$ the subgroup of G consisting of those permutations σ such that $\sigma(i) = i$, we have

$$G_2 = \{1, \ (1 \ 3 \ 4), \ (1 \ 4 \ 3)\},$$

$$G_3 = \{1, \ (1 \ 2 \ 4), \ (1 \ 4 \ 2)\},$$

$$G_4 = \{1, \ (1 \ 2 \ 3), \ (1 \ 3 \ 2)\}.$$

The union $G_1 \cup G_2 \cup G_3 \cup G_4$ is not a subgroup of S_4; however, this set generates the following subgroup:

$$A_4 = \{1, \ (1\ 3\ 4), \ (1\ 4\ 3), \ (1\ 2\ 4), \ (1\ 4\ 2), \ (1\ 2\ 3),$$
$$(1\ 3\ 2), \ (1\ 2)(3\ 4), \ (1\ 3)(2\ 4), \ (1\ 4)(2\ 3)\}.$$

The stabilizer of 1 in A_4 is G_1. Hence $[A_4 : G_1] = 4$ and, by Theorem 8.4, A_4 is transitive. It is the only transitive subgroup of order 12 and degree 4 since any other such group must contain A_4.

For $n \geq 3$ we define the *alternating group* A_n to be the subgroup of S_n generated by the permutations

$$(1\ 2\ 3), \ (1\ 2\ 4), \ \ldots, \ (1\ 2\ n).$$

A permutation of the form

$$(i\ j\ k)$$

with i, j, k distinct integers is called a 3-*cycle*. An arbitrary 3-cycle can be expressed as a product of generators of A_n,

$$(i\ j\ k) = (1\ i\ j)(1\ j\ k) \qquad i, j, k \neq 1,$$

and thus A_n contains all 3-cycles. An arbitrary 3-cycle can also be expressed as

$$(i\ j\ k) = (k\ i)(i\ j).$$

A permutation of the form $(i\ j)$, which just interchanges i and j, is called a *transposition*. A product of an even number of transpositions is called an *even permutation*. Thus every permutation in A_4 is even. Since the identity permutation is a product of two transpositions, for instance

$$1 = (1\ 2)(1\ 2),$$

and since the product of two even permutations is clearly even, it follows that the set of all even permutations is a subgroup of S_n; it is the smallest subgroup containing all the generators of A_n and is therefore precisely A_n.

An alternative equivalent definition of A_n was given in Chapter 7. We leave the proof of this equivalence as an exercise for the reader.

We shall establish a celebrated result about normal subgroups of alternating groups which is due to Evariste Galois. Every group G possesses at least two normal subgroups: the group G itself, and the trivial group $\{1\}$. Groups which possess no other normal subgroups are said to be *simple*.

Theorem 8.5.   *For $n \geq 5$ the alternating group A_n is simple.*

Proof.   Let $n \geq 5$ and let N be a normal subgroup of A_n with $|N| \geq 2$. We must show that $N = A_n$. The proof is broken down into several steps.

1. Suppose that N contains some 3-cycle

$$\alpha = (x \quad y \quad z).$$

We shall show that N then contains all 3-cycles, from which it follows that $N = A_n$. Let

$$\xi = (a, b, c)$$

be an arbitrary 3-cycle. Let σ be any permutation in S_n such that

$$\sigma(x) = a, \qquad \sigma(y) = b, \qquad \sigma(z) = c.$$

Then

$$\xi = \sigma^{-1} \alpha \sigma.$$

Since $n \geq 5$ there are at least two positive integers u, $v \leq n$ which are not included in α. The transposition

$$\tau = (u \quad v)$$

commutes with α, and it follows that

$$\xi = (\sigma\tau)^{-1} \alpha (\sigma\tau).$$

Plainly either σ or $\sigma\tau$ is even and hence in A_n. But N is a normal subgroup of A_n and so ξ lies in N. Hence $N = A_n$.

2. A permutation of the form

$$\sigma = (i_1 \quad i_2 \quad \ldots \quad i_m)$$

in which the i_j are distinct integers is called a *cycle* of *length m*, or an *m-cycle*. Two *m*-cycles are said to be *disjoint* if they have no common integer occurring in them. We shall now assume that N contains the permutation

$$\omega = \gamma\delta\varepsilon \ldots,$$

where γ, δ, ε are disjoint cycles with the length of γ greater than 3, say

$$\gamma = (x_1 \quad x_2 \quad \ldots \quad x_m), \qquad m \geq 4.$$

Now $\sigma = (x_1 \quad x_2 \quad x_3)$ is an even permutation which commutes with all the cycles in ω except the first. Thus

$$\omega_1 = \sigma^{-1} \omega \sigma$$

belongs to N, and so does $\omega_1\omega^{-1}$. We find that

$$\omega_1\omega^{-1} = \sigma^{-1}\gamma\sigma\gamma^{-1}$$

$$= (x_2 \quad x_3 \quad x_1 \quad x_4 \quad \ldots \quad x_m)(x_m \quad x_{m-1} \quad \ldots \quad x_2 \quad x_1)$$

$$= (x_1 \quad x_3 \quad x_m).$$

Hence N contains a 3-cycle, and it follows from 1 that $N = A_n$.

The reader can verify that every permutation is a product of disjoint cycles. So from now on we may assume that all permutations in N are products of disjoint cycles whose lengths are 1, 2, or 3.

3. Suppose N contains a permutation ω which involves at least two 3-cycles, say

$$\omega = \alpha\beta\lambda,$$

where $\alpha = (x_1 \quad x_2 \quad x_3)$ and $\beta = (y_1 \quad y_2 \quad y_3)$, and γ does not depend on x_i or y_i ($i = 1, 2, 3$). Choosing

$$\sigma = (x_2 \quad x_3 \quad y_1)$$

we observe that σ commutes with λ. Hence N contains the element

$$\sigma^{-1}\omega\sigma\omega^{-1} = (\sigma^{-1}\alpha\sigma)(\sigma^{-1}\beta\sigma)\beta^{-1}\alpha^{-1}$$

$$= (x_1 \quad x_2 \quad y_1 \quad x_3 \quad y_3)$$

which contradicts the hypothesis that no cycles of length greater than 3 occur in N.

4. When only a single 3-cycle is permitted amongst the factors, a typical element is of the form

$$\omega = (x_1 \quad x_2 \quad x_3)\lambda,$$

where λ is a product of disjoint transpositions. Thus $\lambda^2 = 1$, and N contains the permutation

$$\omega^2 = (x_1 \quad x_3 \quad x_2),$$

which brings us back to 1.

5. Finally we must discuss the case in which all elements of N, other than the identity, are products of disjoint transpositions. As the number of transposition factors must be even, a typical element of N is of the form

$$\omega = (x_1 \quad x_2)(y_1 \quad y_2)\lambda,$$

where λ does not involve x_1, x_2, y_1, y_2. Since $n \geq 5$ we can choose an integer c distinct from the x_i and y_i. Set $\sigma = (x_2 \quad y_1 \quad y_2)$ and $\delta = (x_1 \quad y_2 \quad c)$. The reader can verify that

$$(x_1 \quad y_2 \quad c) = (\delta^{-1}((\sigma^{-1}\omega\sigma)\omega^{-1})\delta)\omega(\sigma^{-1}\omega^{-1}\sigma),$$

which is in N since N is a normal subgroup. Thus, contrary to our hypothesis, N would contain a 3-cycle. This completes the proof of the theorem.   ∎

Simple groups are the basic building blocks of group theory; their role is somewhat analogous to the role of prime numbers in number theory. To explain the analogy we need to introduce quotient groups.

Let G be an arbitrary group with a normal subgroup N. We denote the collection of cosets of N in G by G/N. The set G/N admits a multiplication:

$$(xN) \circ (yN) = (xy)N$$

for x, y in N. The reader should verify that this multiplication is well defined thanks to the normality of N, and satisfies the axioms of a group. We call G/N a *quotient* group. Much (but in general not all) of the algebraic structure of G is determined by the subgroup N and the quotient group G/N. Any group G which is not simple can thus be 'reduced' to two smaller groups. Simple groups are 'irreducible'.

The complete determination and classification of all *finite* simple groups were recently completed. There are several families of such groups, the alternating groups A_n ($n \geq 5$) being one family, the cyclic groups of prime order being another, and there are 26 *sporadic* finite simple groups which fit into none of the families. Hundreds of mathematicians worked on this classification project from 1950 to 1980. The research papers contributing to the entire classification fill roughly 5000 journal pages. One of the final pieces of work in the classification was completed in early 1980 by Griess. He constructed a predicted monster simple group, the largest of the sporadic groups, of order

$$808\ 017\ 424\ 794\ 512\ 875\ 886\ 459\ 904\ 961\ 710\ 757$$

$$005\ 754\ 368\ 000\ 000\ 000.$$

In any classification of groups, two groups G and G' are considered the same if there is a bijective function $\phi: G \to G'$ satisfying

$$\phi(xy) = (\phi x)(\phi y)$$

for all $x, y \in G$. The function ϕ is called an *isomorphism*, the groups are said to be *isomorphic*, and we write $G \cong G'$. The following two isomorphism theorems are left as difficult exercises for the reader.

First isomorphism theorem.   *Let G be a group with a subgroup A and a normal subgroup H. Let HA be the subgroup of G generated by $H \cup A$. The intersection $H \cap A$ is a normal subgroup of A, H is a normal subgroup of HA, and there is an isomorphism*

$$A/(H \cap A) \cong (HA)/H.$$

Second isomorphism theorem.   *Let H and A be normal subgroups of a group G with H contained in A. Then A/H is a normal subgroup of G/H and there is an isomorphism*

$$(G/H)/(A/H) \cong G/A.$$

From our point of view, normal subgroups are important because of their role in the following definition which we recall from Chapter 7.

A group G is *soluble* if it has a finite series of subgroups

$$\{1\} = G_0 \subseteq G_1 \subseteq \ldots \subseteq G_n = G$$

such that:

(1) G_i is normal in G_{i+1} for $i = 0, \ldots, n-1$;

(2) G_{i+1}/G_i is Abelian for $i = 0, \ldots, n-1$.

Theorem 8.6.   (i) *If N is normal subgroup of a soluble group G then the quotient group G/N is soluble.*

(ii) *Any subgroup H of a soluble group G is also soluble.*

Proof. (i) Let

$$\{1\} = G_0 \subseteq G_1 \subseteq \ldots \subseteq G_n = G$$

be a series of subgroups with G_i normal in G_{i+1} and with Abelian quotient groups G_{i+1}/G_i. Then G/N has a series

$$N/N = G_0 N/N \subseteq G_1 N/N \subseteq \ldots \subseteq G_n N/N = G/N.$$

with G_iN/N normal in $G_{i+1}N/N$. By the isomorphism theorems we have

$$(G_{i+1}N/N)/(G_iN/N) \cong (G_{i+1}N)/(G_iN)$$
$$\cong G_{i+1}/(G_{i+1} \cap (G_iN))$$
$$\cong (G_{i+1}/G_i)/((G_{i+1} \cap (G_iN))/G_i)$$

which is a quotient of an Abelian group G_{i+1}/G_i, so is Abelian. (The reader should verify that any quotient of an Abelian group is Abelian.) Therefore G/N is soluble.

(ii) We leave the proof of this part as an exercise. The isomorphism theorems need to be applied to the series

$$\{1\} = H_0 \subseteq H_1 \subseteq \ldots \subseteq H_n = H$$

where $H_i = G_i \cap H$.   ∎

Theorem 8.7.   *The group S_n is not soluble for $n \geq 5$.*

Proof.   The subgroup A_n is not Abelian and hence, by Theorem 8.5 not soluble. Theorem 8.6 (ii) implies that S_n is not soluble.   ∎

Exercises

1. Let G be the subgroup of S_8 generated by the two permutations $\sigma = (1\ \ 2\ \ 3\ \ 4)(5\ \ 6\ \ 7\ \ 8)$ and $\tau = (1\ \ 6\ \ 3\ \ 8)(2\ \ 5\ \ 4\ \ 7)$.
   (i) List all eight elements of G.
   (ii) Give the multiplication table for G.
   (iii) Give the subgroup lattice for G, indicating conjugate subgroups.

2. Repeat Exercise 1 for the subgroup of S_5 of order 10 generated by the two permutations $\sigma = (1\ \ 2\ \ 3\ \ 4\ \ 5)$ and $\tau = (2\ \ 5)(3\ \ 4)$.

3. Let N be a subgroup of a finite group G with index $[G:N] = 2$. Prove that N must be normal.

4. Determine all of the transitive subgroups of S_4.

5. Let G be a finite group of order p^2 with p a prime, and suppose that G is not a cyclic group. Show that G is generated by two elements x and y, each of order p. Prove that $xy = yx$.

6. Let G be a group. An isomorphism $G \to G$ is called an *automorphism*. Show that the set Aut (G) of all automorphisms is a group under composition of functions. Determine Aut(G) for G a cyclic group of order n.

9 Cryptography

In this chapter we consider some recent developments in cryptography. To explain the basic ideas behind this subject let us consider the situation of an international bank, with branch offices in many of the principal cities of the world, whose head office needs weekly confidential reports from the branches. These reports are sent by fax, and to ensure confidentiality have to be disguised. The problem then is to design a secret code, called a *cryptosystem*, which will resist any code-breaking attempts by the bank's competitors.

The report or message that is to be sent to head office is called *plaintext*, and the disguised message is called *ciphertext*. The plaintext and ciphertext are written in some *alphabet* which we assume to consist of the usual letters A–Z together with possibly punctuation marks, numerals, blanks, and any other symbols used in writing the reports. The process of converting plaintext to ciphertext is called *enciphering*, and the reverse process is called *deciphering*.

One general procedure for enciphering plaintext is to label the letters of our alphabet by the elements of some ring R, that is, to set up a bijection

$$\text{alphabet} \leftrightarrow R,$$

and then to disguise the plaintext by means of some mathematically defined bijective function

$$f: R \to R.$$

The inverse function

$$f^{-1}: R \to R$$

is used to decipher the ciphertext.

As an illustration of this general procedure let us suppose that our alphabet consists of just the twenty-six letters A–Z, and that we have labelled these letters by the elements of the ring $R = \mathbb{Z}_{26}$, the bijection being the obvious one:

$$A \leftrightarrow 1$$
$$B \leftrightarrow 2$$
$$\vdots$$
$$Y \leftrightarrow 25$$
$$Z \leftrightarrow 0.$$

Let us take f to be the function

$$f: \mathbb{Z}_{26} \rightarrow \mathbb{Z}_{26}, \qquad x \mapsto 3x + 4.$$

(Note that f is bijective since 3 is coprime to 26.) Suppose that

HELLO

is the plaintext message to be enciphered. The numerical equivalent of this message is

8   5   12   12   15.

Applying f to each of these five numbers in the ring $\mathbb{Z}_{26}$, we obtain the disguised sequence of numbers

2   19   14   14   23

and consequently the ciphertext

BSNNW.

This ciphertext is deciphered using the function

$$f^{-1}: \mathbb{Z}_{26} \rightarrow \mathbb{Z}_{26}, \qquad x \mapsto 9(x - 4)$$

(in which the number 9 occurs because $3^{-1} = 9$ in $\mathbb{Z}_{26}$).
  There are some remarks to be made about this example.

  1. The example will work for any function

$$f: \mathbb{Z}_{26} \rightarrow \mathbb{Z}_{26}, \qquad x \mapsto \alpha x + \beta$$

with α, β elements in $\mathbb{Z}_{26}$ such that α is a unit. The enciphering procedure can therefore be changed from time to time by varying the parameters α and β. We should always assume that any potential code-breaker knows our choice of ring R, in this case $R = \mathbb{Z}_{26}$, and also knows that the function f is of the form $f(x) = \alpha x + \beta$; the code-breaker's task is simply to determine the pair (α, β) and from this compute the pair $(\alpha^{-1}, -\beta)$. The pair (α, β) is called the *enciphering key*, and the pair $(\alpha^{-1}, -\beta)$ is called the *deciphering key*.

2. By an *affine map* we shall mean a function of the form $f: \mathbb{Z}_N \to \mathbb{Z}_N$, $x \mapsto \alpha x + \beta$ with $\alpha, \beta \in \mathbb{Z}_N$. An enciphering/deciphering procedure, such as the above example, based on an affine map is called an *affine cryptosystem*.

3. The deciphering procedure in any affine cryptosystem is the same as the enciphering procedure, but with the deciphering key used in place of the enciphering key.

4. The deciphering key in an affine cryptosystem is easily deduced from the enciphering key. (In the above example the element α^{-1} can be obtained by using the Euclidean algorithm to find integers m, n such that $1 = \alpha m + 26n$; in $\mathbb{Z}_{26}$ we then have $\alpha^{-1} = m$.)

5. As the ring $\mathbb{Z}_{26}$ has 26 elements, and just 12 invertible elements, there are only $12 \times 26 = 312$ possible enciphering keys in our example. A computer search would instantly yield the correct key. The safety of the cryptosystem could be improved slightly by increasing the number of letters in the alphabet, and consequently replacing $\mathbb{Z}_{26}$ by $\mathbb{Z}_N$ with N a large integer. However, the use of frequency analysis would soon break the improved code. It is known for instance that E is the most frequently occurring letter in English texts, and that T is the second most frequently occurring letter. Suppose that with $N = 26$ as above, an analysis of a large amount of ciphertext shows that S is the most frequently occurring letter, and that L is the second most frequently occurring letter. From the correspondences $E \leftrightarrow 5$, $T \leftrightarrow 20$, $S \leftrightarrow 19$, and $L \leftrightarrow 12$ we can deduce that

$$f(5) = 19 = 5\alpha + \beta$$
$$f(20) = 12 = 20\alpha + \beta.$$

The unique solution to these simultaneous equations over $\mathbb{Z}_{26}$ is $\alpha = 3$ and $\beta = 4$. The enciphering key is thus determined.

There is a simple way to counter the use of frequency analysis. Instead of considering the letters of our alphabet to be the basic building blocks of plaintext, we can consider k-tuples of letters to be the basic building blocks and replace the bijection

$$\text{alphabet} \leftrightarrow R$$

by a bijection

$$k\text{-tuples of letters} \leftrightarrow R.$$

To illustrate this, let us choose $k = 3$. Suppose that our alphabet consists of 28 letters: the usual letters A–Z, the fullstop '.', and the blank ' '. We shall assign the letters A–Z numerical values of 1–26 $(A = 1, B = 2, \ldots, Z = 26)$; we shall assign the full stop the value 27, and blank the value 0. Suppose that the plaintext we wish to encipher is

THE MARKET HAS CRASHED.

We must consider this plaintext as being built up of eight 3-tuples:

THE _MA RKE T_H AS_ CRA SHE D._

In these 3-tuples blanks are represented by an underline. There are $N = 28^3 = 21\,952$ possible 3-tuples of letters, so we shall choose $R = \mathbb{Z}_{21\,952}$, and use the bijection

$$3\text{-tuples of letters} \leftrightarrow \mathbb{Z}_{21\,952},$$

$$XYZ \quad \leftrightarrow 28^2 X + 28 Y + Z.$$

On the right-hand side of this bijection the letters X, Y, Z are understood as having the numerical values assigned to them above. Our plaintext thus corresponds to the following sequence of numbers in $\mathbb{Z}_{21\,952}$:

15909   365   14425   15685   1316   2857   15125   3892.

The enciphering and deciphering can now be carried out as before, using affine maps

$$f : \mathbb{Z}_{21\,952} \to \mathbb{Z}_{21\,952}, \qquad x \mapsto \alpha x + \beta$$

$$f^{-1} : \mathbb{Z}_{21\,952} \to \mathbb{Z}_{21\,952}, \qquad x \mapsto \alpha^{-1}(x - \beta)$$

with suitable $\alpha, \beta \in \mathbb{Z}_{21\,952}$. There are many close contenders for the title of most frequently occurring 3-tuple in English; for this reason it will be difficult to successfully perform a frequency analysis of ciphertext. Of course, by choosing k greater than 3 we can further improve the resilience of the ciphertext to frequency analysis. We shall call an enciphering/deciphering procedure such as this, which is based on an affine map and the use of k-tuples as the basic building block of plaintext, a *k-affine cryptosystem*.

A suitably chosen k-affine cryptosystem could be used by the branch offices of our international bank with reasonable success. The bank's competitors would be assumed to know that a k-affine cryptosystem is in use, and to know the value of k and the number, N, of letters in the alphabet. The enciphering key (α, β) is the only thing that has to be kept secret. To maintain the safety of the cryptosystem the enciphering key would need to be changed every so often. But therein lies a problem. How should the branch offices be notified of any such change? If a potential code-breaker has knowledge of the enciphering key, then a few simple calculations would give her knowledge of the deciphering key. One possibility for notifying branches of changes in the secret enciphering key would be to send new keys by courier, but this may be impractical. Another possibility would be to list the enciphering keys, and the dates when they are to be used, in a book which would be kept safe in each branch office. However, if such a book were to fall into the wrong hands the safety of the cyrptosystem would be jeopardized. There would clearly be little point in using the cryptosystem itself to send enciphered versions of new enciphering keys since a knowledge of the current enciphering key would then give a code-breaker knowledge of the new key.

The difficulties of transmitting the enciphering key of a k-affine code only arise because the deciphering key can be deduced from it. If the the deciphering key could not (easily) be deduced, then there would be no need to keep the enciphering key secret; a knowledge of the enciphering key would not be sufficient to decipher ciphertext. This observation led W. Diffie and M. Hellman, in 1976, to invent the concept of a *public key cryptosystem*. By definition such a cryptosystem is simply an enciphering procedure with the property that someone who knows only how to encipher cannot use the enciphering key to find the deciphering key without a prohibitively lengthy computation. In other words, a public key cryptosystem is based on a function $f: R \to R$ with the property that the inverse function $f^{-1}: R \to R$ cannot be deduced from f without a prohibitively lengthy computation; such a function is called a *trap-door function*.

This definition of a trap-door function is not precise from a mathematical point of view. The only currently known way of computing the inverse of some function $f: R \to R$ may involve a computation which, on the fastest available computer, will take 100 years. It would be reasonable to consider f as being a trap-door function, and to use it in a public key cryptosystem. Unfortunately there is always the possibility that tomorrow someone will devise an ingenious method for computing f^{-1}

which only takes a few minutes. If this possibility were to happen, then f would not be a trap-door function tomorrow, and the safety of any public key cryptosystem based on f would be in jeopardy.

Public key cryptosystems tend to be much slower than k-affine cryptosystems. The slowness is no real problem, however, since public key cryptosystems can be used in conjunction with the faster k-affine cryptosystems: the public key cryptosystem is used to transmit the enciphering key of a k-affine cryptosystem, and thereafter the k-affine cryptosystem is used to convert plaintext into ciphertext.

We shall consider two public key cryptosystems. The first is based on the problem of finding discrete logarithms. Let b be a non-zero element of a finite field $\mathbb{F}$, let y be an element of $\mathbb{F}$ which is a power of b, and let n be an integer such that $y = b^n$. We say that n is the *discrete logarithm* of y to *base b*, and we write

$$\log_b(y) = n.$$

For example, let $\mathbb{F} = GF(2^4)$, let α be a root of $x^4 + x^3 + 1$ in $\mathbb{F}$, and set $b = \alpha^2$. Then from computations in Chapter 3 we have:

$$\log_b(1) = 0, \qquad\qquad \log_b(\alpha^3 + \alpha^3 + 1) = 4,$$
$$\log_b(\alpha^2) = 1, \qquad\qquad \log_b(\alpha^3 + \alpha) = 5,$$
$$\log_b(\alpha^3 + 1) = 2, \qquad\qquad \log_b(\alpha + 1) = 6,$$
$$\log_b(\alpha^3 + \alpha^2 + \alpha + 1) = 3, \qquad \log_b(\alpha^3 + \alpha^2) = 7.$$

In this example certain discrete logarithms, such as $\log_b(\alpha^3)$, are not defined.

Given an element b in a finite field $\mathbb{F}$ of large order q, the computation of discrete logarithms to base b is generally an extremely difficult problem. A trap-door function suitable for a public key cryptosystem can be extracted from this difficulty. To illustrate how, suppose that the head office of our international bank wants to use such a cryptosystem to inform a branch of a new enciphering key (α, β) for some k-affine cryptosystem. Let us suppose that α, β are integers such that $1 \leq \alpha$, $\beta \leq N$. Head office chooses a finite field $\mathbb{F}$ containing at least N non-zero non-zero elements, say $\mathbb{F} = GF(q)$ with $q - 1 \geq N$. The non-zero elements of $\mathbb{F}$ are numbered from 1 to $q - 1$; via this numbering the integers α, β can from now on be thought of as non-zero elements in $GF(q)$. A non-zero element b in $\mathbb{F}$ is also chosen. Head office makes public this choice of $\mathbb{F}$, b, and numbering. The branch office now chooses a secret random integer k in the range $1 < k < q - 1$. This integer k is the secret deciphering key for the public key cryptosystem.

The enciphering key is the element b^k in $\mathbb{F}$. The branch office computes, and makes public, b^k. Head office now chooses a random secret integer n and computes b^{kn} by raising the element b^k to the power n. Head office then converts the plaintext

$$\alpha, \beta$$

into the ciphertext

$$\alpha b^{kn}, \beta b^{kn}$$

and sends this ciphertext, together with the value of b^n, to the branch office. The branch office computes the value of $b^{n(q-1-k)}$ by raising the value of b^n to the power $q - 1 - k$, and then deciphers the ciphertext by computing

$$\alpha = \alpha b^{kn} b^{n(q-1-k)} \qquad \text{and} \qquad \beta = \beta b^{kn} b^{n(q-1-k)},$$

since $b^{q-1} = 1$. The only known way for a code-breaker to break this cryptosystem is for her to compute the discrete logarithm

$$k = \log_b(b^k).$$

Our second example of a public key cryptosystem relies on the extremely difficult problem of factorizing very large integers into prime factors. This is one of the oldest (15 years old) and most popular public key cryptosystems, and has been named the *RSA cryptosystem* after its inventers Rivest, Shamir, and Adleman. To explain this cryptosystem we need to recall details on *Euler's function* $\phi(n)$ (which was introduced briefly in Chapter 4). This function $\phi(n)$ is defined, for each positive integer n, to be the number of positive integers $s \leq n$ such that s is coprime to n. For example, $\phi(3) = 2$ and $\phi(20) = 8$.

Proposition 9.1. (i) $\phi(p) = p - 1$ *for any prime p.*

(ii) $\phi(p^n) = p^n - p^{n-1}$ *for any prime power p^n.*

(iii) $\phi(mn) = \phi(m)\phi(n)$ *for any coprime positive integers m and n.*

(iv) *For any positive integer n and unit a in the ring $\mathbb{Z}_n$ the identity*

$$a^{\phi(n)} = 1$$

holds in $\mathbb{Z}_n$.

Proof. Part (i) is clear. To prove part (ii) it suffices to note that the numbers from 1 to p^n which are not coprime to p^n are precisely those that are divisible by p, and there are p^{n-1} of those. To prove part (iii) let us recall that an *nth root of unity* (over $\mathbb{Q}$) is any complex root of the polynomial $x^n - 1$. An nth root of unity ξ is *primitive* if each other nth root of unity is equal to some power ξ^s of ξ. For example $\xi = \exp(2\pi\sqrt{-1}/n)$ is a primitive nth root of unity; the reader can check that for any positive integer s the power ξ^s is a primitive nth root of unity if and only if s is coprime to n. Thus there are precisely $\phi(n)$ primitive nth roots of unity. We let $P(n)$ denote the set of primitive nth roots of unity. It is routine to verify that for any pair of coprime integers m and n there is a bijection:

$$P(m) \times P(n) \to P(mn), \qquad (\xi, \xi') \mapsto \xi\xi'.$$

Since there are precisely $\phi(m)\phi(n)$ pairs of roots in $P(m) \times P(n)$ and $\phi(mn)$ roots in $P(mn)$ this bijection proves part (iii). To prove part (iv) note that the units in $\mathbb{Z}_n$ are represented by those positive integers $a \leq n$ which are coprime to n. These units form a multiplicative group $\mathbb{Z}_n^*$ of order $\phi(n)$. By Lagrange's theorem (see Chapter 8) we have $a^{\phi(n)} = 1$ for any a in $\mathbb{Z}_n^*$.   ∎

To explain the RSA code let us again suppose that the head office of our bank wants to inform a branch office of a new enciphering key (α, β) with α, β integers in the range $1 \leq \alpha, \beta \leq N$. The branch office chooses two very large primes p and q, and also a random number e which has no common factor with either $p-1$ or $q-1$. The branch computes the product $n = pq$ and makes public the enciphering key (n, e). The number e represents an invertible element in the ring $\mathbb{Z}_{\phi(n)}$. The branch computes

$$\phi(n) = (p-1)(q-1)$$

and

$$d = e^{-1} \text{ modulo } \phi(n)$$

(by which we mean d is an integer representing e^{-1} in $\mathbb{Z}_{\phi(n)}$) and keeps secret the deciphering key (n, d). We can assume that the primes p and q have been chosen large enough (say 100 digits each) so that $N \leq n$, and we can think of α, β as elements in $\mathbb{Z}_n$. The enciphering function used by head office is the function

$$f: \mathbb{Z}_n \to \mathbb{Z}_n, \qquad x \mapsto x^e$$

which raises an element of $R = \mathbb{Z}_n$ to the power e. Thus head office enciphers the plaintext (α, β) into the ciphertext (α^e, β^e). The deciphering function is

$$f^{-1} : \mathbb{Z}_n \to \mathbb{Z}_n, \qquad x \mapsto x^d.$$

Note that $f^{-1}(f(x)) = x^{ed} = x^{1+m\phi(n)} = x(x^{\phi(n)})^m = x$, where m is some integer (here we have invoked Proposition 9.1 (iv)). The deciphering function is only known to the branch office. To discover the deciphering key, given only a knowledge of the enciphering key, a code-breaker would have to compute $\phi(n)$. Since the prime factorization of n is not known to the code-breaker, this would involve a (hopefully) prohibitively lengthy computation.

Any advances in the computation of discrete logarithms or in the factorization of large integers are very much of interest to crytographers. We shall end this chapter with a description of two techniques (one very recent) for factorizing large integers.

The first technique is known as *Pollard's p − 1 method*. This is very successful at finding a factor d of a large integer n if n possesses a prime factor p (as yet unknown) with the property that $p - 1$ has no large prime divisor. An integer B has to be chosen (the larger B is the more likely the method will succeed in producing a factor, but the longer the method will take to work), and the lowest common multiple of all positive integers $\leq B$ is computed and denoted by k. (Alternatively we could take $k = B!$.) Then an integer a in the range $2 \leq a \leq n - 2$ is chosen. Next, the highest common factor

$$d = \mathrm{hcf}(a^k - 1, n)$$

is computed using the Euclidean algorithm. Hopefully d will be a non-trivial factor of n, in which case the method has been successful. If, however, d equals 1 or n then we have to try again with a new value of a and/or k.

To illustrate the method let us use it to find a factor of

$$n = 858\ 058\ 123.$$

Take $B = 14$ and $k = \mathrm{lcm}\ (2, 3, \ldots, 14) = 2^3.3^2.5.7.11.13$, that is

$$k = 360\ 360.$$

Take $a = 2$. A little ingenuity is required to calculate

$$d = \mathrm{hcf}(2^k - 1), n)$$

since $2^k - 1$ is very large. To reduce the size of the numbers involved we can think of 2 as an element of $\mathbb{Z}_n$, and then calculate

$$2^k = 478\,825\,335 \in \mathbb{Z}_n.$$

This means that the integer 2^k is equal to some multiple of n plus $478\,825\,335$. Hence

$$d = \text{hcf}(478\,825\,335, n) = 390\,559.$$

We thus have the factorization

$$n = 390\,559 \times 2197.$$

The reader might like to apply Pollard's method several more times, with the same choice of B, to find the prime factorization

$$n = (13^2 \times 2311) \times (13^3).$$

This example works because all of the prime power divisors of $2310 = 2.3.5.7.11$ and $12 = 2^2.3$ are less than $B = 14$.

To explain when in general Pollard's method will work, suppose that k is divisible by all integers $\leq B$. Suppose also that p is a prime divisor of n such that each prime power divisor of $p - 1$ is less than B. It follows that k is a multiple of $p - 1$. It thus follows from Fermat's little theorem (Exercise 10 of Chapter 2, or a special case of Proposition 9.1 (iv)) that for any integer a in the range $2 \leq a \leq n - 2$ the prime p divides $a^k - 1$. Hence the prime p is a divisor of $d = \text{hcf}(a^k - 1, n)$. The only way that d could fail to be a proper divisor of n is if it happens that $a^k - 1$ is divisible by n.

The main weakness in Pollard's method for factorizing an integer n is that it cannot cope with the situation where each prime divisor p of n has the property that a relatively large prime power divides $p - 1$. From a cryptographer's point of view this weakness is a strength: Pollard's method cannot be used to break the RSA cryptosystem based on two primes p and q chosen such that $p - 1$ and $q - 1$ have large prime power divisors. There are of course other methods for factorizing large integers, and each of these might impose restrictions on the type of primes p and q to be used in the RSA code. One method was recently discovered (1986) by H. W. Lenstra, and is based on the theory of elliptic curves. Although Lenstra's method is better than others in many respects, the improvement in efficiency is not significant enough to pose a threat to existing RSA cryptosystems. Nevertheless, the discovery of an improvement using an unexpected branch of mathematics serves as a warning to cryptographers of possible surprise breakthroughs that might occur in the factorization of integers.

To explain Lenstra's factorization algorithm we need to begin with a few details on elliptic curves. Let K be a field of characteristic different from 2 or 3, and let

$$x^3 + ax + b$$

(where $a, b \in K$) be a cubic polynomial over K with no repeated roots. From Chapter 7 we know that there are no repeated roots if and only if the discriminant

$$4a^3 + 27b^2$$

is non-zero. An *elliptic curve* over K is the set of points (x, y) with x, $y \in K$ which satisfy the equation

$$y^2 = x^3 + ax + b,$$

together with a single element denoted O and called the *point at infinity*. (For fields of characteristic 2 or 3 the general form of the equations of an elliptic curve are $y^2 + y = x^3 + ax + b$ and $y^2 = x^3 + ax^2 + bx + c$, respectively.)

Elliptic curves over $\mathbb{R}$ can be pictured in the usual way. For instance the graphs of the elliptic curves $y^2 = x^3 - x$ and $y^2 = x^3 - x + 1$ over $\mathbb{R}$ are shown in Fig. 9.1.

An important property of the points on an elliptic curve is that they form an Abelian group. To explain how, let P and Q be two points on an elliptic curve E over a field K of characteristic $\neq 2, 3$.

If $P = O$ is the point at infinity then we define

$$-P := O \qquad \text{and} \qquad P + Q := Q;$$

Thus O serves as the group identity element. In the following definitions we shall suppose that neither P nor Q is the point at infinity, and that $P = (x, y)$ and $Q - (x', y')$, where $x, x', y, y' \in K$. We define

$$-P := (x, -y).$$

Clearly $-P$ lies on E. If $Q = -P$ then we define

$$P + Q := O.$$

If however P and Q have different x-coordinates then the reader can verify that the line PQ intersects the curve E in one other point R

(a)

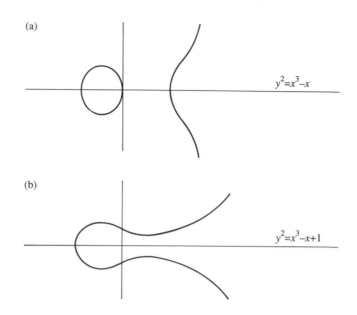

$y^2 = x^3 - x$

(b)

$y^2 = x^3 - x + 1$

Fig. 9.1.

(unless the line is tangent to the curve at P, in which case we set $R := P$, or unless the line is tangent to the curve at Q, in which case we set $R := Q$); we define

$$P + Q := -R.$$

It can (and should) be verified that the coordinates of $P + Q = (x'', y'')$ are given by the formulae

$$x'' = \left(\frac{y' - y}{x' - x}\right)^2 - x - x',$$

$$y'' = \left(\frac{y' - y}{x' - x}\right)(x - x'') - y.$$

(9.1)

Finally, if $P = Q$ then let R be the point, different from P, where the tangent to the curve at P intersects the curve and define:

$$P + Q := -R.$$

The coordinates of $P+Q=(x'',y'')$ in this case are given by the formulae

$$x'' = \left(\frac{3x^2+a}{2y}\right)^2 - 2x,$$

$$y'' = \left(\frac{3x^2+a}{2y}\right)(x-x'') - y.$$

(9.2)

The verification that this algebraic structure on the points of E satisfies the axioms of an Abelian group is quite involved and we shall not give it.

As an illustration consider the points $P=(-3,9)$ and $Q=(6,0)$ on the elliptic curve

$$y^2 = x^3 - 36x$$

over $\mathbb{R}$. The above formulae yield:

$$P+Q=(-2,-8), \qquad 2P=(25/4,-35/8).$$

These computations are represented by Fig. 9.2.

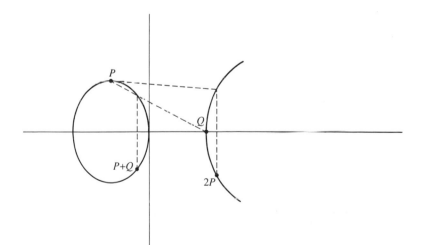

Fig. 9.2.

Lenstra's algorithm for factorizing an integer n involves elliptic curves over the field $\mathbb{Q}$. For any two rational numbers $x, x' \in \mathbb{Q}$ whose denominators are coporime to n we write

$$x \equiv x' \bmod n$$

if the numerator of $x - x'$, written in its lowest terms, is divisible by n. For instance

$$4 \equiv 19 \bmod 5,$$
$$7/6 \equiv 1/3 \bmod 5.$$

For any rational number x with denominator coprime to n there is a unique integer $\bar{x}$, called the *least non-negative residue modulo n*, between 0 and $n - 1$ such that $\bar{x} \equiv x \bmod n$. Given an elliptic curve E over $\mathbb{Q}$ we need to consider the set

$$E \bmod n = \{(\bar{x}, \bar{y}) : (x, y) \in E\} \cup \{O\}$$

of pairs of least residues modulo n together with the point O at infinity. For a point $P = (x, y)$ in E we let $\bar{P}$ denote the pair of residues $(\bar{x}, \bar{y})$ in $E \bmod n$. Two points $\bar{P}$ and $\bar{Q}$ in $E \bmod n$ can be added using the formulae (9.1) and (9.2) provided none of the denominators in these formulae have a common factor with n. It follows that for any prime p the set $E \bmod p$ is an Abelian group.

Lenstra's algorithm for finding a non-trivial factor d of n works as follows. First check to see if either 2 or 3 divide n; we shall suppose that neither do. Choose an integer B (the larger B is the more likely the method will succeed in producing a factor, but the longer the method will take to work), and compute the lowest common multiple of all positive integers $\leq B$. Denote this lowest common multiple by k. Now choose a 'random' elliptic curve E over $\mathbb{Q}$, represented by an equation

$$y^2 = x^3 + ax + b.$$

Compute the highest common factor of the discriminant $4a^3 + 27b^2$ and n:

$$h = \mathrm{hcf}(4a^3 + 27b^2, n).$$

If $h \neq 1$ then set $d = h$. If, as is most likely, $h = 1$ then choose a 'random' point P on E. Now proceed to use the formulae (9.1) and (9.2) to compute, working modulo n, the sum

$$k\bar{P} = \bar{P} + \bar{P} + \cdots + \bar{P}$$

of k copies of P. For instance, if $k = 360\,360 = 2^3.3^2.5.7.11.13$, this computation would be done by computing the following sequence of points, working all the time modulo n:

$$2\bar{P} = \bar{P} + \bar{P}, \, 4\bar{P} = 2\bar{P} + 2\bar{P}, \, 8\bar{P} = 4\bar{P} + 4P,$$
$$3(8\bar{P}) = 8\bar{P} + 8\bar{P} + 8\bar{P}, \, 3^2(8\bar{P}), \dots, k\bar{P}.$$

This computation will hopefully break down at some stage: a partial sum $k_1\bar{P}$ will not be computable because some integer denominator m occurring in either (9.1) or (9.2) has a common factor with n. In using the Euclidean algorithm to try to compute the non-existent inverse m^{-1} of m modulo n, the highest common factor

$$d = \text{hcf}(m, n)$$

is obtained. Now d will be a non-trivial divisor of n unless we have $d = n$. There is a theorem on elliptic curves which implies that $d = n$ if and only if for each prime divisor p of n the point $k_1\bar{P}$ in the group E mod p has order dividing k_1, an unlikely event. If, however, $d = n$ then a new point P and/or curve E have to be chosen and the process repeated.

Exercises

1. An alphabet consisting of the 26 letters A–Z is labelled by the elements of the ring $\mathbb{Z}_{26}$, in the obvious way: $A \leftrightarrow 0, \dots, Z \leftrightarrow 26$. An affine cryptosystem is used to convert a large amount of English plaintext into ciphertext. If the most commonly occurring letter in the ciphertext is A and the next most frequently occurring letter is D, determine the deciphering key of the cryptosystem.

2. Let α be a root in GF(27) of the polynomial $x^3 + x^2 + 2$. Let $b = \alpha + 1$. Compute the discrete logarithm $\log_b(y)$ for each element y in GF(27) for which it is defined.

3. (i) How many integers s are there in the range $1 \le s \le 360\,360$ that are coprime to $360\,360$?
   (ii) What is the smallest positive integer n such that $n + 19^{720\,723}$ is divisible by $360\,360$?

4. Use Pollard's method with $B = 8$ to factorize the integer $540\,143$.

5. With the aid of a computer package such as MAPLE, write a computer program to implement Lenstra's factorization algorithm.

Further reading

In writing this book I have relied heavily on the following texts. These should be consulted for further information on the chapters listed in brackets after them.

Albert, A. A. and Sandler, R. *An introduction to finite projective planes*. Holt, Rinehart and Winston, New York. (Chapters 2 and 6.)

Birkhoff, G. and Bartee, T. C. *Modern applied algebra*. McGraw-Hill, New York. (Chapters 2, 3, 8, and 9.)

Fraleigh, J. B. *A first course in abstract algebra*. Addison-Wesley, Reading, Mass. (Chapters 1, 2, 5, 7 and 8.)

Garling, D. J. H. *A course in Galois theory*. Cambridge University Press, Cambridge. (Chapters 5, 7, and 8.)

Herstein, I. N. *Topics in Algebra*. Wiley, New York. (Chapters 1, 2, 5, 6, 7, 8.)

Hughes, D. R. and Piper, F. C. *Projective planes*. Springer-Verlag, New York. (Chapters 2 and 6.)

Koblitz, N. *A course in number theory and cryptography*. Springer-Verlag, New York. (Chapter 9.)

Ledermann, W. *Introduction to group theory*. Longman, London. (Chapter 8.)

Lidl, R. and Niederreiter, H. *Introduction to finite fields and their applications*. Cambridge University Press, Cambridge. (Chapters 2, 3, 4, 6, 9.)

Stewart, I. *Galois Theory*, Chapman and Hall, London. (Chapters 5, 7 and 8.)

Stewart, I. and Tall, D. *Introduction to algebraic number theory*. Chapman and Hall, London. (Chapter 1.)

Index

Abelian 129, 141
affine cryptosystem 153
algebraic element 55
alternating group 125, 145
associativity 1, 135
automorphism 113, 150
axiom of choice 11

basis 5
BCH code 56
Berlekamp's alogrithm 75
binary symmetric channel 54
bit 51
byte 51

Cauchy's theorem 143
centralizer 104, 142
centre 104, 142
characteristic 33
Chinese remainder theorem 70, 81
ciphertext 151
class equation 142
code 50
codeword 50
combinatorics 25
commutative 2, 129, 141
complete quadrangle 46
complex conjugate 44
congruence 73
conjugacy class 104, 142
conjugate 139, 142
constructible point 84
constructible real number 84
coordinate system 96, 102
coprime 14, 22
coset 35, 48, 130, 140
cryptosystem 151
cubic resolvant 111
cycle 136
cyclic group 129, 141
cyclotomic field 65
cyclotomic polynomial 66

dihedral group 123
deciphering key 153

degree 18, 35, 117, 135
derivative 42
Desargues' theorem 101
diagonal points 46
dimension 7, 50
Diophantine equation 13
discrete logarithm 156
discriminant 125
divide 14, 21
division ring 93

Eisenstein's criterion 91
elliptic curve 161
enciphering key 153
encoding function 50
equivalence class 8
equivalence relation 8
Euclidean algorithm 70
Euclidean domain 19
Euler's function 66, 157
even permutation 145
exponent 141
extension 35

Fermat's little theorem 47
field 2
Frobenius homomorphism 58
$f(x)$-reducing 73

Galois, E. 109
Galois group 116
Gauss' proposition 91
Gaussian integers 18
general linear group 138
generate 6, 20, 45, 47, 141
generating polynomial 55
GF (q) 46
group 116, 118, 135

Hamilton, W. R. 94
Hamming bound 53
Hamming code 52, 63
highest common factor 21
homomorphism 48